SIDREA Series in Accounting and Business Administration

This is the official book series of SIDREA - the Italian Society of Accounting and Business Administration. This book series is provided with a wide Scientific Committee composed of Academics by SIDREA. It publishes contributions (monographs, edited volumes and proceedings) as a result of the double blind review process by the SIDREA's thematic research groups, operating at the national and international levels. Particularly, the series aims to disseminate specialized findings on several topics – classical and cutting-edge alike – that are currently being discussed by the accounting and business administration communities. The series authors are respected researchers and professors in the fields of business valuation; governance and internal control; financial accounting; public accounting; management control; gender; turnaround predictive models; non-financial disclosure; intellectual capital, smart technologies, and digitalization; and university governance and performance measurement. This book series is indexed in Scopus.

Diletta Vito

Corporate Reputation as Strategic Intangible Asset

An analysis of management processes, measurement methods and impact on bank and auditors' decisions

Springer

Diletta Vito
Department of Economics and Management
University of Pisa
Pisa, Italy

ISSN 2662-9879 ISSN 2662-9887 (electronic)
SIDREA Series in Accounting and Business Administration
ISBN 978-3-031-93330-1 ISBN 978-3-031-93331-8 (eBook)
https://doi.org/10.1007/978-3-031-93331-8

This Springer imprint is published by the registered company Springer Nature Switzerland AG
The registered company address is: Gewerbestrasse 11, 6330 Cham, Switzerland

To my family,
always by my side.

Acknowledgements

The process of writing this book proved to be a more challenging and demanding task than expected, and I am incredibly grateful for the support and expertise of those who guided me. I am profoundly grateful to Professor Giuseppe D'Onza whose expert guidance, insightful feedback, and continuous encouragement were central to the completion of this project. His invaluable support not only shaped the development of this book but also significantly influenced my academic growth. My sincere thanks also go to Professor Vincenzo Zarone, whose thoughtful advice and ongoing encouragement have been invaluable and continue to be a source of support throughout this journey into academia and research. Finally, I would like to express my appreciation to all my colleagues for the stimulating discussions, which have enriched my research and broadened my perspective.

Competing Interests The author has no competing interests to declare that are relevant to the content of this manuscript.

Contents

Chapter 1
Introduction to the Book

The way to gain a good reputation is to endeavor to be what you desire to appear.

[Socrates, ancient Greek philosopher].

January 5, 2024—Boeing 737 Max 9 operated by Alaska Airlines experienced a critical failure when a door panel detached mid-flight, causing rapid cabin decompression. The aircraft had to make an emergency landing in Portland, Oregon. It was the last of a long series of incidents involving Boeing. The Federal Aviation Administration (FAA) immediately grounded 171 aircraft, prompting a criminal investigation by the US Department of Justice into Boeing's practices. Financially, Boeing saw a 36% decrease in aircraft deliveries in the first quarter of 2024 compared to the same period the previous year, alongside substantial revenue losses and increased operational costs. It wasn't that long ago that Boeing's reputation was that of a staid industrial giant, known for building the safest, most advanced planes in the sky. It helped introduce the world to commercial jet travel (Chris Isidore, CNN, February 5, 2024). The slogan 'if it's not Boeing, I'm not going', which was common among pilots, others in the industry, and members of the flying public, has lost its meaning. The corporate reputation drastically drops. Boeing spent more than $20 billion in customer compensation, victim compensation, jet storage, added production expenses, software updates, loan interest, and lawsuit settlements (Callum Jones, The Guardian, April 24, 2024), and shares of Boeing have plunged nearly 10% the week following the incidents (Max Zahn, abcNEWS, January 9, 2024).

January 8, 2024—In early 2024, the Milan court announced that the Italian fashion influencer Chiara Ferragni was under investigation for 'aggravated fraud' related to sales of a Christmas cake that was misleadingly linked to fundraising for a children's hospital. She has described the episode as a communication error stating that she had acted in good faith and made herself available to prosecutors to clarify every detail. Despite their statements, Ferragni has lost many partnerships with well-known brands such as Safilo, Coca-Cola, Cartiere Paolo Pigna, and more than

D. Vito, *Corporate Reputation as Strategic Intangible Asset*, SIDREA Series in Accounting and Business Administration,
https://doi.org/10.1007/978-3-031-93331-8_1

200,000 followers since the cake scandals emerged (Angela Giuffrida, The Guardian, January 9, 2024; Lorena Pacho, El Pais, February 12, 2024). Consequently, her societies lost about five million euros in 3 months (Il Messaggero, March 14, 2024).

April 1, 2024—Reuters reported that Tesla's reputation was experiencing a downturn. According to a survey conducted by Caliber, Tesla's scores for 'trust & like' and 'consideration' to buy drastically dropped, showing that consumers' confidence in Tesla and their willingness to recommend or purchase from the company have significantly decreased. Reuters has made known that the percentage of consumers who would consider purchasing a Tesla product fell to 31% in February, less than half its high of 70% in November 2021 when Caliber started tracking consumer interest in the brand. Caliber's CEO Shahar Silbershatz told Reuters that 'it's very likely that Musk himself is contributing to the reputational downfall of Tesla' (Hyunjoo Jin and Nick Carey, Reuters, April 1, 2024). Elon Musk, co-founder and CEO of Tesla, has been at the centre of several controversial public pronouncements that negatively impact his reputation and those of the brands he is associated with. Tesla's stock price dropped by nearly a third in 2024 as the company's sales numbers and profits have disappointed. It has been one of the worst performers in the S&P 500 for the year 2024 (Peter Valdes-Dapena, CNN, April 7, 2024). The reputation of Tesla sharply declined starting in 2022, initially due to Musk openly criticizing COVID-19 restrictions. However, the decline has persisted as Musk has continued to make or support public statements that were perceived as racist, antisemitic, and contrary to supporting inclusion and diversity values. A similar negative impact has been observed with the social media platform X (formerly known as Twitter), which has lost 71% of its value since it was bought by Elon Musk in 2022, according to the mutual fund Fidelity (Adam Gabbatt, The Guardian, January 2, 2024).

These three news releases highlight recent cases that, although seemingly unrelated, underscore the pivotal role of corporate reputation in a company's outcomes.

Defined as *a perceptual representation of a company's past actions and future prospects that describes the firm's overall appeal to all of its key constituents when compared with other leading rivals* (Fombrun, 1996), corporate reputation shapes the firm-stakeholder relationships impacting on firm's ability to attract strategic resources, gain competitive advantage, and create sustainable value. No industry or jurisdiction is immune from inadequate or inappropriate corporate reputation management, which, as shown in the three examples, may provoke several negative consequences. Corporate reputation is a strategic resource that each company potentially can produce and acquire (Hall, 1993; Barney, 1991; Galbreath, 2005; Ambrosini & Bowman, 2009; Kamasak, 2017), whose impact varies based on the effectiveness of its management. All of the above examples underscore the pivotal role reputation plays in shaping a company's economic and financial performance. Each of them—Boeing, Ferragni, and Tesla—highlights a prominent aspect of corporate reputation while also reflecting elements of other key aspects:

- The Boeing case emphasizes the critical role of risk and crisis management in the reputation management process while also illustrating how reputation influences stakeholders' trust and relationships.
- The Ferragni case demonstrates how reputation shapes stakeholders' decisions to engage with and maintain relationships with a specific firm while also underscoring the importance of leadership in defining corporate reputation.
- The Tesla case highlights the direct link between the CEO's reputation and the firm's overall reputation while also demonstrating that mergers and acquisitions, such as Elon Musk's acquisition of Twitter, can serve as vehicles for reputational contagion, whether positive or negative.

The subsequent chapters of this book (Chaps. 3, 4, and 5) delve deeper into each of these aspects, offering a comprehensive analysis of the multifaceted concept of corporate reputation and the key elements that shape it.

Despite scholars producing nearly 6500 research outputs on the topic over the past 70 years,[1] the concept of corporate reputation consistently remains a focal point in scholarly discussions. Numerous companies have experienced reputational damage over the years, negatively impacting their outcomes and stakeholders' expectations. The cases above are just a few examples of significant reputational damage verified in the first months of 2024, resulting in billions of dollars in losses for the financial markets. When considering all the reputational damage that has occurred over the years, the total losses become uncountable.

However, reputational damage is just one potential effect of corporate reputation. In some cases, it serves to underscore the importance of corporate reputation management and fosters awareness of its value within the company. It reflects the common proverb 'You only realize the value of something after you've lost it', highlighting the relevance of caring for it before the worst-case scenario occurs.

Based on this premise, the objective of this book is twofold:

1. It aims to analyse the conceptual aspects of corporate reputation by identifying the main features of corporate reputation through a diachronic analysis of multidisciplinary studies that have explored this concept over time, proposing a theoretical model to outline the key determinants and management processes related to corporate reputation, offering an overview of the outcomes of reputation management, and highlighting the challenges in measuring corporate reputation, including an assessment of the strengths and weaknesses of the measurement methods used in the literature to date.
2. It aims to empirically analyse the impact of corporate reputation on organizational outcomes and stakeholders' decisions to initiate or continue a relationship with the company.

Specifically, the first main aim of the book is divided into several objectives, which form the foundation of the theoretical chapters. Conversely, the second aim guides the analyses presented in the empirical chapter.

[1] According to results form a data query performed in the Scopus Database on June 21, 2024.

Regarding the first main aim, one objective focuses on conducting a diachronic literature review of studies published over the past 50 years across six disciplines (i.e. strategic management, organization theory, accounting, economics, marketing, and sociology). This review aims to highlight how the concept of corporate reputation has evolved and to explore its potential future trajectory. Although a substantial body of literature has examined corporate reputation from various perspectives, the constantly evolving business environment requires a continuous reevaluation of the key aspects of corporate reputation.

The second objective focuses on developing a corporate reputation management framework, defined through a review of existing literature. This framework conceptualizes corporate reputation management as a combination of four processes influenced by determinants that can either positively or negatively impact reputation capital. It builds on previous studies proposing corporate reputation frameworks (e.g. Barnett & Hoffman, 2008; Cuomo et al., 2014; Money et al., 2017) and introduces a stock and flow perspective. In the proposed framework, reputation capital is treated as a stock value, while the processes of reputation building, reputation acquiring, reputational risk management, and crisis management are detected as flow variables. Instead of examining each process in isolation, this work emphasizes a systemic approach to understanding how reputation management operates as a cohesive whole (Marchi, 2014). The framework is informed by earlier research (e.g. Corrado & Hulten, 2010), which indicates that companies are navigating a new phase in the evolution of capitalism, where investments in intangible assets now surpass those in tangible assets. This shift heralds the rise of a knowledge-based economy (Trequattrini et al., 2013). Thus, as organizations transition from traditional economies primarily focused on tangible assets to knowledge-based economies that enhance the role of intangible assets, the management of these assets undergo significant transformation and require particular attention. In this light, the proposed framework aims to provide a comprehensive overview of the determinants and processes involved in corporate reputation management, equipping organizations with the insights needed to navigate this transformation effectively and leverage corporate reputation—a strategic intangible asset—to achieve positive outcomes.

Another objective is to analyse the benefits of adopting full disclosure in corporate communication, emphasizing its role as a determinant of corporate reputation. The recognition that traditional financial disclosure alone is insufficient to fully represent the various dimensions of company management has become widespread (e.g. Giacosa, 2012). There is an increasing acknowledgement of the need for additional non-financial information to evaluate the social and environmental aspects of companies (Kaplan & Norton, 1992; Simnett et al., 2009). This necessity has led companies to voluntarily disseminate non-financial information beyond regulatory requirements (Martínez-Ferrero & García-Sánchez, 2017; Nicolò et al., 2021; Raimo, 2021; Vitolla et al., 2021), willing to engage a broader group of stakeholders and meet their information needs (García-Sánchez et al., 2022). Related to this concept, another related objective is underscoring the importance of transparency and accountability in corporate reputation management (Dando & Swift, 2003; Martins et al., 2021; Mazzola et al., 2006). In an era characterized by increased scrutiny and higher expectations for corporate behaviour, organizations must be proactive in demonstrating their commitment to ethical practices, social responsibility, and sustainable development. This commitment not only enhances corporate reputation but also builds trust and credibility with stakeholders, which are essential for long-term success. Research supports this view, indicating that transparent and accountable practices are fundamental to building and maintaining a positive corporate reputation, thereby confirming the crucial role of communication in this process (Carroll & Olegario, 2020; Swift, 2001). By specifically analysing intentional actions that companies carry out to build reputation, this book intends to shed light on the proactive strategies that companies can implement to answer the continuous pressure the environment puts on them regarding the appropriateness of their actions (Buhmann et al., 2020; Kolk, 2008). Continuing to focus on the determinants of corporate reputation, another objective of the study is to emphasize the central role of the stakeholder in the discussion regarding corporate reputation. Specifically, the study pursues a holistic approach to corporate reputation management that includes various dimensions of stakeholder engagement and information dissemination. This approach answers to the increasing number of stakeholder groups interested in corporate information and results (Raimo et al., 2021; Vitolla et al., 2019). In addition, this study aims also to emphasize the importance of considering specific stakeholders in the analysis. Stakeholders' perceptions and evaluations of an organization's reputation are influenced by a myriad of factors, including corporate actions, communication strategies, and broader socio-economic and cultural contexts. Therefore, understanding the nuances of stakeholder-specific reputation dynamics is critical for developing effective reputation management strategies (Martínez-León et al., 2023; Vito, 2021). For instance, customers' perceptions of corporate reputation are often shaped by their experiences with the company's products and services, as well as the company's commitment to quality, innovation, and customer service. On the other hand, employees' evaluations of corporate reputation are influenced by factors such as organizational culture, leadership, job satisfaction, and opportunities for professional development. Investors and financial analysts, meanwhile, assess corporate reputation based on the company's financial performance, governance practices, and strategic direction. Recognizing these stakeholder-specific nuances, the study seeks to highlight the need for a more detailed and differentiated approach to corporate reputation management.

A further objective related to the first main aim of the study is to provide a comprehensive overview of corporate reputation outcomes. Given the current context marked by a shift from tangible to intangible value creation (Aparicio et al., 2023; Arrighetti et al., 2014), it has become crucial for companies to effectively transform their intangible assets into tangible results to achieve long-term success (Garanina, 2009). Particularly, this study seeks to examine the outcome of corporate reputation from a double perspective, the organization-oriented perspective (in terms of impact on performance) and the stakeholder-oriented perspective (in terms of impact on stakeholder's decision-making). By incorporating a stakeholder-oriented perspective in the analysis of corporate reputation, this study emphasizes the necessity of tailoring reputation management strategies to address the unique needs and expectations of different stakeholder groups. This approach enhances the overall effectiveness of reputation-building efforts.

The last objective of the first aim focuses on examining the reputation measurement methods used in literature to highlight the strengths and weaknesses of each approach. In doing so, the study intends to provide a comprehensive overview that will assist scholars and practitioners in selecting the most suitable methods based on the target stakeholder groups.

The second primary aim of this study is to empirically test the assumptions outlined above regarding the key features and outcomes of corporate reputation. Specifically, the study examines two main areas.

First, it investigates the impact of corporate reputation on a bank's decision to lend to a company and on the cost of debt. This analysis seeks to deepen the understanding of the importance of corporate reputation in a bank-centric financial system such as Italy's.

Second, it explores how corporate reputation influences the relationship between auditors and firms. In particular, it examines its effect on audit fees, the decision to provide non-audit services, and the associated fees for these services. This analysis highlights the broader implications of corporate reputation in influencing auditing practices, including the economic dynamics between auditors and firms, the scope of services offered, and the pricing strategies for both audit and non-audit services.

Through these investigations, the study aims to validate the key characteristic of corporate reputation (specifically, its sensitivity to stakeholders and context) emphasizing that its impact can vary depending on the specific stakeholder group and context under consideration.

Additionally, the final chapter addresses the issue of measurement by empirically analysing whether and how the choice of one measurement method over another affects the outcomes of corporate reputation studies.

By doing so, the empirical section of this book fills important gaps in the literature, which has extensively explored the impact of corporate reputation on certain stakeholder groups (e.g. employees and communities) but has largely overlooked its effects on others, such as banks and auditors.

Figure 1.1 shows the book's structure.

Specifically, Chap. 1 outlines the relevance of the study. Chap. 2 addresses the corporate reputation definition problem. It analyses the definition provided by the literature across three main periods (1973–1997, 1998–2011, and 2012 to present) and within the five research fields identified by Fombrun and van Riel (1997) as distinct literatures that were currently converging in their emphasis on corporate reputations as key factors for company's success (i.e. strategic management, organization theory, accounting, marketing, economics, and sociology). Moreover, this chapter focuses on analysing the strategic role of corporate reputation by drawing on theories such as the resource-based view (Walker, 2010). It concludes by analysing the corporate reputation under the accounting standards lens to explain why it should be considered an intangible asset (Hall, 1993). Chapter 3 focuses on the Corporate Reputation Management Framework by adopting a stock and flow model.

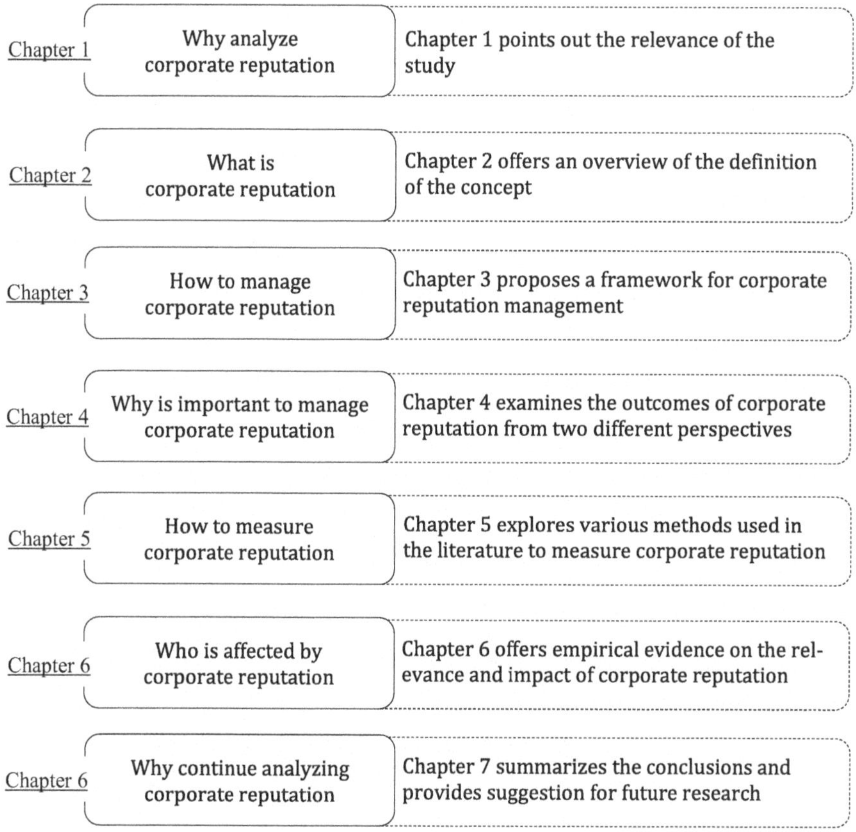

Fig. 1.1 Book overview. Source: author's elaboration

Specifically, it identifies reputational capital as the stock variable, which is fed by positive flow variables consisting of actions aimed at building or acquiring corporate reputation. Conversely, it may be eroded by negative flow variables related to the occurrence of reputational risks or crises. This chapter delves into each element and process involved in the proposed framework. Chapter 4 concludes the corporate reputation management process by incorporating the outcomes into the model. According to Money et al. (2017), the framework uses a dual perspective to analyse potential outcomes: the stakeholder-oriented and the organization-oriented perspectives. Chapter 5 addresses the corporate reputation measurement problem. It introduces an analysis of the most used measurement methods in the literature, highlighting their association with specific stakeholder groups. Specifically, this chapter describes measurement methods based on structured questionnaires, rankings and ratings, indices from third parties, and media coverage. Chapter 6 translates the study into empirical evidence. It begins by examining the impact of corporate reputation on firm-bank relationships, suggesting that it significantly influences a bank's willingness to grant loans to the firm. Additionally, it analyses the role of reputation in firm-auditor relationships, highlighting its impact on auditors' pricing decisions and willingness to offer non-audit services. Finally, Chap. 7 concludes and offers suggestions for future research on the topic.

References

Ambrosini, V., & Bowman, C. (2009). What are dynamic capabilities and are they a useful construct in strategic management? *International Journal of Management Reviews, 11*(1), 29–49. https://doi.org/10.1111/j.1468-2370.2008.00251.x

Aparicio, G., Iturralde, T., & Rodríguez, A. V. (2023). Developments in the knowledge-based economy research field: A bibliometric literature review. *Management Review Quarterly, 73*(1), 317–352. https://doi.org/10.1007/s11301-021-00241-w

Arrighetti, A., Landini, F., & Lasagni, A. (2014). Intangible assets and firm heterogeneity: Evidence from Italy. *Research Policy, 43*(1), 202–213. https://doi.org/10.1016/j.respol.2013.07.015

Barnett, M. L., & Hoffman, A. J. (2008). Beyond corporate reputation: Managing reputational interdependence. *Corporate Reputation Review, 11*(1), 1–9. https://doi.org/10.1057/crr.2008.2

Barney, J. (1991). Firm resources and sustained competitive advantage. *Journal of Management, 17*(1), 99–120. https://doi.org/10.1177/014920639101700108

Buhmann, A., Paßmann, J., & Fieseler, C. (2020). Managing algorithmic accountability: Balancing reputational concerns, engagement strategies, and the potential of rational discourse. *Journal of Business Ethics, 163*(2), 265–280. https://doi.org/10.1007/s10551-019-04226-4

Carroll, C., & Olegario, R. (2020). Pathways to corporate accountability: Corporate reputation and its alternatives. *Journal of Business Ethics, 163*(2), 173–181. https://doi.org/10.1007/s10551-019-04228-2

Corrado, C. A., & Hulten, C. R. (2010). How do you measure a «technological revolution»? *American Economic Review, 100*(2), 99–104. https://doi.org/10.1257/aer.100.2.99

Cuomo, M. T., Metallo, G., & Tortora, D. (2014). *Corporate reputation management: Analisi e modelli di misurazione. Seconda edizione*. G Giappichelli Editore.

Dando, N., & Swift, T. (2003). Transparency and assurance minding the credibility gap. *Journal of Business Ethics, 44*(2), 195–200. https://doi.org/10.1023/A:1023351816790

Fombrun, C. J. (1996). *Reputation: Realizing value from the corporate image*. Harvard Business School Press.

Fombrun, C. J., & van Riel, C. B. M. (1997). The reputational landscape. *Corporate Reputation Review, 1*(1), 5–13. https://doi.org/10.1057/palgrave.crr.1540008

Galbreath, J. (2005). Which resources matter the most to firm success? An exploratory study of resource-based theory. *Technovation, 25*(9), 979–987. https://doi.org/10.1016/j.technovation.2004.02.008

Garanina, T. (2009). The role of intangible assets in value creation: Case of Russian companies. *Perspectives of Innovations, Economics & Business, 3*(3), 92–94.

García-Sánchez, I.-M., Raimo, N., Uribe-Bohorquez, M.-V., & Vitolla, F. (2022). Corporate reputation and stakeholder engagement: Do assurance quality and assurer attributes matter? *International Journal of Auditing, 26*(3), 388–403. https://doi.org/10.1111/ijau.12287

Giacosa, E. (2012). *La Comunicazione Economico-Finanziaria d'Impresa*. G. Giappichelli Editore.

Hall, R. (1993). A framework linking intangible resources and capabiliites to sustainable competitive advantage. *Strategic Management Journal, 14*(8), 607–618. https://doi.org/10.1002/smj.4250140804

Kamasak, R. (2017). The contribution of tangible and intangible resources, and capabilities to a firm's profitability and market performance. *European Journal of Management and Business Economics, 26*(2), 252–275. https://doi.org/10.1108/EJMBE-07-2017-015

Kaplan, R. S., & Norton, D. P. (1992). The balanced scorecard-measures that drive performance. *Harvard Business Review*, 71–79.

Kolk, A. (2008). Sustainability, accountability and corporate governance: Exploring multinationals' reporting practices. *Business Strategy and the Environment, 17*(1), 1–15. https://doi.org/10.1002/bse.511

Marchi, L. (2014). *Introduzione all'economia aziendale: Il sistema delle operazioni e le condizioni di equilibrio aziendale. Nona edizione*. G Giappichelli Editore.

Martínez-Ferrero, J., & García-Sánchez, I.-M. (2017). Sustainability assurance and cost of capital: Does assurance impact on credibility of corporate social responsibility information? *Business Ethics: A European Review, 26*(3), 223–239. https://doi.org/10.1111/beer.12152

Martínez-León, I. M., Olmedo-Cifuentes, I., & Davies, G. (2023). The virtuous circle of internal corporate reputation and financial performance. *Corporate Reputation Review, 26*(2), 97–110. https://doi.org/10.1057/s41299-022-00140-0

Martins, A., Gomes, D., & Branco, M. C. (2021). Managing corporate social and environmental disclosure: An accountability vs. *Impression Management Framework. Sustainability, 13*(1), paper 1. https://doi.org/10.3390/su13010296

Mazzola, P., Ravasi, D., & Gabbioneta, C. (2006). How to build reputation in financial markets. *Long Range Planning, 39*(4), 385–407. https://doi.org/10.1016/j.lrp.2006.09.001

Money, K., Saraeva, A., Garnelo-Gomez, I., Pain, S., & Hillenbrand, C. (2017). Corporate reputation past and future: A review and integration of existing literature and a framework for future research. *Corporate Reputation Review, 20*(3/4), 193–211. https://doi.org/10.1057/s41299-017-0034-3

Nicolò, G., Ricciardelli, A., Raimo, N., & Vitolla, F. (2021). Visual disclosure through integrated reporting. *Management Decision, 60*(4), 976–994. https://doi.org/10.1108/MD-01-2021-0034

Raimo, N. (2021). Integrated reporting: State of play, theoretical underpinnings and empirical insights: The role of corporate governance mechanisms. 1–133.

Raimo, N., Caragnano, A., Zito, M., Vitolla, F., & Mariani, M. (2021). Extending the benefits of ESG disclosure: The effect on the cost of debt financing. *Corporate Social Responsibility and Environmental Management, 28*(4), 1412–1421. https://doi.org/10.1002/csr.2134

Simnett, R., Vanstraelen, A., & Chua, W. F. (2009). Assurance on sustainability reports: An international comparison. *The Accounting Review, 84*(3), 937–967. https://doi.org/10.2308/accr.2009.84.3.937

Swift, T. (2001). Trust, reputation and corporate accountability to stakeholders. *Business Ethics: A European Review, 10*(1), 16–26. https://doi.org/10.1111/1467-8608.00208

Trequattrini, R., Russo, G., & Rosa, L. (2013). Evaluating and measuring relational capital by defining knowledge. *Journal of Modern Accounting and Auditing, 9*(3), 392–397.

Vito, D. (2021). La misurazione della reputazione aziendale: Un'analisi sistematica della letteratura. In P. In Ferretti (Ed.), *La corporate reputation: Alcuni driver di sviluppo* (pp. 1–38). G. Giappichelli Editore.

Vitolla, F., Raimo, N., Rubino, M., & Garzoni, A. (2019). How pressure from stakeholders affects integrated reporting quality. *Corporate Social Responsibility and Environmental Management, 26*(6), 1591–1606. https://doi.org/10.1002/csr.1850

Vitolla, F., Raimo, N., Rubino, M., & Garegnani, G. M. (2021). Do cultural differences impact ethical issues? Exploring the relationship between national culture and quality of code of ethics. *Journal of International Management, 27*(1), 100823. https://doi.org/10.1016/j.intman.2021.100823

Walker, K. (2010). A systematic review of the corporate reputation literature: Definition, measurement, and theory. *Corporate Reputation Review, 12*(4), 357–387. https://doi.org/10.1057/crr.2009.26

Chapter 2
Corporate Reputation: A Literature Review

> *Your reputation is your most valuable asset. Everything else can be taken away from you, but not your reputation.*
>
> *[Jack Welch, Former CEO of General Electric]*

2.1 The Definitional Problem

Starting from the 1970s the study of corporate reputation has witnessed a notable surge in interest in the academic community. Scholars from various fields of studies have examined the reputation of an organization sharing the native idea that it is a social construction and not an objective reality and that it is strongly influenced by a variety of factors shaping the perceptions of company stakeholders (Berens & van Riel, 2004).

One of the first reviews of the corporate reputation literature (Fombrun & van Riel, 1997) identified six distinct disciplines (i.e. strategic management, organization theory, accounting, marketing, economics, and sociology) that have analysed corporate reputation with different research aims, approaches, and perspectives. In doing so, scholars have adopted a definition of corporate reputation that sometimes overlaps, in other cases, differs, or conflicts (Barnett et al., 2006), making corporate reputation a 'foggy' concept (Walsh et al., 2009).

Regarding the semantic problem, Bigus et al. (2024) recently characterized reputation as a 'Gordian'[1] concept, stating that 'despite the rich body of research examining reputation, our ability to conclude what is known about reputation, to generalize empirical findings, and to develop related substantive theory may be built on sand.' The lack of a comprehensive and widely accepted definition of corporate reputation has long been recognized as a challenge, as noted by scholars over the

[1] The term Gordian recall the ancient Greek legend of the Gordian knot. In this context, Bigus et al. (2024) use it metaphorically to describe an intractable problem that can ultimately be solved through innovative thinking or an unconventional approaches, leading to success.

D. Vito, *Corporate Reputation as Strategic Intangible Asset*, SIDREA Series in Accounting and Business Administration,
https://doi.org/10.1007/978-3-031-93331-8_2

years (e.g. Podnar et al., 2012; Dowling, 2016; Bigus et al., 2024). This issue arises from the inherently intangible nature of reputation, which is not only physically invisible but also relies on the subjective judgements of stakeholders. However, despite numerous efforts by scholars to untangle the terminological issues associated with corporate reputation and to establish a common vocabulary (e.g. Gotsi & Wilson, 2001; Walker, 2010), the definition problem remains unresolved.

When discussing corporate reputation, it is crucial to address the definitional challenges associated with the concept. This issue should be introduced at the outset, as the entire trajectory of the research depends on a clear and comprehensive understanding of what reputation entails. Accordingly, this section focuses on analysing the definitional complexities of corporate reputation, emphasizing its evolution over time.

In this regard, I conducted a systematic literature review (SLR) following the three-stage framework drawn by Tranfield et al. (2003):

1. Planning the review.
2. Conducting the review.
3. Reporting and disseminating results.

During the first stage, I developed the SLR protocol in line with prior studies in the fields of accounting and management (Türetken et al., 2020; Kotb et al., 2018). The protocol comprises the following steps:

(a) Conducting a pilot study.
(b) Defining the keywords for the search.
(c) Selecting the database to be consulted.
(d) Establishing inclusion and exclusion criteria.
(e) Extracting papers applying the inclusion and exclusion criteria (*Inc 1*, *Inc 2*, *Inc 3*, *Exc 1*, and *Exc 2*).
(f) Performing a full-text analysis applying the exclusion criterion *Exc 3*.
(g) Analysing and discussing the results.

Following the pilot study, which was conducted to verify the robustness of the identified protocol, I selected the keywords for the search. The string 'corporate AND reputation' has been used for the analysis, as the pilot study indicated that these terms comprehensively capture the relevant literature. Specifically, the search string was applied to papers containing these keywords in the title, abstract, or author-defined keywords. For the database selection, I chose Scopus, which is regarded as the largest database for peer-reviewed literature (Veh et al., 2019). To ensure relevance, I applied specific inclusion and exclusion criteria.

Inclusion Criteria

- *Inc 1*—English-language papers only.

Inc 2—Studies classified under the subject areas of 'business, management, and accounting', 'social science', and 'economics, econometrics, and finance' to maintain alignment with the research aims.

Inc 3—Peer-reviewed papers published in top academic journals.

Exclusion Criteria

Exc 1—Papers published before 1973 or after 2023.

Exc 2—Papers without full-text access.

Exc 3—Papers that do not provide any insights into the corporate reputation definitional problem.

In analysing and discussing results, I adopted a diachronic approach like those developed by Money et al. (2017). Specifically, I identified three distinct periods characterized by different approaches to the study of corporate reputation: 1973–1997, 1998–2011, and 2012–present.

The transitional years (1997 and 2011) were selected because they coincide with significant moments of academic relevance, marked by peaks in the number of publications on corporate reputation, as identified during the systematic literature review. These peaks were observed in the initial analysis of the broader literature, before applying the inclusion and exclusion criteria. This approach ensures a thorough and unbiased representation of the evolution of corporate reputation studies, specifically in terms of the volume of published research over time (Fig. 2.1).

Figure 2.1 shows that the first peak in the publication of papers on corporate reputation occurred in 1997, with a total of 53 papers, more than four times the number of papers published in the previous year (13 studies published in 1996). This year corresponds to the publication of the seminal work titled 'The Reputation Landscape' by Fombrun and van Riel (1997), which laid the groundwork for understanding corporate reputation as a valuable intangible asset and examining its impact on various stakeholders' decision-making processes. In the subsequent years, there was nearly constant growth in research on the topic, with the second peak occurring in 2011 when 242 papers were published. Following the publication of the work titled 'Creating Shared Value' by Porter and Kramer in 2011, a new school of thought emerged, which recent literature defines as 'integrative' (von

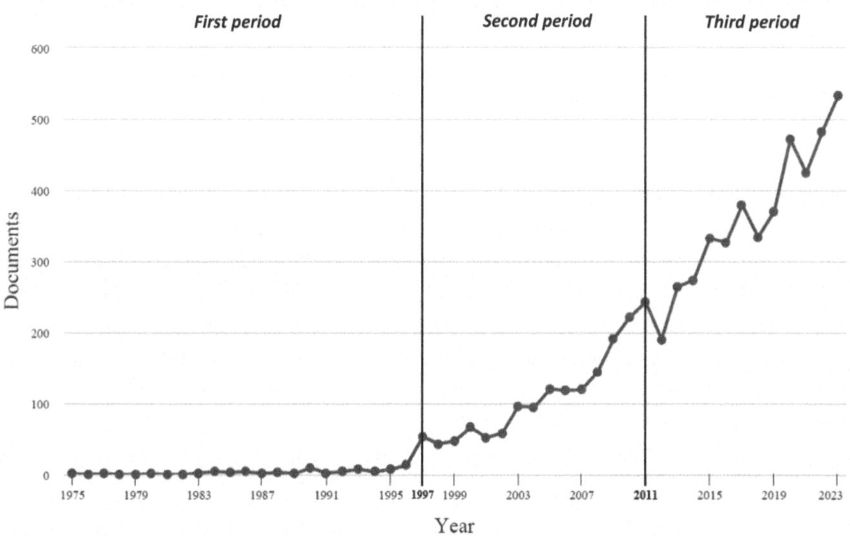

Fig. 2.1 Number of publications on corporate reputation in the last 50 years. (Source: author's elaboration)

Berlepsch et al., 2024) underlying the relevance to examine the construct of corporate reputation from different disciplinary perspectives. Thus, research in recent years adopted a holistic approach that connects reputation with various emerging topics such as Corporate Social Responsibility, non-financial disclosure, and social media management. This integrative view revitalizes the academic interest in corporate reputation, leading to the publication of 532 works in 2023.

After defining the three periods of analysis, I applied the inclusion and exclusion criteria to gather evidence on how the definition of corporate reputation evolves across the periods.

Specifically, I extracted 647 papers that meet the inclusion and exclusion criteria *Inc 1*, *Inc 2*, *Inc 3*, *Exc 1*, and *Exc 2*. Then, I conducted the full-text analysis to apply the exclusion criterion *Exc 3*. Thus, I obtained the final sample of 97 papers.[2]

The analysis results are consistent with those of Money et al. (2017) and confirm the prevalence of strategic, relational, and strategic-relational perspectives across the three periods.

The first period, spanning from 1973 to 1997, is marked by a prevailing strategic perspective, wherein corporate reputation is perceived as an intangible asset that serves as a signal of an organization's capability to generate value. During this phase, Money et al. (2017) indicate that there is a predominant inclination to view corporate reputation as a unidirectional construct, emanating from organizations and influencing stakeholders. Consequently, the focus of analysis primarily centres on the organizations themselves.

In the second period, covering the years 1998–2011, there is a notable shift from a strategic perspective to a relational perspective of reputation. Reputation is conceptualized as an aggregate of perceptions held by diverse stakeholders regarding an organization. Consequently, the focus of analysis moves from organizations to individuals. In this period, stakeholders are recognized as 'guardians' of corporate reputation, emphasizing their role as opinion leaders. Within this perspective, stakeholders possess power and legitimacy, thereby potentially influencing public opinion concerning the reputation of a given organization (Zyglidopoulos & Phillips, 1999).

The third period, which started in 2012, shows a recognition of the essential coexistence of both the strategic and relational perspectives of corporate reputation. During this phase, there is an increased emphasis on investigating the antecedents and consequences of reputation to comprehensively understand its underlying causes and effects. Scholars devote greater attention to exploring the factors that shape corporate reputation as well as the outcomes and impacts associated with it. This period reflects a more integrated and holistic approach to studying corporate reputation, acknowledging the multifaceted nature of the concept and its implications for organizations and stakeholders.

[2] While the primary objective of the SLR is to explore the evolution of the corporate reputation concept from a semantic perspective, the same process was employed to collect and analyse evidence on the determinants, outcomes, and measurement methods of corporate reputation. These aspects are discussed in detail in the subsequent chapters (Chaps. 3–5, respectively).

The following subsections review the literature to summarize how corporate reputation has been defined across the three periods highlighted in Fig. 2.1 and within the five research fields suggested by Fombrun and van Riel in 1997 (i.e. strategic management, organization theory, accounting, marketing, economics, and sociology). In doing so, the aim is to clarify this study's subject matter, help its contextualization in management and accounting research, and prepare the field for the research problem formulation (Ferraris Franceschi, 1978; Fattore, 2005).

2.1.1 The Reputational Landscape in the Earliest Studies

In the strategic management research field, corporate reputation is considered both an asset and a mobility barrier. Fombrun and Shanley (1990) define *reputation as assets in which individuals and firms invest*, specifying that it is *the outcome of competitive process in which firms signal their key characteristics to constituents to maximize their social status*. Moreover, they defined reputation as the *partly reflections of publics' interpretation of the merits of a firm's strategic postures* compared to those of competing firms, and thus, it is described as a mobility barrier as it may inhibit the mobility of rivals in an industry.

Furthermore, reputation is a unique internal feature that is difficult to duplicate as it *is a set of attributes ascribed to a firm, inferred from the firm's past action* and interactions with stakeholders (Weigelt & Camerer, 1988). In this period, strategic management literature looks at reputation also as a highly firm-specific asset, non-tradeable, inimitable, and non-substitutable as internally accumulated. In this regard, Dierickx and Cool (1989) define corporate reputation as a strategic intangible asset that favours the sustainability of a privileged asset position and supports the success of the implementation of a corporate strategy.

In the realm of organization theory research, scant scholarly attention was devoted to the concept of corporate reputation during the nascent stages of its literature development. Most early researchers synthesized organizational reputation with the term trust, albeit acknowledging the problematic nature of defining trust due to the wide variety of approaches to the concept (Husted, 1989). In this regard, Hosmer (1995) defines reputation (in terms of a company's trust) *as the optimistic expectation by one person, group, or firm of the behaviour of another person, group, or firm in a common endeavour or economic exchange, under conditions of vulnerability and dependence on the part of the trusting party, for the purpose of facilitating cooperation between both parties that will result in an ultimate joint gain but, given the lack of effective contractual, hierarchical, legal, or social enforcement methods, with reliance upon a voluntarily accepted duty by the trusted party to protect the rights and interests of all others engaged in the endeavour or exchange*. In the latter years of this initial period, research in the organization theory field began to focus on reputation as a condensation of internal stakeholders' perceptions, especially those of employees, and more specific definitions began to emerge.

One of the most relevant definitions was proposed by Koys (1997), who defined corporate reputation as *the firm's ability to attract, develop, and retain key personnel*.

Corporate reputation has garnered significant attention from accounting scholars and practitioners since the 1980s. However, this interest experienced rapid growth after the 2000s. Like strategic management, accounting literature regards reputation as a valuable intangible asset that companies should measure and manage due to its impact on the company's outcomes (Deephouse, 1997). In this early stage, much of the work focuses on the auditing field by analysing the concept of reputational capital of auditing firms (Balvers et al., 1988; Beatty, 1989). For instance, Beatty (1989) describes reputational capital as an unobservable and non-operationalizable aspect of an audit firm. Moizer (1997), while describing what reputation entails, delineates what it is not and asserts that reputation should not be confined solely to the quality of services that a company delivers. Instead, he underscores that reputation is a multidimensional construct that should encompass how the company is generally perceived in the financial community.

The description of a reputation as an intangible asset is confirmed also by economists. For instance, Wilson (1985) describes a firm's reputation as an important asset that can be built, maintained, or even exploited and that can influence the decision-making process of both firms and their stakeholders. During this period, economists have started to consider corporate reputation through the lens of the signalling theory. For instance, Brucato and Smith (1997) refer to reputation as a *reliable signal*, which is a signal that should be confirmed by future information releases. Moreover, reputation is not an unvarying asset as it may change over time as firms make 'investments' by signalling consistently. According to Shapiro's (1982) definition, reputation is an *imperfect attribute* because there is always a time lag effect between firms' behaviours and changes in perceived reputation. Shapiro specifies that this effect is mainly due to the speed of information flow and the speed of learning by stakeholders, which, in that period, were much slower than they are nowadays.

In the marketing research field, scholars frequently refer to reputation as a construct strongly related to corporate image and link it to the perceptions that consumers hold regarding a company's products (Markwick & Fill, 1997). Marketing scholars consider both corporate image and reputation as external perceptions of the firms, even though they underline some differences between them. Specifically, corporate image is defined as the firm's portrait made in the mind of a consumer, while corporate reputation is associated with the degree of trust (or distrust) in a firm's ability to meet customers' expectations on a given attribute. Marketing studies suggest that a two-sided relationship exists between these two concepts. On one side, scholars indicate that corporate reputation is the general outcome of the process of building a corporate image (Allen, 1984). On the other side, they indicate that a good reputation may help a pioneer firm build an innovative image in the industry (Porter, 1985).

Finally, sociologists describe corporate reputations as the aggregated assessments of a firm's institutional prestige built on the stratification of the social system surrounding firms and industries (Shapiro, 1987; DiMaggio & Powell, 1983).

The year 1997 holds significant importance in the advancement of corporate reputation literature. This pivotal period saw the publication of the seminal work by Fombrun and van Riel (1997) titled 'The Reputation Landscape'. Concurrently, the academic community witnessed the establishment of the Corporate Reputation Review journal, dedicated to disseminating empirical and conceptual research on reputation management and its associated domains. Thus, 1997 can be considered a milestone in the development of corporate reputation research.

At the end of this first period, Fombrun and van Riel (1997) offer a combined view of the corporate reputation concept by jointly considering the five academic literatures highlighted in Table 2.1.

Starting from the six key characteristics listed below, they proposed one of the first comprehensive descriptions of corporate reputation, which is still one of the most cited today: *a corporate reputation is a collective representation of a firm's past actions and results that describes the firm's ability to deliver valued outcomes to multiple stakeholders. It gauges a firm's relative standing both internally with employees and externally with its stakeholders, in both its competitive and institutional environments.* More in detail:

- Reputations are derivative, second-order characteristics of an industrial system that crystallize the emergent status of firms in an organization field.
- Reputations are the external reflection of a company's internal identity—itself the outcome of sense-making by employees about the company's role in society.
- Reputations develop from firms' prior resource allocations and histories and constitute mobility barriers that constrain both firms' actions and rivals' reactions.
- Reputations summarize assessments of past performance by diverse evaluators who assess firms' ability and potential to satisfy diverse criteria.
- Reputations derive from multiple but related images of firms among all a firm's stakeholders and inform about their overall attractiveness to employees, consumers, investors, and local communities.

Table 2.1 Definition of corporate reputation by research fields

Discipline	Definition
Strategic management	Reputation is an intangible asset that is difficult for rivals to imitate, acquire, or substitute, and so creates mobility barriers that provide their owners with a sustained competitive advantage
Organization theory	Reputation is viewed as the sense-making experiences of employees or the perception of the organization held by an organization's internal stakeholders
Accounting	Reputation is one of many types of intangible assets that are difficult to measure but create value for companies
Economics	Reputation is traits or signals that describe a company's probable behaviour in a particular situation
Marketing	Reputation is viewed from the customer or end-user's perspective and concentrates on the way reputations are formed
Sociology	Reputation is viewed as an aggregate assessment of a firm's performance relative to expectations and norms in an institutional context

Source: Fombrun and Van Riel (1997)

- Reputations embody two fundamental dimensions of firms' effectiveness: an appraisal of firms' economic performance and an appraisal of firms' success in fulfilling social responsibilities.

2.1.2 The Growth of Corporate Reputation Literature

Following the seminal work of Fombrun and van Riel (1997), scholars have made concerted efforts over time to improve clarity around the concept of corporate reputation, which has historically been fragmented due to widespread interest in the concept across several research disciplines.

In the second period of this analysis (1998–2011), differences and similarities among definitions persist.

Strategic management studies confirm the strategic role of corporate reputation as *an asset of considerable interest and importance* (Chun et al., 2002). Moreover, scholars confirm that it contributes significantly to the long-run competitive advantages of organizations as it is a *critical resource* for companies (Dowling, 2006; Rose & Thomsen, 2004). However, an important strand in this literature starts to describe reputation as *social responsiveness* and points out that it plays a crucial role in influencing perceptions of organizations in the eyes of society (Brammer & Pavelin, 2004). In this period scholars from strategic management propose more complex definitions of corporate reputation pointing the focus on the relational perspective. In this regard, Romenti (2008) defines reputation as the results of a firm's effectiveness in managing relationships with stakeholders. It originates from the social processes (interactions) between firms and stakeholders and develops with them.

Focusing on the concept of reputation in organization theory, in the early years of this second period, studies continue to mainly focus on the internal stakeholders' perceptions, especially those of employees (Helm, 2011). In this respect, some scholars emphasized the role that employees play in corporate reputation management by suggesting that reputation does not result by fiat; rather, it is the output of management leadership and concerted efforts by everyone in the corporation (Cravens & Oliver, 2006; Harris & de Chernatony, 2001). Others consider the improvement of employer attractiveness as one of the most prominent aspects of corporate reputation (Cappelli, 2001; Maxwell & Knox, 2009), and thus, it is defined as a *crucial resource* to overcome the constant war over talent in several industries (Fishman, 1998; Sivertzen et al., 2013). In this second view, scholars consider corporate reputation as *a source of information flow* towards potential employees, which allows them to know more about working conditions in different organizations (Cable & Turban, 2003). In the final years of this second period, scholars in organizational studies approach a more comprehensive definition of reputation. Francesconi and Dossena (2009) describe corporate reputation as the perception that stakeholders have of a firm depending on the credibility of its communication activities, the quality and reliability of its products and services, and the legitimacy and responsibility of its actions. Thus, also organization theory studies move from considering reputation in relation to a single stakeholder (i.e. the employee) and come closer to the multi-stakeholder view.

In this second period, there is a consistent consensus among accounting scholars regarding the definition of corporate reputation as an intangible asset. Toms (2002) asserts that *reputation is arguably the most significant among intangible assets*, emphasizing that reputation-based intangible assets are increasingly crucial contributors to firm performance. By confirming that reputation influences the firm's performance, Gazzola (2006) refers to corporate reputation as the *social value* of a firm describing it as an index of the overall quality of an organization. She suggests that reputation is the outcome of a firm's investment in quality (i.e. quality of procedures, products, and behaviours) that improves the market perception of the value, trust, and loyalty of the company. Another similar approach that incorporates both the accounting and strategic management views refers to corporate reputation as 'reputational capital', highlighting its nature as a stock. In this regard, Petrick et al. (1999) state that *reputational capital is that portion of the excess market value that can be attributed to the perception of the firm as a responsible domestic and global corporate citizen*.

Economists continue to build on signalling theory and define reputations as either traits or signals. Moreover, they underline its relevance in the case of information asymmetry between an organization and its stakeholders (Fombrun et al., 2000a). In this research field, scholars assign a functional role to reputation by assuming that it generates perceptions among employees, customers, investors, competitors, and the community about what a company is, what it does, and what it stands for.

In the marketing field, Weiss et al. (1999) depart from delineating reputation solely as corporate image and propose that it encompasses *a global perception of the degree to which an organization is esteemed or regarded highly*. They specify that an organization garners public esteem or high regard when it is perceived as both visible and credible, such as being established, professional, and a stable player in the marketplace.

Sociologists introduce the reference to the neo-institutionalism approach by connecting reputation to social legitimacy, which firms should acquire not only by fulfilling the social expectation of economic efficiency but also by satisfying other normative expectations (Hiss, 2009). Mutti (2008) and Catino (2010) move closer to strategic management and accounting views and introduce the concept of *reputation capital* in the sociology field. According to Mutti's definition, reputation capital is the *temporal stabilization of expectations among a plurality of agents regarding certain qualities (positive or negative) of specific individuals, groups, and institutions*.

Considering together those characterizations of reputation in the five academic literature, Gotsi and Wilson (2001) identify and emphasize the fundamental attributes associated with corporate reputation to offer a comprehensive definition of the concept:

- Corporate reputation is a dynamic concept.
- It is built over time.
- There is a bilateral relationship between corporate reputation and corporate image: corporate reputation is closely dependent on the everyday image that stakeholders form of a company based on its behaviour, communication, and symbolism, while at the same time corporate reputations can influence stakeholders' everyday images of a firm.
- Corporate reputation crystallizes a company's perceived ranking in a field of other rivals.
- The corporate reputation may vary depending on the based on the economic, social, and personal background of the different categories of stakeholders considered.

Based on these attributes, they propose the following comprehensive definition: *a corporate reputation is a stakeholder's overall evaluation of a company over time. This evaluation is based on the stakeholder's direct experiences with the company, any other form of communication, and symbolism that provides information about the firm's actions and/or a comparison with the actions of other leading rivals.*

Following Gotsi and Wilson's work, Walker (2010) conducts an updated systematic analysis of the literature on corporate reputation. His study aims to examine the distinctions between the concepts of organizational identity, organizational image, and corporate reputation, which are frequently used interchangeably by different scholars. Walker (2010) concludes that these three concepts differ primarily in terms of the stakeholders they pertain to. Notably, *organizational identity* is associated with internal stakeholders, while *organizational image* emerges among external stakeholders. In contrast, *corporate reputation* is a broader concept that encompasses the perceptions of both internal and external stakeholders.

Based on his analysis of the definitions provided by various scholars, Walker (2010) revises the attributes that prior literature ascribed to corporate reputation. Then, he specifies that:

1. Corporate reputation is a construct that relies on perceptions.
2. Reputation, being a social and collective concept, encompasses the cumulative perceptions of different stakeholder groups defined by shared interests, such as environmental responsibility, social responsibility, profitability of the company, or employee welfare.
3. Evaluating reputation entails making comparisons, both in terms of space and time.
4. Reputation can manifest as either positive or negative.
5. Reputation is not a definitively defined, stable, or enduring concept; rather, it is subject to changes, sometimes occurring rapidly

Expanding the Fombrun and van Riel's seminal definition of reputation, Walker (2010) defines corporate reputation as a *relatively stable and issue-specific aggregate perceptual representation of a company*. It encompasses the composite evaluation of a company's past and future actions, which are assessed in comparison to some predetermined standards. This definition underscores the enduring nature of reputation as well as its focus on specific aspects of a company's performance and behaviour. By aggregating stakeholders' perceptions, reputation becomes a comprehensive construct that reflects how a firm's conduct in the past and its potential for the future are perceived by its various stakeholders (Walker, 2010).

Subsequently, Lange et al. (2011) attempt to establish a definitive conceptualization of corporate reputation by conducting a new extensive review of the literature. Their comprehensive analysis offers the identification of three distinct dimensions that contribute to the understanding of reputation: *being known*, *being known for something*, and *generalized favourability*. Within the first dimension (*being known*), the authors posit that a company's corporate reputation is strengthened when it gathers widespread recognition among stakeholders or within society at large. Additionally, the presence of a distinct perception held by individuals, regardless of its positive or negative nature, is viewed as relevant. Notably, within the academic literature, this dimension has been named by various synonymous terms. For instance, Rindova et al. (2005) use the term prominence to describe this dimension, Shamsie (2003) and Barnett et al. (2006) prefer the concept of awareness, while Yang (2007) opts for the term familiarity. However, it is worth noting that considering familiarity as one dimension of corporate reputation lacks universal consensus. Scholars such as Brooks et al. (2003) and Turban (2001) argue that familiarity should be viewed as an antecedent rather than as a way to describe corporate reputation.

The second dimension (*being known for something*) refers to the definition of corporate reputation based on the value that stakeholders associate with an organization's capacity to fulfil their interests or meet their expectations in specific domains. In contrast to the first dimension, *being known for something* involves a judgement on the organization itself, its outputs, and its actions. Rindova et al. (2005) refer to this dimension as perceived quality, while Love and Kraatz (2009) use the concept of technical effectiveness to capture this notion. Pfarrer et al. (2010) associate the dimension of *being known for something* with stakeholders' evaluation of the company's demonstrated ability to generate value.

Lastly, the third dimension highlighted by Lange et al. (2011) is *generalized favourability*. It denotes an overall positive evaluation of the company, making it preferable or attractive compared to its competitors in a general sense. Unlike the dimension of *being known for something*, this third dimension does not solely rely on the expectations of specific stakeholder groups but encompasses the collective and general assessment of multiple organizational attributes by the broader community.

Despite the growing academic efforts towards comprehensively defining corporate reputation during this second period, it remains a 'foggy' concept that continues to inspire a significant amount of research, even in recent years.

2.1.3 Corporate Reputation Research in Recent Years

The third period of this analysis (2012–present) has witnessed exponential growth in the importance of reputation in academic literature and this is reflected in the growing number of publications on this topic (see Fig. 2.1).

In recent years, strategic management studies have reconsidered the reputation in the era of media, data, and accelerating information flow. Hutt (2016) uses the term *visibility* to describe reputation in this era of global connectedness. He specifies that *corporate reputation is a complex concept describing how positively, or negatively, a company is perceived by its key stakeholders such as employees, customers, investors, the media, suppliers, and financial analysts. Reputation is central to the company's competitiveness and profitability as an intangible asset along with customer relationships, human capital, innovation, and patents. It is fragile and sometimes easily damaged.* In this period, globalization, social media, and the availability of abundant information led many empirical academics to move their focus from the definition problem to the management issue (Lamboglia, 2018). The relevance of reputation management arises also from the definitions proposed by academics in the strategic management and accounting field during this third period. For example, Lamboglia (2018) describes corporate reputation as a determinant of corporate success that must be appropriately managed through a designed, formalized, and shared management policy with two main aims: (1) creating a reputational capital over time and (2) protecting the reputational capital from risks that may erode it.

Meanwhile, this period witnesses a growing interest among scholars in the analysis of reputation in relation to emerging topics such as Corporate Social Responsibility (CSR) and environmental, social, and governance (ESG) practices. Thus, definitions of corporate reputation proposed in the third period encompass this evolving scenario. For instance, Melo and Garrido-Morgado (2012) define reputation as *one of the consequences of a variety of management practices and behaviours* and specify that with the term 'practices' they prominently refer to those associated with CSR engagement.

Similarly, also in accounting studies, the definition of reputation reflects this evolving global scenario. Cao et al. (2012), building on the prior definition of the concept (e.g. Barnett et al., 2006), describe corporate reputation as *observers' collective judgement of a corporation based on assessments of the financial, social, and environmental impacts attributed to the corporation over time.*

By focusing on CSR disclosure, these third-period scholars introduce a new term to identify reputation: *credibility*. Specifically, Odriozola and Baraibar-Diez (2017) describe corporate reputation as the *credibility of the information disclosed by a company*. On the contrary, they suggest that companies should be aware of what they disclose because they may give rise to a so-called credibility gap, defined as a situation in which what someone says is not believed or trusted due to the difference between what is said and what seems to be true. This situation negatively impacts on the reputation of companies.

Referring to the economic view, scholars in the third period do not move away from the origins of corporate reputation research in the economic field and confirm the connection with signalling and game theory. By relying on the game-theoretic perspective and the signalling perspective, economic studies see reputation as a reliable information mechanism that reduces information asymmetry and enhances the predictability of economic exchanges (Ravasi et al., 2018).

Similarly to strategic management, accounting, and economic fields, marketing studies point to the focus on reputation as the credibility of a firm (Boateng & Okoe, 2015). In the years when social media advertising is still in its early stages, Boateng and Okoe (2015) posit that reputation is both the ability and the intention of a company to fulfil its promises. Thus, the concept remains connected to the trustworthiness of information disseminated by a company.

The organization theory studies also introduce CSR into the new definition of corporate reputation by suggesting that it may be defined as *the green attitude* of a company (Scipioni, 2021).

Finally, sociologists introduce the social identity theory in the realm of corporate reputation studies. Recently, Frare and Beuren (2021) posit that, under the possible lenses through which the corporate reputation can be interpreted, one concerns the social identity theory since the corporate reputation permeates the collective beliefs about the company's interest and ability to meet the wishes of the stakeholders. For instance, by specifically focusing on employees, they suggest that stakeholders start to express the feeling of belonging, in line with the organization's reputation and to the detriment of the internal and external context.

Taken together, the prior sections emphasize that each of these disciplines views reputation differently and depending on the discipline, reputation may represent an intangible asset, a resource, a signal, an image, a brand, an identity, or an observer's judgement.

Even though some similar characteristics can be identified along the different approaches (e.g. reputation as a vantage and information mechanism), a comprehensive definition of corporate reputation seems to be lacking.

Consequently, literature reviews emerged to provide orientation in the extensive field of research on corporate reputation and to advance the scholarly understanding of the concept (e.g. Bigus et al., 2024; Esenyel, 2020; Gatzert, 2015; Money et al., 2017; Veh et al., 2019).

One of the most notable studies is by Money et al. (2017), which presents a comprehensive framework of the concept (Fig. 2.2).

The framework developed by Money et al. (2017) serves as a comprehensive model valuable for future research in the field of corporate reputation. The authors successfully integrate both the strategic perspective, which views reputation as an asset, and the relational perspective, which emphasizes stakeholders' perceptions of reputation.

The framework goes beyond mere description and delves into the identification of causes and consequences of corporate reputation. As the authors suggest, the framework can be explored from an organization-oriented perspective as well as from a stakeholder-oriented perspective. Focusing on the causes of corporate

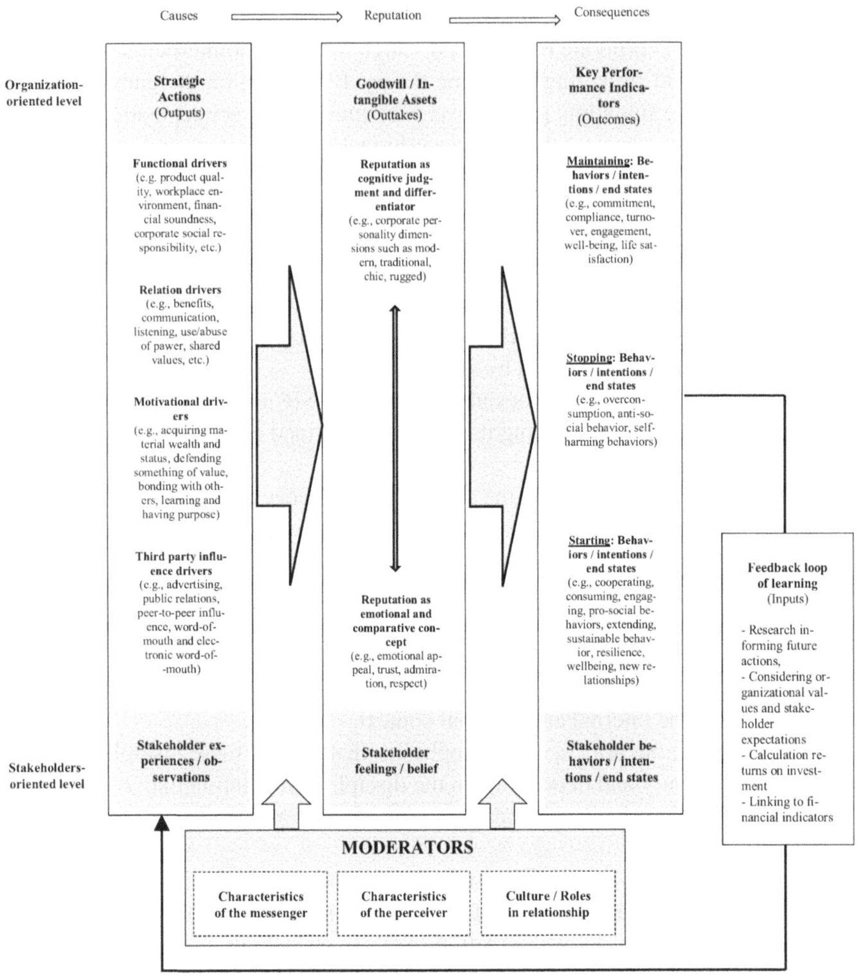

Fig. 2.2 Corporate reputation framework. (Source: Money et al., 2017)

reputation, the organization-oriented perspective interprets them as strategic actions undertaken by the organization, whereas the stakeholder-oriented perspective views them as experiences or observations that are, in some way, connected to these strategic actions. Moving to reputation definition, from the organization-oriented perspective, it may be considered as 'goodwill' or as an 'intangible asset', while from the stakeholder-oriented perspective, it can be compared to trust, admiration, and stakeholder esteem. Finally, in terms of consequences, from the organization-oriented perspective, reputation outcomes are related to sustainable consumption, employee engagement, or community well-being, while from the stakeholder-oriented perspective, they are stakeholders' behaviours, states, and intentions towards the firm.

The framework is further enriched by the inclusion of moderating variables that play a significant role in shaping reputation. These additional factors are organizational characteristics, stakeholder characteristics, and factors arising from the relationship between them.

This framework contributes to advancing the understanding of corporate reputation by providing a comprehensive model that integrates different perspectives, identifies key factors, and incorporates moderating variables. It may serve as a valuable tool for researchers and practitioners seeking a structured approach to studying and conceptualizing corporate reputation, leading to a more holistic view of this construct. Overall, the framework proposed by Money et al. (2017) highlights the contextual nature of reputation and makes clear its complexity due to the interplay of several variables.

In conclusion, the concept of corporate reputation, although varying in its definitions, consistently underscores the pivotal role of stakeholders as 'guardians' of the reputation. In other words, stakeholders are crucial in defining the reputation of an organization, according to their interests, perceptions, judgements, and emotions.

The next sections delve into the consideration of corporate reputation as a strategic resource and intangible asset pointing out its strategic role for corporate competitive advantage.

2.2 The Strategic Role of Corporate Reputation

Several authors have argued that corporate reputation plays a key role in strategic management processes as it can become a source of sustainable competitive advantages for firms having a positive reputation. This role arises from strategic management studies, which is one of the fields mentioned in Sect. 2.1 (Aqueveque, 2005; Baldarelli & Gigli, 2014; Dierickx & Cool, 1989; Dowling, 2006; Roberts & Dowling, 2002; Rumelt, 2005; Weigelt & Camerer, 1988).

The intangible nature of reputation, its rareness and social complexity, make it difficult to trade and imitate. As a result, reputation can contribute significantly to differentiating performance among organizations by favouring a sustainable competitive advantage (Barney, 1991; Peteraf, 1993). Furthermore, the strategic view of reputation underlines that it has an inertial effect, suggesting that reputation, once acquired, appears to be maintained over time despite the actual behaviour of its owner (Fasaei et al., 2014).

In literature, scholars adopt three prevailing theoretical frameworks to justify the strategic role of corporate reputation: the resource-based view theory, the signalling theory, and the institutional theory (Walker, 2010).

The resource-based view theory is the most common theoretical framework adopted in strategic management and accounting studies. According to the resource-based view theory proposed by Barney (1991), organizations possessing resources that are valuable, rare, and difficult to imitate or substitute can achieve sustained competitive advantages. In turn, these competitive advantages can create superior performance for an organization relative to its rivals that lack resources (e.g. Barney, 1991; Deephouse, 2000; Dowling, 2006; Hall, 1993; Milgrom & Roberts, 1982; van Riel, 1997).

Starting from the 1980s, studies in the field of strategic management proposed the resource-based view theory, which emphasized the distinction between resources and capabilities. According to this perspective, resources, together with several other internal elements of a company, form a unique and cohesive entity, ultimately aimed at achieving the company's objectives (Bertini, 1990).

According to strategic management studies, firm resources include assets, capabilities, organizational processes, firm attributes, information, knowledge, etc. controlled by a firm that enable the firm to elaborate and realize strategies that improve its efficiency and effectiveness (Daft, 1983). This view originates from traditional strategic research that considers firm resources as strengths that allow to conceive and implement corporate strategies (Learned et al., 1969; Porter, 1981).

More recent academic literature (e.g. Bianchi Martini, 2009; Bruni & Garzoni, 1999; Galeotti & Garzella, 2013; Grant, 1991) classifies resources into:

- *Tangible*, related to physical and financial assets.
- *Intangible*, related to technologies, corporate reputation, and organization culture.
- *Human*, related to knowledge, skills, attitude, and motivation of human resources.

It is worth noting that not all firm resources possess the potential to provide sustained competitive advantages. According to Barney (1991), for a resource to have this potential, it must meet four specific attributes, collectively known as the VRIN criteria. Specifically, a firm resource must be:

- Valuable.
- Rare.
- Imperfectly imitable.
- Non-substitutable.

Firm resources are valuable when they exploit opportunities or neutralize threats in a firm's environment. However, valuable firm resources possessed by many competing or potentially competing firms cannot be sources of either a competitive advantage or a sustained competitive advantage. Thus, a firm's valuable resources must be unique among a set of competing or potentially competing firms to be able to generate at least a competitive advantage and have the potential to generate a sustained competitive advantage. Moreover, valuable and rare firm resources can only be a source of sustained competitive advantage if firms that do not possess these resources cannot obtain them. More specifically, firm resources must be imperfectly imitable, and this is possible for one or a combination of three reasons: (a) the ability of a firm to obtain a resource is dependent upon unique historical conditions, (b) the link between the resources possessed by a firm and a firm's sustained competitive advantage is causally ambiguous, or (c) the resource generating a firm's advantage is socially complex. Finally, firm resources must be not strategically equivalent to valuable resources that are themselves either not rare or imitable.

Building on Barney (1991), Bianchi Martini (2009) makes a distinction between resource attributes that contribute to generating a competitive advantage and resource attributes that support that competitive advantage over time. The firsts are similar to those proposed by Barney (1991): rareness, uniqueness, competitive value, and synergistic ability to connect with other resources. The latter refers to durability. Specifically, by introducing the concept of durability, Bianchi Martini (2009) assumes that the longer lasting a resource is, the more valuable it will be. The durability attribute expresses also the 'decay process' of all the other attributes that the resource must have to generate and sustain a competitive advantage. This term indicates the deterioration or degradation of a resource within an organization over time, leading to a decrease in its value or effectiveness in generating and sustaining a competitive advantage.

Extensive literature suggests that intangible resources are the most likely resources to create competitive advantage or the most probable sources of superior firm performance as they have greater potential to meet the VRIN criteria (Barney, 1991; Galbreath, 2005; Ambrosini & Bowman, 2009; Kamasak, 2017). Therefore, according to the resource-based view theory, corporate reputation may be considered a firm's critical resource as it respects all the attributes highlighted above. This assumption is also proposed by Hall (1993) who suggests that corporate reputation has been identified to be one of the most critical strategic resources a company can possess because of its intangible nature, its rareness, its imperfect imitability, and its social complexity.

More on this point, Walker (2010) points out that studies adopting the resource-based view as the theoretical framework to investigate reputation often focus on analysing how reputation is a valuable and rare resource that leads to a sustained competitive advantage. Furthermore, he suggests that the resource-based view theory seems to be particularly suitable in research analysing the outcomes of the reputation management process (i.e. the *post-action stage*).

Besides the resource-based view theory, scholars use the signalling theory by focusing on how firms portray the 'good things' about their organization, especially in the economic field. This theoretical framework not only examines strategic signals sent out by firms but also examines stakeholder interpretations of these signals. Walker (2010) suggests that signalling theory is often applied at an *action stage* of reputation management indicating that it is useful in analysing the effort that firms make to maintain and defend a reputation based on projected organizational images. Therefore, signalling theory considers social performance as an antecedent to corporate reputation.

Furthermore, Deephouse (2000) suggests that firms make strategic choices in determining which 'true' attributes reveal, using these as signals to stakeholders to reduce information asymmetry and mitigate market uncertainty. As a result, this theoretical framework underlines the reduction effect of corporate reputation on the stakeholders' concern about the firm's ability and trustworthiness.

Contrariwise, institutional theory is applied to examine the actions that a firm takes to build its reputation by gaining legitimacy within its institutional context and thus benefit from its consequences. Walker's (2010) study shows that scholars adopting institutional theory to explain the strategic role of reputation often focus on decisions aimed at building a good reputation (i.e. the *pre-action stage*). Moreover, Deephouse et al. (2016) point out that institutional theory is a very appropriate lens for explaining differences in corporate reputation across countries. Indeed, much research demonstrates how corporate behaviour is influenced by national institutions through the influence they have on stakeholders' expectations (Brouthers, 2013; Crossland & Hambrick, 2011; Nell et al., 2015; Peng et al., 2008). This implies that, according to institutional theory, companies who want to build a valuable reputation should prefer some actions rather than others based on the characteristics of their home environments.

Taken together, these theoretical frameworks are based on a common idea: reputation functions as capital. It must be cultivated. One can invest in one's reputation and it may yield additional revenues as a result. Companies that are respected can find supporters more easily, exercise influence, and have more opportunities to realize their strategic goals. Hence, building and cultivating a reputation must be part of strategic actions (Voswinkel, 2011).

Figure 2.3 summarizes the main contribution, focus, and stage of studies adopting the three theoretical frameworks highlighted above as suggested by Walker (2010).

Figure 2.3 and the preceding analysis of the three theoretical frameworks suggest the existence of a two-sided relationship between corporate reputation and corporate strategies. On one side, companies may define strategies aimed to build and bolster the corporate reputation; on the other side, corporate reputation may influence the strategic outcomes of a company.

Referring to the definition of reputation-building strategies, Goldberg et al. (2003) conceptualized four general strategic actions companies may carry out. First, looking at long-term investment, companies should develop core competencies to build a reputation based on 'years of demonstrated superiority'. Second, as a short-term strategy, companies should focus on image management by investing in

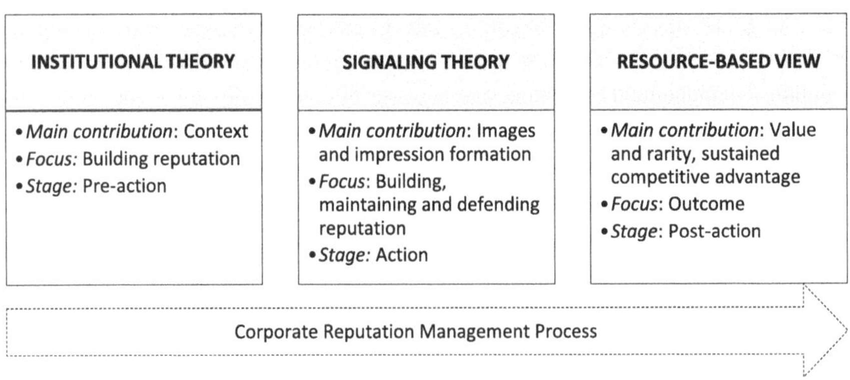

Fig. 2.3 The three most used theoretical frameworks in corporate reputation studies. (Source: adapted from Walker, 2010)

symbols of quality and indicators of a successful enterprise. Finally, a positive reputation also may be sought through strategic alliances.[3] This strategy seems to be particularly useful for small businesses that can benefit from a long-term cooperative relationship with, for example, a well-known multinational company. However, Goldberg et al. (2003) specify that each strategy must be seen as a mixed blessing, as each alternative can lead to both positive and negative consequences that influence the future performance of a firm.

Moving on to the strategic outcomes related to corporate reputation, Caves and Porter (1977) suggest that it protects firms' profitability by creating barriers to competitive threats, thus strengthening the company's strategic position in the competition. Schmalensee (1982) and Tetrault Sirsly and Lamertz (2008) support the view that corporate reputation supports firms by favouring a first-mover advantage. For example, they suggest that when a company has a positive reputation, it is often seen as more trustworthy and credible. This trust can be crucial when being the first to enter a particular market, introduce a new product or technology, or establish a new business model. Moreover, a company with a positive reputation may find it easier to secure resources, such as financing or partnerships, to support its first-mover initiatives. Sánchez and Sotorrío (2007) show that corporate reputation may improve the effectiveness of a firm's differentiation strategy by making their customers identify their offer as distinct from that of their competitors. They suggest that corporate reputation fosters trust. When customers trust a company, they are more willing to try new and differentiated products or services offered by that company. Trust reduces the perceived risk of trying something new. Consequently, companies with a strong reputation may be able to command premium prices for their differentiated offerings due to the significant customer loyalty it generates. However, on this latter point, the literature also presents opposing views. For instance, Williams et al. (2005) argue that corporate reputation alone does not necessarily determine the success of a diversification strategy, specifying that, in some cases, reputation can act as a hindering factor. This perspective emphasizes the need to consider reputation as a resource that functions in synergy with other firm resources. In other words, Williams et al. (2005) argue that reputation is an integral component of a firm's overall resource base, and when effectively combined with other assets, it can contribute significantly to the firm's long-term success. However, when considered in isolation, reputation may not have a positive and significant impact.

Finally, just as reputation can influence strategic changes, strategic changes can also affect corporate reputation. In this regard, reputation is a crucial factor for firms to consider before implementing major strategic shifts, as such changes have the potential to negatively impact its value. To mitigate the risk of reputational erosion, firms may take proactive steps during the planning phase, minimizing associated costs and safeguarding their competitive advantage.

In conclusion, the literature has extensively examined the impact of reputation on corporate strategies and *vice versa*. While a positive reputation can create and

[3] For more details on strategic alliances as determinants of corporate reputation, refer to Sect. 3.2.3.

support opportunities for organizations, a damaged reputation can lead to strategic setbacks. Similarly, although companies' strategies may enhance reputation positively, other actions, whether voluntary or involuntary, may diminish it. Thus, corporate reputation possesses the capacity to yield future benefits, yet it remains subject to fluctuation in value. These characteristics justify considering corporate reputation as an intangible asset. Despite extensive literature referring to reputation as such, accounting standards do not classify corporate reputation within this specific category.

The next section delves deeper into this intricate issue.

2.3 Corporate Reputation as an Intangible Asset

Companies typically possess a combination of tangible and intangible resources, irrespective of their size or industry. However, in the last decade, several studies (e.g. Corrado & Hulten, 2010) have revealed that we are facing a new phase in the evolution of the capitalistic system, where investments in intangibles have overcome those on tangibles.

While some intangible resources, such as patents, copyrights, and other forms of intellectual property, may be explicitly reported on a firm's financial statements, others are more challenging to categorize and assess. Specifically, when evaluating resources, intangible ones are frequently referred to as 'assets'. This term directly pertains to economic elements within a company's holdings that are acknowledged for their capacity to yield future benefits.

Several authors have argued that corporate reputation should be included in the class of intangible assets, as evidence shows that it significantly contributes to firm performance and value creation. This assumption arises from strategic management, accounting and economic studies that are three out of the six fields mentioned in Sect. 2.1 (e.g. Dierickx & Cool, 1989; Hutt, 2016; Toms, 2002; Wilson, 1985).

The category of intangible assets encompasses both tangible resources (e.g. trademarks and patents) that are readily identifiable due to specific legal regulations governing them and resources whose assessment is more uncertain. This uncertainty may arise from factors such as the lack of legal protection or the absence of an objectively defined economic value. This second category of intangible resources refers to all non-monetary, non-physical production conditions whose participation in the production process extends over multiple accounting periods and is not acquired externally, hence lacking a certain cost component.

The international accounting standard IAS 38 defines an 'intangible asset' as an identifiable non-monetary asset without physical substance controlled by an entity as a result of past events, from which future economic benefits are expected to flow to the entity. Furthermore, IAS 38 points out that a resource that meets the definition of an intangible asset should be non-monetary, identifiable, under the control of the firm, and able to produce future economic benefits. More specifically, regarding identifiability, the international standard states that *an asset is identifiable if it either: (a) is separable, i.e. is capable of being separated or divided from the entity and sold, transferred, licensed, rented or exchanged, either individually or together with a related contract, identifiable asset or liability, regardless of whether the entity intends to do so; or (b) arises from contractual or other legal rights, regardless of whether those rights are transferable or separable from the entity or from other rights and obligations* (IAS 38, p. 12). As for controllability, the standards specify that '*an entity controls an asset if the entity has the power to obtain the future economic benefits flowing from the underlying resource and to restrict the access of others to those benefits. The capacity of an entity to control the future economic benefits from an intangible asset would normally stem from legal rights that are enforceable in a court of law. [...]. However, legal enforceability of a right is not a necessary condition for control because an entity may be able to control the future economic benefits in some other way* (IAS 38, p. 13). Finally, according to the standard, *the future economic benefits flowing from an intangible asset may include revenue from the sale of products or services, cost savings, or other benefits resulting from the use of the asset by the entity* (IAS 38, p. 17).

Additionally, intangible assets can be separately acquired, acquired in a business combination, or internally generated. Even if standard rules about recognition criteria apply to all those cases, the IAS 38 admitted that it is sometimes difficult to assess whether an internally generated intangible asset qualifies for recognition. However, to comply with the general rules for the recognition and initial measurement of an intangible asset, an entity must apply the requirements and guidance that IAS 38 defined: first, the firm should determine the cost of the asset generation process to recognize the asset in the balance sheet. Particularly, the cost of an internally generated intangible asset is the sum of expenditure incurred from the date when the intangible asset first meets the recognition criteria listed by the international standard.

These requirements complicate the assessment of corporate reputation as an intangible asset, leading to its omission or underestimation on the balance sheet. In July 2012, the Chairman of the International Accounting Standards Board (IASB), Mr. Hans Hoogervorst, acknowledged this potential issue by stating that *intangible assets often go unrecorded (or under-recorded) on the balance sheet... we know that the [accounting] standard [IAS 38] is rudimentary because it is based on historical cost, which may not reflect the true value of the intangible asset.*

Even though the IASB Chairman did not directly refer to corporate reputation, prior academic research makes it clear that corporate reputation can be considered one of the resources that suffers from this measurement weakness (e.g. Zambon, 2013).

In this regard, scholars have been reflecting on the possibility of including corporate reputation in the challenging category of intangible assets for decades, emphasizing the difficulty of measuring it (Cravens et al., 2003).

Nowadays, it is widely accepted in accounting and management literature that corporate reputation is an intangible asset (Barney, 1991; Ferguson et al., 2000; Fombrun et al., 2000b; Fombrun, 1996; Aqueveque & Ravasi, 2006). Consistent with this perspective, reputation is a socially complex intangible resource that is valuable and non-transferable, where time plays a substantial role in its creation (Mahon, 2002). As such, it has been proven to lead to persistent performance differences (Carmeli & Tishler, 2004; Roberts & Dowling, 2002).

This current view of corporate reputation as an intangible asset is motivated by the idea that it creates value and generates economic benefits for the firm (Barnett & Pollock, 2012; Barney, 1991; Dierickx & Cool, 1989; Fombrun, 1996). This assumption is broadly accepted and generated a broad body of research demonstrating the effect of corporate reputation on performance (see Chapter 4 for more details).

More on this issue, Hall (1993) suggested that reputation could be considered an intangible asset because it shares certain characteristics with them, such as a sense of 'belongingness'. However, unlike intangible assets like trademarks, reputation does not have the same property rights. While reputation can be defended against attacks like libel, it lacks the clear legal protections and definable economic value associated with trademarks.

Fombrun (2005) suggests that reputation has intrinsic economic value because it affects a company's bottom-line performance; thus it can be considered a firm's asset.

Barnett and Pollock (2012) specify that reputation can be classified as an intangible asset based on specific characteristics it has:

6. *Asset specificity*. The authors refer to asset specificity as the extent to which firms vary in their desire to shape the perceptions of specific stakeholders and their willingness to make costly investments to do so. The more firms target a specific group of stakeholders, and the more they focus their investments on signalling information to this stakeholder group, the higher the level of specificity that their reputation assets are likely to have.
7. *Asset accumulation*. The asset accumulation quality refers to the level of accumulation of reputation by a firm within its organizational field. Thus, it characterizes the degree of recognition and attention among diverse groups of stakeholders that interact with each other and with the firm within a given organizational field. In other words, the asset accumulation characteristic is defined by the size of the audience that is focused on a given firm, as well as the relative salience of the firm in the collective attention of the audience. This characteristic has distinct and important value-creating effects (e.g. asset accumulation enhances economic performance through scale effect and facilitates asset growth).
8. *Asset breadth of appeal*. The breadth of appeal is the scale of applicability of the asset that is affected by the heterogeneous perceptions that make up a firm's reputation. A reputational asset has a high degree of attractiveness when the invariable heterogeneous perception that surrounds the firm is anchored in predominantly positive, general opinions, beliefs, and assessments. The generalized nature of favourable perceptions is important in characterizing the value of a firm's reputation as an asset because it requires less investment in reputation maintenance and can be leveraged across a broader variety of situations (e.g. from stakeholders' points of view, generalized reputation reduce monitoring

costs, as generalized beliefs reduce the attention paid to specific occurrences, and predispose observers to integrate current information to fit with pre-existing beliefs).

9. *Asset codification.* Authors refer to asset codification as the designation of a position in a reputational ranking. The asset codification characteristics give the reputation a social facticity that increases stakeholder reliance on it in decision-making. The ranking is essentially a socially constructed cognitive shortcuts that allow the assessment and discussion of reputation by firms and stakeholders (e.g. being a 'Big Four' accounting firm immediately indicates the relative standing of the organization to its stakeholders, with consequent implications for its economic exchange with it).

In conclusion, while scholars emphasize the importance of considering corporate reputation as an intangible asset and recognizing its value (Barnett & Pollock, 2012; Fombrun, 1996), others highlight its lack of clear and distinct attributes compared to other intangible assets (Cravens et al., 2003). This discrepancy makes it challenging to include reputation in financial statements or assign a specific monetary value to it for accounting purposes. Zambon (2013) and Girella and Zambon (2014) refer to this challenge as the 'intangibles problem,' suggesting that it extends beyond accounting concerns.

2.4 Key Concepts of Corporate Reputation

In summary, the concept of corporate reputation, while often approached from distinct disciplinary perspectives, has been combined into a multifaceted construct recognized across strategic, relational, and cognitive dimensions. Initially framed as an asset for competitive differentiation, reputation was seen primarily through the lens of strategic management, where it served as an intangible barrier against rivals and a symbol of competitive advantage. As research evolved through the relational and integrative phases, reputation began to encompass the aggregated perceptions of stakeholders who assess an organization based on its symbolic and social standing. This broader view highlights that reputation is not static or unidirectional but rather a social construction, dynamically shaped by the interactions and judgements of various stakeholder groups. By embodying both an internal identity marker and an external judgement of organizational legitimacy, reputation has developed into an invaluable asset that is deeply integrated with the operational and social practices of firms.

Throughout its evolution, reputation has consistently demonstrated several core features. Specifically, it is:

- *Socially constructed.* Reputation arises from stakeholder perceptions rather than from objective, quantifiable metrics, making it inherently intangible.

- *Historically rooted.* As an 'accumulated asset,' reputation builds over time based on an organization's past actions, providing a historical narrative that informs stakeholders' current and future judgements.
- *Strategically valuable.* It acts as a durable competitive asset that is challenging to replicate, contributing to long-term performance and providing a strategic advantage through stakeholder trust, loyalty, and legitimization.
- *Stakeholder sensitive.* Reputation is highly responsive to the diverse expectations, interests, and values of different stakeholder groups, resulting in varying perceptions and judgements that potentially generate differing valuations of corporate reputation based on specific audiences.
- *Contextually sensitive.* Reputation is contingent on context, meaning that the same actions or attributes may be viewed differently across varying cultural, economic, and institutional settings.
- *Multidimensional and dynamic.* Comprising both cognitive elements (recognition, awareness) and affective components (trust, admiration), reputation adapts as stakeholder expectations evolve and as organizations respond to social and economic pressures.

In recent years, reputation has solidified its role as a dynamic, multi-stakeholder evaluation that serves not only as a gauge of trustworthiness but also as a resource for navigating complex social and market landscapes. This integrative view reflects cumulative insights from strategic, organizational, economic, and sociological perspectives, each contributing to a holistic understanding of reputation.

Corporate reputation today, therefore, can be described as:

1. *A perception-based construct.* Corporate reputation relies on subjective stakeholder evaluations rather than concrete financial metrics, situating it within a relational and interpretive framework.
2. *A strategic asset.* It represents an enduring competitive advantage, as it is resistant to replication and enhances organizational stability and stakeholder willingness to be engaged with the company.
3. *A relationally derived resource.* It is an outcome of continuous interactions and communications with stakeholders, reinforcing or reshaping their perceptions over time.
4. *An indicator of legitimacy.* Corporate reputation serves as a 'license to operate', signifying an organization's alignment with stakeholder expectations, which is essential for engaging with them.

To conclude, both scholars and companies recognize the strategic importance of corporate reputation assets for driving corporate growth, influencing consumer behaviour, enhancing brand loyalty, fostering investor confidence, and ultimately ensuring overall business success (Zambon, 2013). However, the strategic role of reputation, when considered alongside the complexity of its construct, necessitates that companies focus on implementing effective reputation management processes. Only a reputation management strategy that fosters positive perceptions and mitigates negative ones can yield beneficial outcomes associated with corporate reputation.

In this light, the next chapter examines the processes involved in corporate reputation management, aiming to highlight the factors that can enhance reputational capital as well as those that can diminish it.

References

Allen, F. (1984). Reputation and product quality. *RAND Journal of Economics, 15*(3), 311–327.

Ambrosini, V., & Bowman, C. (2009). What are dynamic capabilities and are they a useful construct in strategic management? *International Journal of Management Reviews, 11*(1), 29–49. https://doi.org/10.1111/j.1468-2370.2008.00251.x

Aqueveque, C. (2005). Signaling corporate values: Consumers' suspicious minds. *Corporate Governance: The International Journal of Business in Society, 5*(3), 70–81.

Aqueveque, C., & Ravasi, D. (2006). Corporate reputation, affect, and trustworthiness: An explanation for the reputation-performance relationship. In *10th Annual Corporate Reputation Institute Conference, New York, NY*. http://www.repman.com.tr/tr/wp-content/uploads/user/makaleler/corporate-reputation-affect-and-trustworthiness.pdf

Baldarelli, M.-G., & Gigli, S. (2014). Exploring the drivers of corporate reputation integrated with a corporate responsibility perspective: Some reflections in theory and in praxis. *Journal of Management and Governance, 18*(2), 589–613. https://doi.org/10.1007/s10997-011-9192-3

Balvers, R. J., McDonald, B., & Miller, R. E. (1988). Underpricing of new issues and the choice of auditor as a signal of investment banker reputation. *The Accounting Review, 63*(4), 605–622.

Barnett, M. L., & Pollock, T. G. (2012). *The Oxford handbook of corporate reputation*. OUP.

Barnett, M. L., Jermier, J. M., & Lafferty, B. A. (2006). Corporate reputation: The definitional landscape. *Corporate Reputation Review, 9*(1), 26–38. Scopus. https://doi.org/10.1057/palgrave.crr.1550012

Barney, J. (1991). Firm resources and sustained competitive advantage. *Journal of Management, 17*(1), 99–120. https://doi.org/10.1177/014920639101700108

Beatty, R. P. (1989). Auditor reputation and the pricing of initial public offerings. *The Accounting Review, 64*(4), 693–709.

Berens, G., & van Riel, C. B. M. (2004). Corporate associations in the academic literature: Three main streams of thought in the reputation measurement literature. *Corporate Reputation Review, 7*(2), 161–178. https://doi.org/10.1057/palgrave.crr.1540218

Bertini, U. (1990). *Il sistema d'azienda. Schema di analisi (I)*. G. Giappichelli Editore.

Bianchi Martini, S. (2009). *Introduzione all'analisi strategica dell'azienda (I)*. G. Giappichelli Editore.

Bigus, J., Hua, K. P. M., & Raithel, S. (2024). Definitions and measures of corporate reputation in accounting and management: Commonalities, differences, and future research. *Accounting and Business Research, 54*(3), 304–336. https://doi.org/10.1080/00014788.2022.2149458

Boateng, H., & Okoe, A. F. (2015). Consumers' attitude towards social media advertising and their behavioural response: The moderating role of corporate reputation. *Journal of Research in Interactive Marketing, 9*(4), 299–312. https://doi.org/10.1108/JRIM-01-2015-0012

Brammer, S., & Pavelin, S. (2004). Building a good reputation. *European Management Journal, 22*(6), 704–713. https://doi.org/10.1016/j.emj.2004.09.033

Brooks, M. E., Highhouse, S., Russell, S. S., & Mohr, D. C. (2003). Familiarity, ambivalence, and firm reputation: Is corporate fame a double-edged sword? *The Journal of Applied Psychology, 88*(5), 904–914. https://doi.org/10.1037/0021-9010.88.5.904

Brouthers, K. D. (2013). Institutional, cultural and transaction cost influences on entry mode choice and performance. *Journal of International Business Studies, 44*(1), 1–13.

Brucato, P. F., Jr., & Smith, D. M. (1997). An analysis of the role of firm reputation in the market's reaction to corporate dividends. *Quarterly Review of Economics and Finance, 37*(3), 647–665. Scopus. https://doi.org/10.1016/s1062-9769(97)90015-6

Bruni, M., & Garzoni, A. (1999). *Risorse e competenze aziendali nella sostenibilità del vantaggio competitivo*. EGEA.
Cable, D. M., & Turban, D. B. (2003). The value of organizational reputation in the recruitment context: A brand-equity perspective. *Journal of Applied Social Psychology, 33*(11), 2244–2266. https://doi.org/10.1111/j.1559-1816.2003.tb01883.x
Cao, Y., Myers, L., & Omer, T. (2012). Does company reputation matter for financial reporting quality? Evidence from restatements. *Contemporary Accounting Research, 29*(3), 956-+. https://doi.org/10.1111/j.1911-3846.2011.01137.x
Cappelli, P. (2001). Making the most of on-line recruiting. *Harvard Business Review, 79*, 139–146, 166.
Carmeli, A., & Tishler, A. (2004). The relationships between intangible organizational elements and organizational performance. *Strategic Management Journal, 25*(13), 1257–1278. Scopus. https://doi.org/10.1002/smj.428
Catino, M. (2010). Gatekeepers miopi? Aspetti organizzativi nel fallimento dei controlli.
Caves, R. E., & Porter, M. E. (1977). From entry barriers to mobility barriers: Conjectural decisions and contrived deterrence to new competition. *The Quarterly Journal of Economics, 91*(2), 241–261. https://doi.org/10.2307/1885416
Chun, R., Silva, R. D., Davies, G., & Roper, S. (2002). *Corporate reputation and competitiveness*. Routledge. https://doi.org/10.4324/9780203218112
Corrado, C. A., & Hulten, C. R. (2010). How do you measure a "technological revolution"? *American Economic Review, 100*(2), 99–104. https://doi.org/10.1257/aer.100.2.99
Cravens, K. S., & Oliver, E. G. (2006). Employees: The key link to corporate reputation management. *Business Horizons, 49*(4), 293–302. https://doi.org/10.1016/j.bushor.2005.10.006
Cravens, K., Goad Oliver, E., & Ramamoorti, S. (2003). The reputation index: Measuring and managing corporate reputation. *European Management Journal, 21*(2), 201–212. https://doi.org/10.1016/S0263-2373(03)00015-X
Crossland, C., & Hambrick, D. C. (2011). Differences in managerial discretion across countries: How nation-level institutions affect the degree to which CEOs matter. *Strategic Management Journal, 32*(8), 797–819. https://doi.org/10.1002/smj.913
Daft, R. L. (1983). Learning the craft of organizational research. *The Academy of Management Review, 8*(4), 539–546. https://doi.org/10.2307/258255
Deephouse, D. L. (1997). Part IV: How do reputations affect corporate performance?: The effect of financial and media reputations on performance. *Corporate Reputation Review, 1*(1), 68–72. https://doi.org/10.1057/palgrave.crr.1540019
Deephouse, D. L. (2000). Media reputation as a strategic resource: An integration of mass communication and resource-based theories. *Journal of Management, 26*(60), 1091–1112.
Deephouse, D. L., Newburry, W., & Soleimani, A. (2016). The effects of institutional development and national culture on crossnational differences in corporate reputation. *Journal of World Business, 51*(3), 463–473. https://doi.org/10.1016/j.jwb.2015.12.005
Dierickx, I., & Cool, K. (1989). Asset stock accumulation and sustainability of competitive advantage. *Management Science, 35*(12), 1504–1511.
DiMaggio, P. J., & Powell, W. W. (1983). The iron cage revisted: Institutional isomorphism and collective rationality in organizational fields. *American Sociological Review, 48*, 147–160. https://doi.org/10.17323/1726-3247-2010-1-34-56
Dowling, G. (2006). How good corporate reputations create corporate value. *Corporate Reputation Review, 9*(2), 134–143. https://doi.org/10.1057/palgrave.crr.1550017
Dowling, G. R. (2016). Defining and measuring corporate reputations. *European Management Review, 13*(3), 207–223. https://doi.org/10.1111/emre.12081
Esenyel, V. (2020). Corporate reputation as a strategic management tool: Through the lens of employees. *International Journal of Management and Sustainability, 9*(1), 24–42. Scopus. https://doi.org/10.18488/journal.11.2020.91.24.42
Fasaei, H., Jansen, J. J. P., & Tempelaar, M. P. (2014). The inertial effect of good corporate reputation on exploration-exploitation interplay. *Academy of Management Proceedings, 2014*(1), 11563. https://doi.org/10.5465/ambpp.2014.11563abstract
Fattore, G. (2005). *Metodi di ricerca in economia aziendale*. EGEA.

Ferguson, T. D., Deephouse, D. L., & Ferguson, W. L. (2000). Do strategic groups differ in reputation? *Strategic Management Journal, 21*(12), 1195–1214. Scopus. https://doi.org/10.1002/1097-0266(200012)21:12<1195::AID-SMJ138>3.0.CO;2-R

Ferraris Franceschi, R. F. (1978). *L'indagine metodologica in economia aziendale*. Giuffrè.

Fishman, C. (1998). The war of talent. *Fast Company, 16*(104).

Fombrun, C. J. (1996). *Reputation: Realizing value from the corporate image*. Harvard Business School Press.

Fombrun, C. J. (2005). A world of reputation research, analysis and thinking—Building corporate reputation through CSR initiatives: Evolving standards. *Corporate Reputation Review, 8*(1), 7–12. https://doi.org/10.1057/palgrave.crr.1540235

Fombrun, C., & Shanley, M. (1990). What's in a name? Reputation building and corporate strategy. *Academy of Management Journal, 33*, 233–258. https://doi.org/10.2307/256324

Fombrun, C., & van Riel, C. (1997). The reputational landscape. *Corporate Reputation Review, 1*(2), 5–13. https://doi.org/10.1057/palgrave.crr.1540024

Fombrun, C. J., Gardberg, N. A., & Barnett, M. L. (2000a). Opportunity platforms and safety nets: Corporate citizenship and reputational risk. *Business and Society Review, 105*(1), 85–106. https://doi.org/10.1111/0045-3609.00066

Fombrun, C. J., Gardberg, N. A., & Sever, J. M. (2000b). The Reputation QuotientSM: A multi-stakeholder measure of corporate reputation. *Journal of Brand Management, 7*(4), 241–255. https://doi.org/10.1057/bm.2000.10

Francesconi, A., & Dossena, C. (2009). L'IT per l'analisi e la gestione della web corporate reputation. Un caso aziendale. In *10o Workshop di Organizzazione Aziendale "Per lo sviluppo, la competitività e l'innovazione del sistema economico: il contributo degli studi in organizzazione aziendale"*, Cagliari.

Frare, A. B., & Beuren, I. M. (2021). Effects of corporate reputation and social identity on innovative job performance. *European Journal of Innovation Management, 25*(5), 1409–1427. https://doi.org/10.1108/EJIM-02-2021-0071

Galbreath, J. (2005). Which resources matter the most to firm success? An exploratory study of resource-based theory. *Technovation, 25*(9), 979–987. https://doi.org/10.1016/j.technovation.2004.02.008

Galeotti, M., & Garzella, S. (2013). *Governo strategico dell'azienda (I)*. G. Giappichelli Editore.

Gatzert, N. (2015). The impact of corporate reputation and reputation damaging events on financial performance: Empirical evidence from the literature. *European Management Journal, 33*(6), 485–499. Scopus. https://doi.org/10.1016/j.emj.2015.10.001

Gazzola, P. (2006). CSR e reputazione nella creazione di valore sostenibile. EconomiaAziendale 2000 web, 2. https://doi.org/10.13132/2038-5498/2006.2.27-45

Girella, L., & Zambon, S. (2014). Varieties of capitalism vs. varieties of "soft regulatory" theories: A discussion on the case of intangibles reporting in Japan and Germany. In *Intellectual capital in organizations*. Routledge.

Goldberg, A. I., Cohen, G., & Fiegenbaum, A. (2003). Reputation building: Small business strategies for successful venture development. *Journal of Small Business Management, 41*(2), 168–186. https://doi.org/10.1111/1540-627X.00074

Gotsi, M., & Wilson, A. M. (2001). Corporate reputation: Seeking a definition. *Corporate Communications: An International Journal, 6*(1), 24–30. Scopus. https://doi.org/10.1108/13563280110381189

Grant, R. M. (1991). The resource-based theory of competitive advantage: Implications for strategy formulation. *California Management Review, 33*(3), 114–135. https://doi.org/10.2307/41166664

Hall, R. (1993). A framework linking intangible resources and capabiliites to sustainable competitive advantage. *Strategic Management Journal, 14*(8), 607–618. https://doi.org/10.1002/smj.4250140804

Harris, F., & de Chernatony, L. (2001). Corporate branding and corporate brand performance. *European Journal of Marketing, 35*(3/4), 441–456. https://doi.org/10.1108/03090560110382101

Helm, S. (2011). Employees' awareness of their impact on corporate reputation. *Journal of Business Research, 64*(7), 657–663. https://doi.org/10.1016/j.jbusres.2010.09.001

Hiss, S. (2009). From implicit to explicit corporate social responsibility: Institutional change as a fight for myths. *Business Ethics Quarterly, 19*(3), 433–451.
Hosmer, L. T. (1995). Trust: The connecting link between organizational theory and philosophical ethics. *Academy of Management Review, 20*(2), 379–403. https://doi.org/10.5465/amr.1995.9507312923
Husted, B. W. (1989). Trust in business relations: Directions for empirical research. *Business and Professional Ethics Journal, 8*(2), 23–40. https://doi.org/10.5840/bpej1989827
Hutt, R. W. (2016). Reputation on the line: The Starbucks cases. *Journal of Business Strategy, 37*(1), 19–26. https://doi.org/10.1108/JBS-11-2014-0134
Kamasak, R. (2017). The contribution of tangible and intangible resources, and capabilities to a firm's profitability and market performance. *European Journal of Management and Business Economics, 26*(2), 252–275. https://doi.org/10.1108/EJMBE-07-2017-015
Kotb, A., Halabi, H., & Elbardan, H. (2018). The auditor-to-client revolving door: A structured literature review. *International Journal of Auditing, 22*(3), 464–485. https://doi.org/10.1111/ijau.12132
Koys, D. J. (1997). Human resource management and fortune's corporate reputation survey. *Employee Responsibilities and Rights Journal, 10*(2), 93–101. https://doi.org/10.1023/A:1025632711742
Lamboglia, R. (2018). La corporate social responsibility e la reputazione aziendale: Le principali relazioni. In *L'azienda e la corporate social responsibility. Approfondimenti dottrinali e riflessioni gestionali* (pp. 43–64). Franco Angeli. https://ricerca.uniparthenope.it/handle/11367/71363
Lange, D., Lee, P. M., & Dai, Y. (2011). Organizational reputation: A review. *Journal of Management, 37*(1), 153–184. Scopus. https://doi.org/10.1177/0149206310390963
Learned, E. P., Christensen, C. R., Andrews, K. R., & Guth, W. D. (1969). *Business policy: Text and cases*. Richard D. Irwin, Incorporated.
Love, E. G., & Kraatz, M. (2009). Character, conformity, or the bottom line? How and why downsizing affected corporate reputation. *Academy of Management Journal, 52*(2), 314–335. https://doi.org/10.5465/AMJ.2009.37308247
Mahon, J. (2002). Corporate reputation: Research agenda using strategy and stakeholder literature. *Business & Society, 41*,415–445. https://doi.org/10.1177/0007650302238776
Markwick, N., & Fill, C. (1997). Towards a framework for managing corporate identity. *European Journal of Marketing, 31*(5–6), 396–409. Scopus. https://doi.org/10.1108/eb060639
Maxwell, R., & Knox, S. (2009). Motivating employees to "live the brand": A comparative case study of employer brand attractiveness within the firm. *Journal of Marketing Management, 25*(9–10), 893–907. https://doi.org/10.1362/026725709X479282
Melo, T., & Garrido-Morgado, A. (2012). Corporate reputation: A combination of social responsibility and industry. *Corporate Social Responsibility and Environmental Management, 19*(1), 11–31. https://doi.org/10.1002/csr.260
Milgrom, P., & Roberts, J. (1982). Limit pricing and entry under incomplete information: An equilibrium analysis. *Econometrica, 50*(2), 443–459. https://doi.org/10.2307/1912637
Moizer, P. (1997). Auditor reputation: The international empirical evidence. *International Journal of Auditing, 1*(1), 61–74. https://doi.org/10.1111/1099-1123.00013
Money, K., Saraeva, A., Garnelo-Gomez, I., Pain, S., & Hillenbrand, C. (2017). Corporate reputation past and future: A review and integration of existing literature and a framework for future research. *Corporate Reputation Review, 20*(3/4), 193–211. https://doi.org/10.1057/s41299-017-0034-3
Mutti, A. (2008). *Finanza sregolata?* Le dimensioni sociali dei mercati finanziari. https://www.mulino.it/isbn/9788815128324?forcedLocale=itandfbrefresh=CAN_BE_ANYTHING
Nell, P. C., Puck, J., & Heidenreich, S. (2015). Strictly limited choice or agency? Institutional duality, legitimacy, and subsidiaries' political strategies. *Journal of World Business, 50*(2), 302–311. https://doi.org/10.1016/j.jwb.2014.10.007
Odriozola, M. D., & Baraibar-Diez, E. (2017). Is corporate reputation associated with quality of CSR reporting? Evidence from Spain. *Corporate Social Responsibility and Environmental Management, 24*(2), 121–132. https://doi.org/10.1002/csr.1399

Peng, M. W., Wang, D. Y. L., & Jiang, Y. (2008). An institution-based view of international business strategy: A focus on emerging economies. *Journal of International Business Studies, 39*(5), 920–936. https://doi.org/10.1057/palgrave.jibs.8400377

Peteraf, M. A. (1993). The cornerstones of competitive advantage: A resource-based view. *Strategic Management Journal, 14*(3), 179–191. https://doi.org/10.1002/smj.4250140303

Petrick, J. A., Scherer, R. F., Brodzinski, J. D., Quinn, J. F., & Ainina, M. F. (1999). Global leadership skills and reputational capital: Intangible resources for sustainable competitive advantage. *Academy of Management Perspectives, 13*(1), 58–69. https://doi.org/10.5465/ame.1999.1567322

Pfarrer, M. D., Pollock, T. G., & Rindova, V. P. (2010). A tale of two assets: The effects of firm reputation and celebrity on earnings surprises and investors' reactions. *Academy of Management Journal, 53*(5), 1131–1152. https://doi.org/10.5465/amj.2010.54533222

Podnar, K., Tuškej, U., & Golob, U. (2012). Mapping semantic meaning of corporate reputation in global economic crisis context: A Slovenian study. *Public Relations Review, 38*(5), 906–915. https://doi.org/10.1016/j.pubrev.2012.08.003

Porter, M. E. (1981). The contributions of industrial organization to strategic management. *The Academy of Management Review, 6*(4), 609–620. https://doi.org/10.2307/257639

Porter, M. E. (1985). *Competitive advantage of nations: Creating and sustaining superior performance*. The Free Press.

Ravasi, D., Rindova, V., Etter, M., & Cornelissen, J. (2018). The formation of organizational reputation. *Academy of Management Annals, 12*(2), 574–599. https://doi.org/10.5465/annals.2016.0124

Rindova, V. P., Williamson, I. O., Petkova, A. P., & Sever, J. M. (2005). Being good or being known: An empirical examination of the dimensions, antecedents, and consequences of organizational reputation. *Academy of Management Journal, 48*(6), 1033–1049. https://doi.org/10.5465/AMJ.2005.19573108

Roberts, P. W., & Dowling, G. R. (2002). Corporate reputation and sustained superior financial performance. *Strategic Management Journal, 23*(12), 1077–1093. https://doi.org/10.1002/smj.274

Romenti, S. (2008). Corporate governance e reputazione: Dallo stakeholder relationship management allo stakeholder engagement, 2.

Rose, C., & Thomsen, S. (2004). The impact of corporate reputation on performance: Some Danish evidence. *European Management Journal, 22*, 201–210. https://doi.org/10.1016/j.emj.2004.01.012

Rumelt, R. P. (2005). Theory, strategy, and entrepreneurship. In S. A. Alvarez, R. Agarwal, & O. Sorenson (A c. Di), Handbook of Entrepreneurship Research: Interdisciplinary Perspectives (pp. 11–32). Springer US. https://doi.org/10.1007/0-387-23622-8_2

Sánchez, J. L. F., & Sotorrío, L. L. (2007). The creation of value through corporate reputation. *Journal of Business Ethics, 76*(3), 335–346. https://doi.org/10.1007/s10551-006-9285-0

Schmalensee, R. (1982). Product differentiation advantages of pioneering brands. *The American Economic Review, 72*(3), 349–365.

Scipioni, S. (2021). Circular Corporate Reputation nelle piccole e medie imprese: Il caso di una good practice italiana. In P. Ferretti (Ed.), *La Corporate Reputation. Alcuni driver di sviluppo*. G. Giappichelli Editore.

Shamsie, J. (2003). The context of dominance: An industry-driven framework for exploiting reputation. *Strategic Management Journal, 24*, 199–215. https://doi.org/10.1002/smj.291

Shapiro, C. (1982). Consumer information, product quality, and seller reputation. *The Bell Journal of Economics, 13*(1), 20. https://doi.org/10.2307/3003427

Shapiro, S. P. (1987). The social control of impersonal trust. *American Journal of Sociology, 93*(3), 623–658. https://doi.org/10.1086/228791

Sivertzen, A.-M., Nilsen, E. R., & Olafsen, A. H. (2013). Employer branding: Employer attractiveness and the use of social media. *Journal of Product and Brand Management, 22*(7), 473–483. https://doi.org/10.1108/JPBM-09-2013-0393

Tetrault Sirsly, C.-A., & Lamertz, K. (2008). When does a corporate social responsibility initiative provide a first-mover advantage? *Business and Society, 47*(3), 343–369. https://doi.org/10.1177/0007650307299221

Toms, J. S. (2002). Firm resources, quality signals and the determinants of corporate environmental reputation: Some UK evidence. *The British Accounting Review, 34*(3), 257–282. https://doi.org/10.1006/bare.2002.0211

Tranfield, D., Denyer, D., & Smart, P. (2003). Towards a methodology for developing evidence-informed management knowledge by means of systematic review. *British Journal of Management, 14*(3), 207–222. https://doi.org/10.1111/1467-8551.00375

Turban, D. B. (2001). Organizational attractiveness as an employer on college campuses: An examination of the applicant population. *Journal of Vocational Behavior, 58*(2), 293–312. https://doi.org/10.1006/jvbe.2000.1765

Türetken, O., Jethefer, S., & Ozkan, B. (2020). Internal audit effectiveness: Operationalization and influencing factors. *Managerial Auditing Journal., 35*(2), 238–271. https://doi.org/10.1108/MAJ-08-2018-1980

van Riel, C. B. M. (1997). Research in corporate communication: An overview of an emerging field. *Management Communication Quarterly, 11*(2), 288–309. https://doi.org/10.1177/0893318997112005

Veh, A., Göbel, M., & Vogel, R. (2019). Corporate reputation in management research: A review of the literature and assessment of the concept. *Business Research, 12*, 315–353. https://doi.org/10.1007/s40685-018-0080-4

von Berlepsch, D., Lemke, F., & Gorton, M. (2024). The importance of corporate reputation for sustainable supply chains: A systematic literature review, bibliometric mapping, and research agenda. *Journal of Business Ethics, 189*, 9–34. https://doi.org/10.1007/s10551-022-05268-x

Voswinkel, S. (2011). Reputation: A sociological view. In S. Helm, K. Liehr-Gobbers, & C. Storck (Eds.), *Reputation management* (pp. 31–45). Springer. https://doi.org/10.1007/978-3-642-19266-1_5

Walker, K. (2010). A systematic review of the corporate reputation literature: Definition, measurement, and theory. *Corporate Reputation Review, 12*(4), 357–387. https://doi.org/10.1057/crr.2009.26

Walsh, G., Mitchell, V.-W., Jackson, P. R., & Beatty, S. E. (2009). Examining the antecedents and consequences of corporate reputation: A customer perspective. *British Journal of Management, 20*(2), 187–203. https://doi.org/10.1111/j.1467-8551.2007.00557.x

Weigelt, K., & Camerer, C. (1988). Reputation and corporate strategy: A review of recent theory and applications. *Strategic Management Journal, 9*(5), 443–454.

Weiss, A. M., Anderson, E., & MacInnis, D. J. (1999). Reputation management as a motivation for sales structure decisions. *Journal of Marketing, 63*(4), 74–89. https://doi.org/10.2307/1251975

Williams, R. J., Schnake, M. E., & Fredenberger, W. (2005). The impact of corporate strategy on a firm's reputation. *Corporate Reputation Review, 8*(3), 187–197. Scopus. https://doi.org/10.1057/palgrave.crr.1540249

Wilson, R. (1985). Reputations in games and markets. In A. E. Roth (Ed.), *Game-theoretic models of bargaining* (pp. 27–62). Cambridge University Press.

Yang, S.-U. (2007). An integrated model for organization—Public relational outcomes, organizational reputation, and their antecedents. *Journal of Public Relations Research, 19*, 91–121. https://doi.org/10.1080/10627260701290612

Zambon, S. (2013). Research forum on "intangibles". *Financial Reporting, 3*, 13–17. https://doi.org/10.3280/FR2013-003002

Zyglidopoulos, S., & Phillips, N. (1999). Responding to reputational crises: A stakeholder perspective. *Corporate Reputation Review, 2*(4), 333–350. https://doi.org/10.1057/palgrave.crr.1540090

Chapter 3
Corporate Reputation Management Process

It takes 20 years to build a reputation and five minutes to ruin it.

[Warren Buffet, Co-founder, Chairman and CEO of Berkshire Hathaway]

3.1 Corporate Reputation Management Framework

Starting from the early stage of the development of literature on corporate reputation, accounting studies introduce the concept of reputational capital to underline the similarities of the concept's attributes to those of a company's traditional assets (e.g. Beatty, 1989; Petrick et al., 1999). Chapter 2 points out that, in some cases, literature considers corporate reputation and reputation capital as synonymous concepts. In other cases, scholars suggest that the first acts like an antecedent of the latter (e.g. Lamboglia, 2018).[1] However, both views assume that corporate reputation represents one of the rarest and most difficult to imitate competitive resources (Barney, 1991; Dierickx & Cool, 1989). They consider reputation as an intangible asset whose value is intricately linked to stakeholders' perception, evaluation, and trust in a company (Weigelt & Camerer, 1988; Fombrun & van Riel, 1997). Moreover, both views indicate that corporate reputation implicitly promises improved performance and significantly contributes to the creation of value for stakeholders (Fombrun, 1996; Fombrun & van Riel, 1997, 2004; Weiss et al., 1999; Bennett & Kottasz, 2000; Mahon & Wartick, 2003).

Based on the resource-based view theory, studies recognized that corporate reputation possessed all the VRIN criteria that makes it strategic to gain and sustain the competitive advantage of a firm (see Sect. 2.2 for more details). Specifically, the rareness and the imperfect imitability attributes seem to be strictly related to the

[1] In this work we use the terms 'corporate reputation' and 'reputational capital' interchangeably.

D. Vito, *Corporate Reputation as Strategic Intangible Asset*, SIDREA Series in Accounting and Business Administration,
https://doi.org/10.1007/978-3-031-93331-8_3

specific nature of the construct. As Sect. 2.1 emphasizes, literature considers corporate reputation as a multidimensional construct (e.g. Moizer, 1997), which is determined by a complex mix of factors that cannot be perfectly identified as they depend on the firm's past and present activities and behaviours, signals intentionally or unintentionally sent to stakeholders, industry context, actions of rivals, external events, and many other potentially and unobservable elements (Basdeo et al., 2006). These elements are defined determinants of corporate reputation, shaping it through a highly firm-specific mix that may vary over time. This variation contributes to strengthening the imperfect imitability of corporate reputation. In some cases, these determinants originate from actions that the company intentionally undertakes to bolster corporate reputation. Literature across various fields of research (e.g. strategic management, accounting, marketing) emphasizes the relevance of corporate communication (e.g. Francesconi & Dossena, 2009; Romenti, 2008; van Riel & Fombrun, 2007) and corporate reporting (e.g. Allegrini, 2003; Coda, 1991; Corvi, 1997; Di Stefano, 1990; Michelon, 2011; Quagli, 2008) as 'signal' that firms send to stakeholders with the aims of influencing their perceptions. In other cases, determinants may originate from actions that do not directly aim to build corporate reputation. For example, the literature includes in this latter group the firm's performance and market actions (Basdeo et al., 2006), product and process innovation activities (Basir, 2020), or employee behaviours (Helm, 2011).

Just like any firm's intangible assets, the reputational capital can be internally generated or externally acquired (IAS 38). In this regard, firms may invest in strategic alliances or merger and acquisition operations to improve their reputation by 'acquiring' that of the partner (Gibbs & Humphries, 2009).

As corporate reputation building and acquisition contribute to enhancing the value of reputational capital, it's important to acknowledge that other factors may have a negative impact. For instance, the occurrence of events, internal or external to the organization, may lead to a deterioration of stakeholders' opinions about the company, thus lowering its reputational capital (Lamboglia & D'Onza, 2014). In some cases, firms may proactively adopt actions to lower the risk of reputation damage (i.e. reputation risk management); in other cases they can just define activities and strategies to repair reputation damage (i.e. crisis management).

The framework in Fig. 3.1 summarizes these assumptions.

It indicates that reputational capital is a 'stock' variable, which is enhanced and diminished through temporal 'flow' sequences (Love & Kraatz, 2009) varying its value over time. Thus, as suggested by Lamboglia (2018), companies must effectively manage corporate reputation through a designed, formalized, and shared strategy to create reputational capital over time and protect it from risks that may erode it. By undertaking a series of actions aimed at achieving the goal of creating and safeguarding the corporate reputation, a firm develops a process that can be termed the *corporate reputation management process* (see Sect. 4.1 for more details on the definition of corporate reputation management as a process).

The following Sects. 3.2 and 3.3 examine the elements included in the proposed framework. Specifically, Sect. 3.2 focuses on the analysis of actions that allow companies to enhance the value of their reputational capital (i.e. positive flows), while

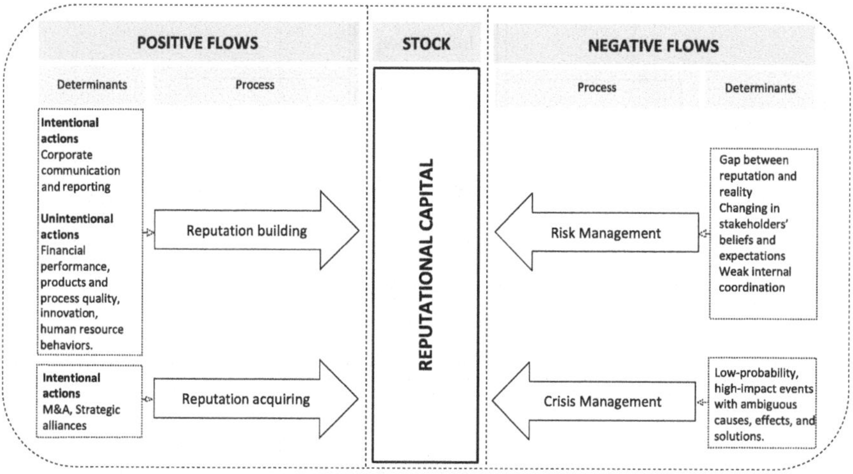

Fig. 3.1 Corporate reputation management framework. Source: author's elaboration

Sect. 3.3 investigates elements and events that may provoke a loss of reputational capital (i.e. negative flows).

3.2 Creating and Acquiring the Reputational Capital

3.2.1 Creating Reputational Capital Through Intentional Action

Corporate Communication in Reputation Building

The building of corporate reputation is intricately tied to a competitive process wherein companies actively communicate their key characteristics to various stakeholders (Fombrun & Shanley, 1990). Dowling (2006) was one of the first scholars to posit that companies should use communication to complement their reputation-building efforts. He suggested that the role of corporate communication is to explain the behaviour of a company in terms of its mission and morality and in this way create an emotional bond with key stakeholders that will help to foster their trust and support. Greater trust and support will help stakeholders to better appreciate the company's activities and behaviours.

Traditionally, corporate communication can be controlled and regulated both when directed internally and especially when directed outside the boundaries of the company. It effectively represents how the firm can address its various stakeholders with information and resource requests, thereby influencing their perceptions and attitudes towards it. From the firm's point of view, corporate communication is one of the key elements of strategic management (Coda, 1991). It aids in resource

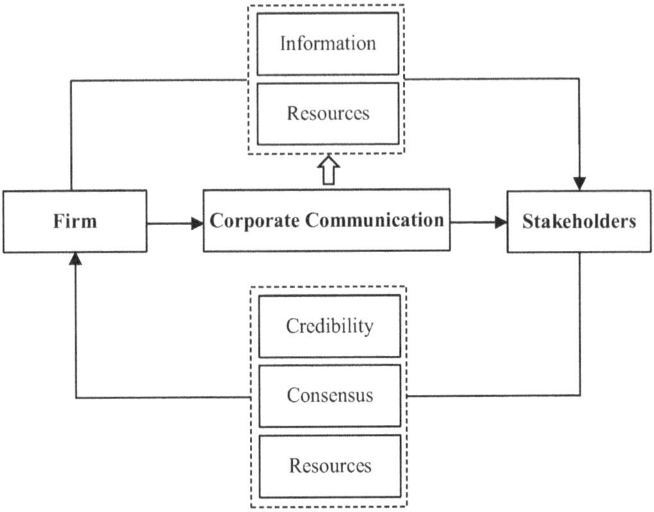

Fig. 3.2 Communication process: from firm to stakeholders and from stakeholders to firm. Source: adapted from Giacosa (2012)

acquisition by attracting valuable human and financial resources and enhancing customer loyalty, thus positively impacting the firm's value. From the stakeholder's point of view, corporate communication is valuable for extracting insights into the company's capabilities, credibility, strategic attributes, and ability to deliver value (Basdeo et al., 2006; Clark & Montgomery, 1998; Rindova & Fombrun, 1999).

As illustrated in Fig. 3.2, communication can be understood as an interactive, bidirectional, and cyclical process. This process involves the transmission of informational flows between the firm and its stakeholders (Shannon & Weaver, 1971). Through corporate communication, the firm delivers information and resources to stakeholders to mitigate information asymmetry and enhance their decision-making processes. In return, stakeholders provide the firm with credibility, consensus, and resources. Moreover, stakeholders' responses influence the nature and volume of information disseminated by the firm, as it tailors its information flows according to stakeholder preferences and evolving perceptions, thereby perpetuating the cycle.

Specifically, firms investing in corporate communication generally have three main aims: (1) enhancing corporate credibility (Coda, 1991), (2) fostering trust (Gulati & Wohlgezogen, 2023), and (3) building consensus among stakeholders (Reilly & Di Angelo, 1990; Salvioni, 2003). By doing so, firms may succeed in promoting strong connections with stakeholders and facilitating the acquisition of resources, thus contributing to achieving sustainable success (Salvioni, 2002; Bertinetti, 1996).

The relevance of corporate communication is strictly related to the stakeholder's need for information regarding the company's actions and behaviours. An improved information flow allows stakeholders to better evaluate the company's credibility and the opportunity to create or maintain relationships with it. In this regard,

Giannessi (1960), Bandettini (1978), and Marchi and Mancini (1999) concur in assuming that stakeholders require a proper evaluation of circumstances and an unbiased formulation of judgements, not distorted by a lack of information, to engage in a decision-making process aimed at building relationships with an organization. The communication process aims to address this potential lack of information by conveying not only the actions taken but also the corporate values, mission, and, generally, the role in the business landscape (Garzella, 2005).

Additionally, corporate communication can be defined as the result of a corporate strategic decision that starts with the identification of the information beneficiaries (i.e. the stakeholders). According to the characteristics of the identified beneficiaries, the firm defines the content, quantity, vehicle, and timing of dissemination of the information. In defining those elements, companies should consider the purpose of the information flows, which can be directed towards building or improving a good reputation (Giacosa, 2012).

Focusing on communication content, some authors posit that communication should shed light on a company's mission and morality and how they help to create value for stakeholders (e.g. Dowling, 2006). Others suggest that communication should also emphasize the company's value, goals, and commitment to sustainability and corporate social responsibility initiatives (e.g. Dutot et al., 2016; Eberle et al., 2013).

Regarding communication quantity, excessive information can be detrimental, just as insufficient information can pose challenges. By not disseminating enough information, the company may fail to satisfy stakeholders' needs and thus neglect to address information asymmetry. However, an abundance of information may also lead to negative consequences. In this regard, the issue of information overload has become increasingly prevalent over the past decade (Laud & Schepers, 2009). The term 'overload' stems from psychological research and it is defined as a state in which informational input exceeds human information processing capacity (Eppler & Mengis, 2004), resulting in ineffective information processing (Schmitt et al., 2018). Consequently, as stakeholders are inundated with new and vast volumes of data daily, each company should discern which types of data are valuable to mitigate the risk that the volume and complexity of its communication flow overshadow the intelligibility and usefulness of the information disseminated (Laud & Schepers, 2009).

Referring to the communication vehicle, much literature has shed light on the relevance of the Internet and social media as emerging communication channels (e.g. Etter et al., 2019). Kaul et al. (2015) state that the Internet and social media have transformed the business and communication landscape by shaping patterns of communication, collaboration, consumption, and innovation. Before the Internet, the only ways to communicate directly with more than a small number of stakeholders located, for example, in a small geographical area were to own a means of publishing, broadcasting to them, or having a physical presence. Now, through social media, newsgroups, websites, bulletin boards, chatrooms, instant messaging, e-mail, and mailing lists, anybody with Internet access can have a worldwide presence and potentially find a worldwide audience for the cost of a local phone call (Bunting &

Lipski, 2000). Consequently, new domains of interactivity for companies and stakeholders have emerged. Companies recognize that the Internet acts as an indispensable vehicle for improving reputation and they are implementing tailored strategies to establish a presence in this challenging domain. The Internet and its channels (e.g. networks and e-mail) have opened the path for the personalization of information flows and concrete interaction with stakeholders that could lead to a better fit between stakeholders' expectations and firms' attributes (Dutot et al., 2016)[2] with a positive impact on the reputation of the firm.

Finally, the timing of communication is another crucial aspect the firm needs to consider in defining its communication strategy to build its reputation. Timely communication ensures that the message reaches stakeholders when it is most pertinent and can address current concerns or events (e.g. Mariconda et al., 2023; Smith & Grimm, 1991). In case of positive events or a firm's achievements, timely communication allows companies to capitalize on them by maximizing their impact on stakeholders and enhancing their reputation. Meanwhile, in case of negative events or crises, prompt communication can help mitigate reputational damage by providing transparent and timely updates, demonstrating accountability, and showcasing efforts to address the issue.

In conclusion, corporate communication plays a pivotal role in reputation building and management. By strategically conveying key messages, fostering stakeholder engagement, and navigating the complexities of modern communication channels, companies can enhance their reputation, build trust, and create lasting value. Organizations must prioritize transparency, authenticity, and timely responsiveness in their communication efforts while also adapting to evolving stakeholder expectations and industry trends. Ultimately, by recognizing the intrinsic link between communication and reputation, companies can leverage communication as a powerful tool to achieve their strategic objectives and build and maintain a positive and resilient reputation in today's dynamic business landscape.

Corporate Reporting in Reputation Building

Corporate communication, when referring to the formal or regulated release of information, is known as reporting. It differs from the above-described corporate communication as corporate reporting is standardized, regulated, scheduled, quantitative, and often audited (Gibson, 2001). It represents an organized exchange of information provided by the firm to the external environment (von Alberti-Alhtaybat et al., 2012) and is widely observed as the primary source of information that stakeholders consult when seeking insights about companies. It aims to ensure transparency and accountability, facilitate comparisons between companies, and highlight

[2] Some authors use the term e-reputation as synonymous of reputation when it is built from the set of perceptions that stakeholders will create from any element circulating on the Internet (Maltese et al., 2017).

aspects that regulators consider to be of common interest, ultimately safeguarding investors and market stability (Healy & Palepu, 2001).

Even though corporate reporting provides largely standardized information, the literature recognizes its significant role in building the corporate reputation as it legitimizes a company's behaviour in the eyes of stakeholders, educates them about the company's practices, informs them of relevant developments, and ultimately shapes their perceptions and expectations (Adams & Larrinaga-González, 2007; Adams & McNicholas, 2007; Michelon, 2011). The identification of reporting as a determinant of reputation is explained through various theoretical frameworks in literature. For instance, legitimacy theory, stakeholder theory, and signalling theory are prominent frameworks that highlight the role of corporate reporting in fostering dialogue between a company and its stakeholders.

Specifically, legitimacy theory posits that corporate reporting follows environmental factors (economic, social, political) and favours the legitimization of a company's actions (Patten, 1991; Hogner, 1982; Lindblom, 1993). This theory is based upon the assumption that business operates in society via a 'social contract' where it agrees to perform various socially desired actions in return for approval of its objectives, other rewards, and its ultimate survival. It therefore needs to report enough social information for society to assess whether it is a good corporate citizen. In legitimizing its actions via reporting, the firm hopes ultimately to justify its continued existence (Guthrie & Parker, 1989).

Referring to the accountability variant of stakeholder theory proposed by Deegan and Unerman (2006) and Gray et al. (1996), a company has 'the duty to provide an account (not necessary a financial one) or reckoning of those actions for which it is held responsible' (Gray et al., 1996). As highlighted by Dameri and Ferrando (2021), Freeman's stakeholder theory should be applied to both financial and non-financial reporting. This dual application enables companies to address criticisms that arise from focusing reporting primarily on investors while neglecting other stakeholder groups. By doing so, companies can fully harness the potential of reporting to build and maintain their reputation.

Finally, signalling theory suggests that reporting acts as a signal that companies send to their stakeholders (Axjonow et al., 2018). This theory is particularly relevant in scenarios where two parties (individuals and organizations) have access to different information. In these cases, one party, referred to as the sender, must decide whether and how to disclose (or signal) that information, while the other party, the receiver, interprets the signal (Connelly et al., 2011). In this regard, Baumgartner et al. (2022) highlight that stakeholders often struggle to evaluate a company's reputation due to insufficient information regarding its actions, behaviours, and values (Raithel & Schwaiger, 2015). Thus, building on signalling theory, companies can bridge this information gap by signalling comprehensive details about their actions, thereby reducing existing information asymmetries (Connelly et al., 2011; Spence, 1973, 1974) and promoting greater transparency through clear, quantitative, and certified data. As a result, stakeholders interpret and utilize these signals to make informed decisions (Connelly et al., 2011; Toms, 2002; Hasseldine et al., 2005). According to Gabbioneta et al. (2007), stakeholders tend to focus on signals that align with their specific interests and values, drawing inferences about a company's trustworthiness, reliability, and social responsibility based on observable and quantifiable behaviours.

All these theories share a common prerequisite: stakeholders must perceive corporate reporting to be reliable. Specifically, the academic literature suggests that corporate reporting gains value when recipients trust the credibility of the information provided (Hosmer, 1995; Odriozola & Baraibar-Diez, 2017). This perception of reliability is generally met in corporate mandatory reporting, given its mandatory statutory audits. However, for voluntary reporting, achieving similar credibility presents a challenge. In this case, companies may choose to obtain assurance for their reports. Brown et al. (2009) argue that enhancing corporate reputation and gaining greater stakeholder consensus are key objectives for companies that seek assurance for their voluntary disclosures. To provide empirical support, Brown et al. (2009) analysed 604 multinational corporations between 2011 and 2017. Their findings confirm that assurance services for voluntary reports increase stakeholder trust, foster dialogue between the company and its stakeholders, and improve the company's reputation. In a similar vein, Simnett et al. (2009) examined 2113 companies across 31 countries that produced voluntary reports between 2002 and 2004 to explore the motivations behind obtaining assurance for these reports. Their results suggest that companies view assurance as an investment in reputational capital. The study also shows that companies with a higher need for credibility are more likely to seek assurance for voluntary reports, supporting the idea that assurance serves as a tool to strengthen stakeholder trust.

Corporate reporting encompasses a wide range of disclosures in addition to the cited mandatory reporting and voluntary reporting. It includes narrative, financial and non-financial, mandatory and voluntary, as well as printed and online formats (Ali et al., 2007; Xiao, 2020). Among these, mandatory financial reporting is traditionally the most frequently consulted report (Gigler & Hemmer, 1998). Consequently, companies and managers can use financial statements to send signals that meet the stakeholders' expectations and address their information needs. Gigler and Hemmer (1998) emphasize the confirmatory role of mandatory financial reporting suggesting that stakeholders use financial statements to evaluate the truthfulness of management's past disclosures (i.e. to 'confirm' that they are indeed truthful). Moreover, the authors assume that financial reporting may be useful in creating an environment in which management can credibly communicate their more value-relevant information, which is not directly verifiable. It is important to note, however, that financial statements do not provide new, substantial, transparent, or direct insights into corporate reputation. Although corporate reputation is frequently described by scholars and practitioners as an intangible asset, it is not recognized or reported as such within financial statements. This omission arises because the necessary recognition criteria, as required by IAS 38.63, are not fulfilled (see Sect. 2.3 for further details). It assumes a relevant role in building a reputation as it confirms information contained in earlier disclosures and communications, thus establishing the credibility of management's provisions and actions. In doing so, it influences the company's ability to attract stable and lasting resources and support from its environment while also showcasing its economic dynamics to external audiences (Allegrini, 2003).

Some authors have criticized the role of mandatory financial reporting in building corporate reputation, arguing that financial reports primarily contain backwards-looking information, which may lack relevance for stakeholders assessing a company's economic and social prospects and potential for engagement (Eccles & Krzus, 2010; Francis & Schipper, 1999; Gibson, 2001).

In response, they advocate for a more comprehensive approach that integrates financial and non-financial, mandatory and voluntary reporting to provide stakeholders with future-oriented and value-relevant disclosure. In this light, the concepts of *full disclosure* and *integrated reporting* arise.

Full disclosure refers to the practice of providing comprehensive and transparent information about an organization's activities, financial performance, governance practices, risks, and other relevant matters to stakeholders. It includes both mandatory and voluntary reporting and aims to inform stakeholders of both the present and future company's results. With a focus on the contents of full disclosure, Giacosa (2012) suggests that it should embrace economic and financial data, performance measurement information, and results from prospective analyses (Fig. 3.3).

Regarding economic and financial information flow, the company should enhance its reporting of results at the global, divisional, or unit levels, going beyond what is typically included in financial statements to encompass both monetary and non-monetary results. Performance measurement information flow entails providing data on the factors influencing these results to outline the company's potential, strengths, and weaknesses. This includes information on technical and physical performance, the extent of investment in intangible capital, and policies and outcomes in social and environmental areas. Prospective results information flow involves providing insights into the likely evolution of management and its impact on company performance, as well as the potential risk system affecting the business. For more accurate forecasting, the firm should focus on a reasonably limited timeframe, as longer horizons can reduce forecast precision and mislead stakeholders in their decision-making processes.

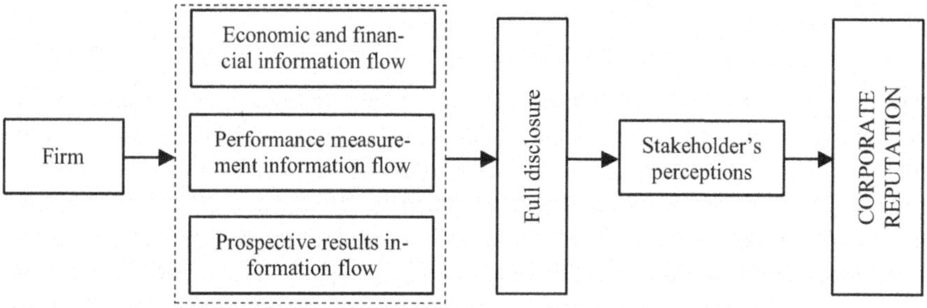

Fig. 3.3 The relationship between full disclosure and reputation. Source: adapted from Giacosa (2012)

Similarly, integrated reporting aims to address the shortcomings of traditional reporting practices, which often entail the dissemination of separate annual, environmental, and social reports, thereby lacking a comprehensive overview of the organization's overall performance and impact. By presenting distinct types of disclosures in isolation, companies typically strive to meet the diverse interests of various stakeholders. However, this fragmented approach can lead to increased publication costs and information overload, ultimately undermining the effectiveness of communication with stakeholders (Hoque, 2017). In response to these challenges, the International Integrated Reporting Council developed the integrated reporting framework in 2010. This framework facilitates the creation of a consolidated report, allowing companies to synthesize all reporting concerns and performance indicators relevant to stakeholders. Known as an integrated report, this document combines financial and narrative information from a company's annual report with non-financial data, such as environmental, social, and governance issues, and the narrative information typically found in a company's CSR or sustainability report (Eccles & Krzus, 2010). In this regard, Busco et al. (2013) defined the integrated report as 'a process that results in communicating value creation over time'. It is a concise communication about how an organization's strategy, governance, performance, and prospects, in the context of its external environment, lead to the creation of value over the short, medium, and long term. Integrated reporting should be designed to benefit all stakeholders interested in an organization's ability to create value over time. Its key objective is to enhance accountability and stewardship concerning the broad base of six kinds of capital (i.e. financial, manufactured, intellectual, human, social, relational, and natural) and promote understanding of their interdependencies. In doing so, integrated reporting builds a corporate reputation as well as favours the company's relationship with stakeholders (Busco et al., 2013; Hoque, 2017).

Building upon this premise, the EU Directive 2022/2464 on Corporate Sustainability Reporting (CSRD) introduces enhanced reporting requirements that align with the principles of integrated reporting. By mandating comprehensive disclosures that reflect both the impact of corporate activities on society and the environment and the influence of these factors on business performance, the CSRD underscores the necessity of integrating financial and non-financial reporting. This approach ensures that organizations provide a complete picture of their performance, enhancing transparency and accountability and ultimately enhancing corporate reputation and stakeholder trust. According to what the CSRD declares, these new requirements 'can provide a basis for better dialogue and communication between undertakings and their stakeholders and can help undertakings to improve their reputation' (Directive (EU) 2022/2464, introduction section p. 12). Specifically, the CSRD drew attention to and expanded articles 19a(1) and 29a(1) of Directive 2013/34/EU highlighting that companies are required to 'include in the report information necessary to understand the undertaking's impact on sustainability matters, and information necessary to understand how sustainability matters affect the undertaking's development, performance and position'. This approach is known as

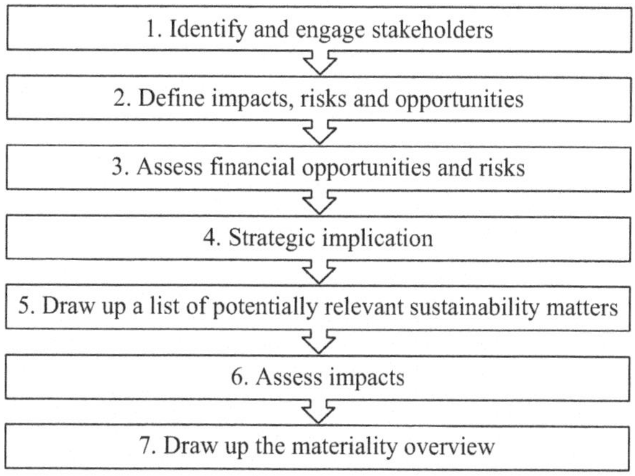

Fig. 3.4 Double materiality assessment process. Source: author's elaboration

double materiality assessment, which incorporates both an inside-out view and an outside-in view, and it is one of the most prominent novelties introduced by CSRD.

Organizations can follow the double materiality assessment by following the process in Fig. 3.4.

Under the double materiality concept, a non-financial matter can be material from an impact point of view and/or from a risk and opportunity perspective. In this light, CSRD improves corporate reputation disclosure as it requires assessing risk and focusing on the topics that are most relevant for the organization and its stakeholders. By doing that, companies can deal with reputational risk. Indeed, the outcomes of the process described in Fig. 3.4 support the functioning of the five-step process suggested by Eccles et al. (2007) through which companies should manage the reputational risk (for more details see Sect. 3.3.1).

Particularly, the double materiality assessment can enhance a company's reputation among stakeholders in several ways. First, it supports the identification and engagement of relevant stakeholders, ensuring their perspectives are considered in decision-making processes. Second, it aids in evaluating the company's true character by defining and assessing its impacts, risks, and opportunities concerning sustainability issues. Finally, it facilitates the monitoring of evolving beliefs and expectations by comparing double materiality assessments over the years, allowing companies to adapt and respond effectively to stakeholder concerns and societal changes.

To summarize, corporate communication and reporting are crucial to building corporate reputation, representing deliberate actions that companies take to enhance their reputational capital. By effectively communicating their values, performance, and impacts, organizations shape stakeholder perceptions, foster trust, and ultimately strengthen their reputation. Importantly, these actions also help mitigate reputational risk (see Sect. 3.3.1 for details on reputational risk). Academic studies, including those by Bebbington et al. (2008) and Michelon (2011), emphasize that well-managed communication and reporting are essential for reducing reputational vulnerabilities, enhancing transparency, and aligning with stakeholder expectations. This dual role underscores the strategic importance of communication and reporting in both building and protecting reputation.

For example, Gray et al. (1995) argue that sustainability reporting promotes a socially responsible image, enhancing legitimacy and supporting better reputational risk management (Fombrun et al., 2000; Bebbington et al., 2008). Recently, Lavorato et al. (2021) confirmed this positive association by reviewing the literature on the topic. They conclude that environmental and social reporting plays a significant role in mitigating reputation risk (Brivot et al., 2017; Lemke & Petersen, 2013; Pineiro-Chousa et al., 2017) and managing crises (Bebbington et al., 2008; Hogan & Lodhia, 2011).

However, corporate communications and reporting can also worsen corporate reputation, particularly when they do not align with stakeholder information needs. Providing information that is overly generic, irrelevant, or misleading can create a 'credibility gap' eroding trust and damaging stakeholder perceptions (Adams, 2004; Baier et al., 2022; Boiral, 2013; Torelli et al., 2020). While overly generic or irrelevant information can pose a reputation risk that can be managed, as outlined in Sect. 3.3.1, misleading communication represents a practice of 'false signalling', where the signaller intentionally sends a misleading signal about a quality they do not possess (Connelly et al., 2011). Overly generic or irrelevant information may stem from a lack of understanding of stakeholders' beliefs and expectations, whereas misleading information involves a deliberate effort to misrepresent the truth. Both cases have a potential negative impact on the corporate reputation. Specifically, while the former generates reputation risk, the latter can lead to a reputation crisis when discovered (see Sect. 3.3.1 for more details on reputation risk management and Sect. 3.3.2. for reputation crisis management).

A pertinent example of misleading communication is greenwashing, which refers to misleading practices concerning environmental issues intended to shape stakeholder perceptions and influence their decision-making. In this regard, Torelli et al. (2020) empirically confirm that the effects of greenwashing on stakeholders' perceptions can negatively impact corporate reputation when such practices are uncovered.

Thus, corporate communications and reporting can be seen as a double-edged sword: they can build and protect corporate reputation, but they can also damage it if not properly managed or tailored to stakeholder information needs.

The following sections explore additional determinants of corporate reputation, including those related to managing reputational risk and crisis.

3.2.2 *Creating Reputational Capital Through Unintentional Actions*

The preceding section highlights how firms actively engage in intentional actions to build and enhance their reputation. However, corporate reputation is also influenced by various aspects and outcomes of the firm's operations that, while not primarily aimed at bolstering reputation, can significantly impact stakeholder perceptions

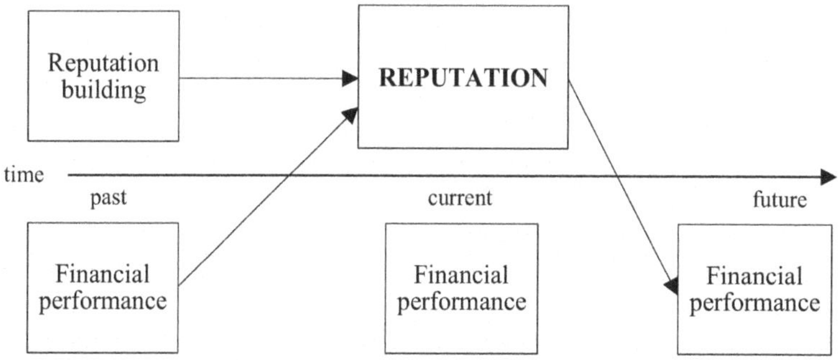

Fig. 3.5 Framework of reputation-financial performance dynamics. Source: Roberts and Dowling (2002).

regarding the firm's ability to meet its needs. These factors include financial performance, quality of products and processes, and human resource behaviours.

Starting with economic and financial performance, research suggests that the relationship between corporate reputation and financial performance is bidirectional. In this regard, McGuire et al. (1990) were the first to point out that a firm's financial performance affects its reputation, and conversely, its reputation affects its performance. Drawing on the assumption proposed by McGuire et al. (1990), Roberts and Dowling (2002) undertake an analysis of the relationship between corporate reputation and the dynamics of financial performance using two complementary dynamic models. They propose the framework in Fig. 3.5 to support their analysis.

The authors assume that a company's past financial performance can shape stakeholders' perceptions of the company as being 'good' or successful. In other words, when a company performs well financially, stakeholders (such as investors, customers, or the public) are likely to view the company positively, associating its financial success with its overall reputation. Furthermore, the authors argue that this perception creates a self-reinforcing dynamic, which means that a strong corporate reputation, built on past financial performance, can lead to continued financial success. As stakeholders continue to view the company positively, it may attract more investment, customers, or support, which in turn contributes to future financial performance. This cycle of positive financial results and enhanced reputation can reinforce each other over time, creating a feedback loop where good financial performance strengthens the company's reputation, and a strong reputation supports further financial success. Other studies (e.g. Hammond & Slocum, 1996) suggest that metrics like return on assets, sales growth, and asset growth positively affect subsequent corporate reputation. Conversely, risk measures exert a negative impact. Thus, firms with low risk and high return on assets will later have an image of high-reputation firms. This association is also confirmed by Laskin (2013), who expanded the analysis including the role of corporate communication in the process. As what counts is how the financial performance is being interpreted by the company's stakeholders, communication about the company's financial performance is as important or even more important than the financial performance itself in building reputation (see Sect. 3.2.1 for more details on the role of communication in the reputation building process). Studies often refer to the reputation created by financial performance as 'financial reputation' (Deephouse, 1997; Roberts and Dowling, 2002). Specifically, financial reputation is the general evaluation of a company's financial prospects made by the financial rating industry. This general evaluation is the result of expectations for profitability, stability, and growth (Fombrun, 1996). It can be considered a component of the overall reputation of a firm. Deephouse and Carter (2005) agree on including financial performance on antecedents of corporate reputation. In addition, they suggest that normal fluctuations in performance are likely not the basis of changes in the reputation of firms. For example, a for-profit business that reports a lower quarterly profit is not necessarily viewed as a low-reputation company. Although the firm may not have met the expectations of certain stakeholders who benefit, such as investors, it will not be perceived as any less qualified to remain in business.

Similarly, the perceived quality of products and processes also impacts corporate reputation (Zeithaml et al., 1996). This assumption is mainly expressed in research focusing on customers as principal stakeholders and conducting studies on the customer-behaviour-related antecedents of corporate reputation. In this regard, Walsh et al. (2009) explain the quality-enhancing effect of reputation by the fact that companies offering good product quality will be favoured by customers, who will engage in positive word of mouth. Conversely, companies offering poor product quality will be penalized by customers, who will engage in negative word of mouth. Moreover, Sundaram et al. (1998) suggest that customers who perceive the company as having good-quality products and processes are more willing to engage in positive word of mouth than those customers who do not perceive the company to have a good reputation. This effect helps companies with good-quality products and processes to create a goodwill reservoir for themselves, which can involve customers acting as advocates of the company.

More recently, literature has highlighted innovations as an important determinant of corporate reputation. Henard and Dacin (2010) emphasize products, positing that firms can cultivate a distinct reputation for pioneering product innovations, referred to as 'reputation for product innovation'. Similarly, Höflinger et al. (2018) focus on technological innovation and introduce the notion of 'reputation for technological innovation'. Both these reputations—reputation for product innovation and reputation for technological innovation—constitute components of the multifaceted constructs of reputation (Rindova et al., 2005). Throughout, the authors argue that a firm's innovative endeavours can influence how consumers perceive its proactive ability to cater to their needs through innovative products or services.

Another factor influencing corporate reputation is the behaviour of the firm's human resources, with a substantial body of research focusing on the CEO. Management studies suggest that top leaders influence how stakeholders see their firm (Love et al., 2017). Thus, corporate leaders can be defined as the 'face of the firm', appearing as the human force behind the firm's actions and outcomes (Cannella et al., 2009). A growing body of research asserts that the CEO is crucial in shaping their firm's reputation, whether in routine management or during crises (Kitchen & Laurence, 2003; Gaines-Ross, 2000). CEO ensures the coordination of several organizational functions, deals with the development of the reputational risk strategy, monitors in advance external threats, and manages reputation in crisis conditions. CEO that holds the greatest responsibility in the management of reputation is defined in terms of the Chief Reputation Officer (Conte, 2018). Consequently, CEOs play a pivotal role in various dimensions of corporate reputation management and simultaneously influence it through their personal reputation.

To confirm the influence of CEO reputation on corporate reputation, Love et al. (2017) conducted a study on 372 large US firms listed in Fortune magazine's annual 'Most Admired Company' survey from 1991 to 1997. Their findings suggest that highly reputed CEOs can enhance their firm's reputation, sometimes substantially, whereas CEOs with negative reputations can significantly damage it. Conte (2018) confirms this finding relating to the Italian context by supporting the central underlying idea that the firm is a reflection of its leaders (Hambrick & Mason, 1984; Ireland & Hitt, 1999). Weng and Chen (2017) analyse the same relationship within the Taiwanese context and arrive at similar conclusions. Moreover, they emphasize that in certain industries (such as the electronics industry), the reputation of the CEO can overshadow that of the firm itself. They find that the impact of CEO reputation on firm performance is often more significant than that of corporate reputation.

This evidence draws on the upper echelons theory. The fundamental idea of this theory is captured well by the seminal paper by Hambrick and Mason (1984) on the upper echelons perspective. The authors suggest that the organization is a reflection of its top managers (the so-called upper echelons). The theory acknowledges that individual top managers heavily influence organizational outcomes by the choices they make, which are—in turn—affected by the managers' characteristics.

However, corporate reputation can also be influenced by other aspects of human resource behaviours, not solely those of the CEO or top management. For instance, a different research stream has investigated the role of employees in building corporate reputation (Dowling, 2002; Harris & de Chernatony, 2001). In this regard, Helm (2011) describes all activities or behaviours employees exhibit to contribute to the formation of corporate reputation with the terms 'internal reputation building'. He suggests that employees can directly or indirectly, voluntarily or involuntarily, affect reputation by any act that is transmitted to, and communicated by, external audiences who evaluate corporate conduct. Recent studies emphasize that this relationship is particularly significant in the age of connectivity (Schaarschmidt & Walsh, 2020). Employees often serve as brand ambassadors, promoting company products and services through their personal social media channels (Dreher, 2014). However, their social media activity can also pose risks (Miles & Mangold, 2014). When employees use their real names and mention their employer, each pos, whether positive or negative, can influence public perception of the company. Inappropriate statements in employee posts can jeopardize corporate reputation and potentially lead to legal consequences for the organization (Schaarschmidt & Walsh, 2020).

Finally, it is worth noting that all the corporate reputation determinants analysed here (financial performance, product and process quality, innovation, and human resource behaviours) positively interact with each other and with other prominent firm features or actions. This interaction creates a virtuous cycle that enhances the positive impact each determinant has on corporate reputation due to their synergistic effects (Podolny, 1993). However, in some cases, this virtuous cycle can turn into a vicious cycle, where the interaction of these determinants leads to reputational losses. Therefore, companies should include these aspects, referred to as unintended actions, in a comprehensive reputation management process to ensure its effectiveness.

3.2.3 Acquiring Reputational Capital

Besides intentional and unintentional actions, a new approach to enhancing corporate reputation has emerged: external acquisition. Specifically, building on literature that suggests corporate reputation can be considered an intangible asset (see Sect. 2.3 for further details), this section posits that corporate reputation also aligns with the acquisition criteria outlined in IAS 38 for intangible assets. Therefore, just as corporate reputation can be internally generated, it can also be externally acquired. Section 3.2.2 provided an in-depth analysis of how companies may internally generate corporate reputation. This section focuses on the issue of externally acquired corporate reputation, examining the two primary paths available to companies: engaging in merger and acquisition agreements and opting for strategic alliances.

Mergers and Acquisitions

Mergers and acquisitions (M&A) are important strategies employed by companies in today's business environment (Edi et al., 2020; Garzella & Fiorentino, 2017). Typically, companies engage in M&A to create value, which arises from the realization of synergies defined as the combination of two firms' assets that are more valuable together than separately. Scholars from multiple disciplines, including strategic management, financial economics, and accounting, have analysed synergies using various theoretical perspectives, such as the resource-based view, industrial organization economics, and behavioural theory (Haspeslagh & Jemison, 1991; Shaver & Mikulincer, 2006). These fields of literature generally agree on classifying synergies into two categories: operating and financial synergies.

Operating synergies are those that allow firms to increase their operating income from existing assets, increase growth, or both. They include economies of scale, greater pricing power, a combination of different functional strengths, or higher growth in new or existing markets (Devos et al., 2009). Financial synergies are those that allow firms to increase cash flows and lower the cost of capital or both. They include diversification, tax benefits, or increased debt capacity (Leland, 2007).

Recently, strategic management literature has advanced the existing conceptualization of synergy uncovering novel synergy sources. Specifically, Feldman and Hernandez (2022) identify more than two synergy types by conducting a systematic review of the literature on value and synergy in M&A. Specifically, they suggest that synergy sources can be classified as internal, market power, relational, network, and nonmarket. They define internal synergy as a combination of resources or capabilities that the acquirer and target own and control directly, not shared with another party, that jointly enhance revenues or lower costs. This type of synergy creates value arising from improved efficiency. According to their view, market power synergy is a combination of assets and industry positions that give the combined firm power in competitive interactions, such as eliminating or weakening a rival, increasing buying power, or increasing pricing power. In defining internal and market power synergies, Feldman and Hernandez (2022) specify that they represent a redefinition of the common operating and financial synergies based on two underlying dimensions: the level of analysis at which valuable activities occur and the orientation by which those activities are governed. However, the real novelty of their work lies in recognizing relational, network, and nonmarket synergies as sources of value creation in M&A activities. Fig. 3.6 shows the three new synergies and their origin from M&A.

Specifically, Feldman and Hernandez (2022) define relational synergies as the enhancement of assets shared with an individual third party made possible by the combination of the acquirer and target. The third party typically has a contractual relationship with the merged firm, which could be a vertical (supplier or buyer) or horizontal (alliance partner) relationship. In this case, the value arises from partner-specific assets such as mutual trust, governance routines, contracting capabilities, or knowledge-exchange capacity collaboratively shared with other firms.

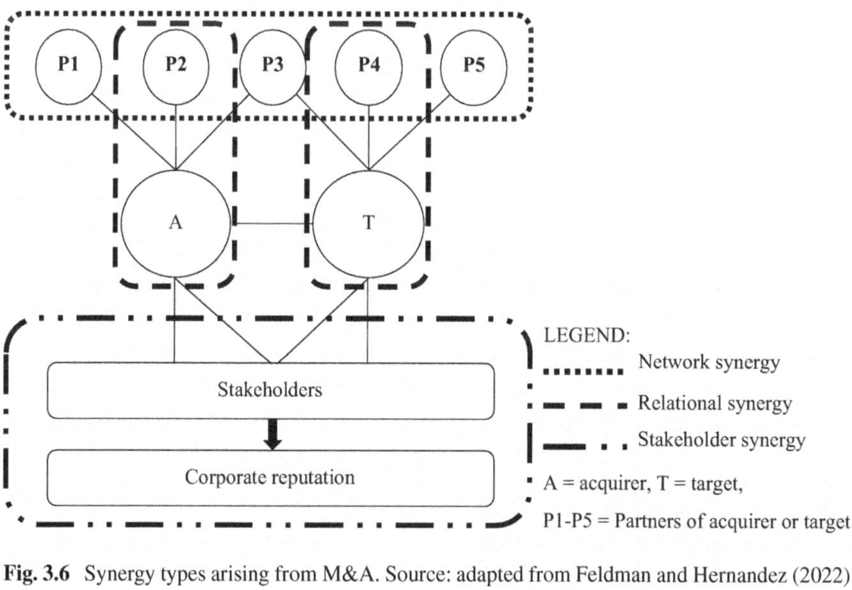

Fig. 3.6 Synergy types arising from M&A. Source: adapted from Feldman and Hernandez (2022)

Referring to network synergies, the value created through M&A activities can arise from the structural positions a firm occupies in the network generated by the totality of a firm's direct and indirect ties. Specifically, network synergies are defined as the combination of the acquirer's and target's pre-acquisition ego networks that improve the combined firm's structural position (e.g. centrality, structural holes, status). The ego network comprises the combining firms' direct and indirect (second-order) ties. While value lies in cooperative external ties for both network and relational synergies, these differ in their levels of analysis. Relational synergies enhance the gains from individual direct ties. Network synergies improve the acquirer's position in a network encompassing all the direct ties and indirect ties of the combined firms.

Finally, the nonmarket synergies consider the interaction between firms and various stakeholders in the nonmarket environment (Baron, 1995). In this case, the value arises from legitimacy gained with good relationships with them (Ahuja and Yayavaram, 2011; DiMaggio & Powell, 1983). Through M&A firms can redefine the expectations and rules of engagement with stakeholders (Krishnan, 2005) that impact on the value of the reputational capital of firms (Freeman & McVea, 2001). Feldman and Hernandez (2022) also refer to nonmarket synergies as stakeholder synergies, emphasizing that they arise when firms gain influence over or approval from their stakeholders. Since corporate reputation is defined as *stakeholders' overall evaluation of a company over time* (Gotsi & Wilson, 2001), the value created through stakeholder synergies can be seen as an acquisition of corporate reputation. In other words, Feldman and Hernandez (2022) indirectly acknowledge that a firm can enhance its corporate reputation through M&A that positively influences stakeholder perceptions. Moreover, their analysis suggests that building a corporate reputation through M&A requires a greater level of integration compared to pursuing other types of synergies. This is because it involves both internal changes and external integrations, with external integration being particularly time-consuming. On one hand, firms should align their internal organization, values, and behaviour to redefine the expectations and rules of engagement with stakeholders in the nonmarket environment. On the other hand, they should invest time and consistent effort into cultivating and sustaining strong, trustworthy relationships with their stakeholders to turn this reputation into a long-lasting source of advantage. Together, these efforts create a unified approach to stakeholder engagement that leverages stakeholders' priorities and needs to address social challenges collaboratively. This ensures the firm's actions align with stakeholder expectations in the long period.

Consequently, acquiring a corporate reputation through M&A has a very long timeline for initial synergy realization, combined with medium control over value-creating activities, making it a challenging outcome to pursue. Once acquired, a firm can benefit from a good corporate reputation in the medium term. However, to sustain and enhance this reputation, the firm must continuously invest in building relationships with stakeholders and developing the necessary skills to address social issues effectively. Corporate reputation, built through stakeholder synergy, remains vulnerable to conflicts or controversies surrounding the issues stakeholders prioritize. When firms' behaviours and stakeholders' expectations do not align, the process of value creation may halt, and in some cases, dis-synergies can occur. This suggests that, even though M&A can be intentional activities undertaken to acquire reputation, they do not ensure the sustainability of reputational capital. Corporate reputation sustainability requires their integration with internally generated corporate reputation activities and other complementary endeavours.

This assumption aligns with the literature on M&A, which suggests that the value created through the synergies arising from these activities is not often long-lasting (Agrawal & Jaffe, 2000).

In addition, the analysis of externally acquired corporate reputation through M&A activities must also consider the costs that the acquirer must cover. Eccles et al. (1999) suggest that most cases of M&A failures occur because the price of the deals is too high. Setting the right price for an M&A deal is not without challenges, as it depends on the purpose the acquisition will serve (Christensen et al., 2011). In today's market, the purchase price of an acquisition will almost always exceed the intrinsic value of the target company. The intrinsic value represents the net present value of expected future cash flows, completely independent of any acquisition, assuming the company continues under current management with anticipated revenue growth and performance improvements already factored in by the market.

Often, the price of an M&A activity carries a premium on the intrinsic value of the target. As this premium allocates some of the future benefits of the combination to the target shareholders, without a premium, most target shareholders would refuse to sell. In this regard, the acquirer should carefully evaluate the maximum level of premium price that it can bear. This level of premium price should not surpass the synergy value of the M&A, which is defined as the net present value of the cash flow resulting from improvements made when the companies are combined. These improvements go beyond those anticipated by the market if the acquisition didn't occur since those are already incorporated into the intrinsic value of each company (Christensen et al., 2011).

Given that the key to the success of an acquisition lies in proper pricing, when firms engage in M&A activities to acquire reputation, they should conduct thorough due diligence and valuation assessments. This ensures that the price paid aligns with the expected benefits and is sustainable in the long term. This aspect sheds light on a problem already evident in the literature: the correct valuation and measurement of corporate reputation (see Chap. 5 for more details on challenges in evaluating and measuring corporate reputation). Indeed, this may render the path to acquiring corporate reputation through M&A riskier and more expensive compared to internally building corporate reputation (see Sect. 3.2.1 for more details on creating reputational capital through intentional actions) or acquiring corporate reputation through strategic alliances. The following part of this section focuses on this latter aspect in greater detail.

Strategic Alliances

The second path a firm can follow to acquire a corporate reputation is engaging in strategic alliances. Strategic alliances are becoming more and more prominent in the global economy as they are considered an efficient approach that organizations may use to achieve their goals (Elmuti & Kathawala, 2001). Peter Drucker, who has been called the father of the management theory, states 'The greatest change in corporate culture, and the way business is being conducted, may be accelerating growth of relationships based not on ownership, but on partnerships' (Drucker, 1996). Indeed, strategic alliances allow an organization, in a strategic context, to advance in the direction of their purposes and significantly reduce the efforts of an individual approach in acquiring strategic resources (Harrigan, 2017). They are partnerships of two or more corporations or business units that work together to achieve mutually beneficial and strategically significant objectives (Elmuti & Kathawala, 2001). As M&A, strategic alliances are externally oriented corporate development efforts to achieve economies of scale, scope, market share, prestige, survival, and other outcomes essential to temporary or sustained competitive advantage. During this decade, both M&A and strategic alliances have achieved unprecedented growth (Shi et al., 2012). Prior research suggests that a focal firm prefers an alliance to an acquisition if the focal firm does not have enough information about the potential target (Balakrishnan & Koza, 1993) or if the potential target possesses some assets that are not separable from the assets the focal firm would like to acquire (Hennart, 1988). Other evidence points out that firms choose between those two corporate strategies for combining their resources based on resource similarity and complementarity between the two firms. Specifically, higher levels of resource similarity between two firms are more likely to prompt firms to choose acquisition. Conversely, high levels of resource complementarity led firms to opt for an alliance (Wang & Zajac, 2007). Thus, based on firms' characteristics, strategic alliances may be an alternative corporate strategy used to acquire a corporate reputation.

The term 'strategic alliances' can be considered an umbrella term that involves several forms by which two or more organizations can pursue a strategic alliance. In this regard, Todeva and Knoke (2005) identify at least 13 basic forms of inter-organizational relations:

1. *Hierarchical relations*: one firm takes full control of another's assets and coordinates actions by the ownership rights mechanism.
2. *Joint ventures*: two or more firms create a jointly owned legal organization that serves a limited purpose for its parents, such as R&D or marketing.
3. *Equity investments*: a majority or minority equity holding by one firm through a direct stock purchase of shares in another firm.
4. *Cooperatives*: a coalition of small enterprises that combine, coordinate, and manage their collective resources.
5. *R&D consortia*: interfirm agreements for research and development collaboration, typically formed in fast-changing technological fields.
6. *Strategic cooperative agreements*: contractual business networks based on joint multi-party strategic control, with the partners collaborating over key strategic decisions and sharing responsibilities for performance outcomes.
7. *Cartels*: large corporations collude to constrain competition by cooperatively controlling production and/or prices within a specific industry.

8. *Franchising*: a franchisor grants a franchisee the use of a brand-name identity within a geographic area, but retains control over pricing, marketing, and standardized service norms.
9. *Licensing*: one company grants another the right to use patented technologies or production processes in return for royalties and fees.
10. *Subcontractor networks*: inter-linked firms where a subcontractor negotiates its suppliers' long-term prices, production runs, and delivery schedules.
11. *Industry standards groups*: committees that seek the member organizations' agreements on the adoption of technical standards for manufacturing and trade.
12. *Action sets*: short-lived organizational coalitions whose members coordinate their lobbying efforts to influence public policy-making.
13. *Market relations*: arm's-length transactions between organizations coordinated only through the price mechanism.

Those forms of strategic alliances vary based on the integration and formalization in the governance of their inter-organizational relationships.

Strategic alliances can be divided into two groups depending on the type of partner: horizontal and vertical collaborations. The first group includes alliances with competitors, while the second one identifies alliances with suppliers and/or customers. Specifically, whereas vertical interfirm relations are seen as spanning differentiated organizations that combine symbiotically to achieve collective ends, horizontal interfirm relations span similar organizations that combine commensalistically[3] to also aim at achieving collective ends (Baum & Ingram, 2002; Belderbos et al., 2012).

Even though the reasons for establishing strategic alliances may be varied, the literature identifies several recurring purposes. For example, some of the primary motivations for forming strategic alliances include pursuing growth strategies, entering new markets, acquiring new technologies, ensuring superior quality or lower costs, reducing financial risk, sharing research and development costs, and achieving or maintaining a competitive advantage (Elmuti & Kathawala, 2001). Traditionally, research on alliances has focused primarily on the role of tangible resource exchanges in explaining how partnerships favour competitive advantage. After the growth of corporate reputation literature, an increasingly common perspective in strategic management and organizational theory addresses how organizational decisions are affected by intangible considerations by including in these decisions also the strategic alliances. In this respect, Olk and Ring (1997) have addressed the issue of how threats to, or the desire to change, organizational image, reputation, and legitimacy provide explanations for an organization's strategy to enter alliances.

---

[3] The word 'commensalistically' is derived from 'commensalism', a term introduced by zoologist and paleontologist Pierre-Joseph van Beneden in 1876. In biological science, commensalism refers to a long-term biological interaction in which members of one species benefit, while those of the other species neither benefit nor are harmed. Baum and Ingram (2002) used this term to describe collaborations between firms, as it effectively captures the concept underlying horizontal interfirm relationships.

This stream of literature underlines that enhancing or acquiring corporate reputation may also be a reason for forming strategic alliances, as it serves as a strategic resource that contributes to creating a sustainable competitive advantage (see Sect. 2.2 for more details on corporate reputation as a strategic resource).

In this regard, it is worthy to note that the relationship between corporate reputation and strategic alliance is bidirectional, complex, and dynamic.

It is bidirectional because corporate reputation influences strategic alliances, and strategic alliances, in turn, influence corporate reputation. A positive corporate reputation may facilitate agreements between the economic units involved in the alliance, while a negative reputation may impede such agreements. Conversely, alliances can enhance the partners' reputations or cause reputational damage (Todeva & Knoke, 2005).

This relationship is complex because it indirectly impacts other elements crucial to a firm's sustainable value creation: social capital and social liabilities. Specifically, the relationship can have both positive and negative effects on a firm's goals. When strategic alliances bring benefits, they generate social capital in the form of organizational prestige, reputation, status, and brand name recognition. Conversely, when strategic alliances bring disadvantages, the relationship may create social liabilities (Leenders & Gabbay, 1999).

Additionally, the relationship between corporate reputation and strategic alliances is dynamic as it evolves over time. A company's reputation can change due to various factors, including the outcomes of its strategic alliances, which in turn can affect future alliances (Gotsi & Wilson, 2001).

Understanding this bidirectional, complex, and dynamic relationship is crucial for companies aiming to build reputation through strategic alliances or leverage their reputation to form effective alliances. It requires a comprehensive approach to managing both corporate reputation and the elements of social capital and social liabilities within the framework of strategic alliances. Figure 3.7 graphically illustrates the relationship between corporate reputation and strategic alliances, highlighting all the major elements involved in the framework.

The following part of this section delves into each of the relationships shown in the figure, analysing the influence of corporate reputation on strategic alliances, the influence of strategic alliances on corporate reputation, and the consequences of this relationship on social capital and social liability.

The Influence of Corporate Reputation on Strategic Alliances

Corporate reputation has a significant impact on the decision to proceed with a strategic alliance (Dollinger et al., 1997), and it is an important criterion for partner selection and increases significantly the likelihood of forming a strategic alliance (Franco & Haase, 2020).

The relevance of corporate reputation in this context is grounded in several theoretical models, such as resource-based view theory, transaction cost theory, signalling theory, game theory, and theories of organizational effectiveness.

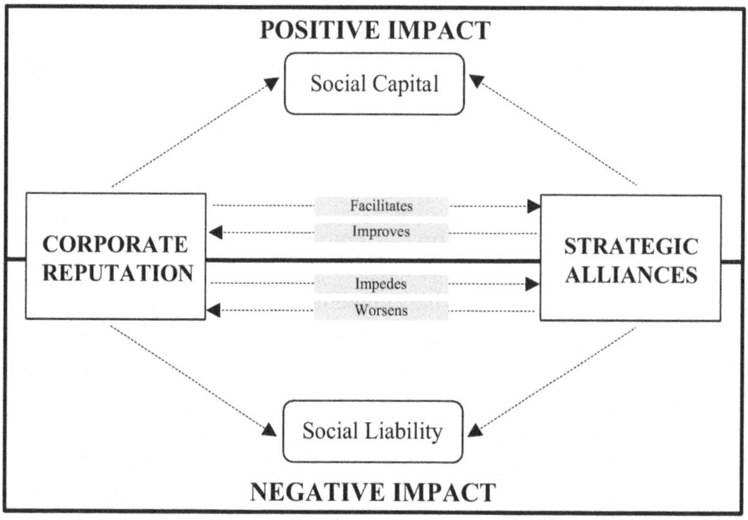

Fig. 3.7 The relationship between corporate reputation and strategic alliances. Source: author's elaboration

From the perspective of resource-based theory, reputation is seen as an intangible resource and contributes significantly to different levels of performance among firms because intangible resources are rare, socially complex, and difficult to exchange and imitate (Rao, 1994). Thus, corporate reputation seems to be able to attract new resources (and partners) and the better the reputation the more likely a strategic alliance will be successful (Dollinger et al., 1997; Arend, 2009).

According to transaction cost theory (Williamson, 1975), a positive reputation can reduce transaction costs when forming a cooperation agreement between partners. In other words, a partner's positive reputation indicates trustworthiness, which helps reduce the costs associated with selecting that partner.

Regarding signalling theory, corporate reputation can be considered a signal that a firm sends to a potential partner to communicate its capacity to create value based on its characteristics and qualities.

From a game theory perspective (Dollinger et al., 1997), corporate reputation acts as a cue for the target's game behaviour. Specifically, according to this view, forming an alliance adds value and transforms a zero-sum game into a positive-sum game. However, for the game to result in the total maximum utility over the length of the relationship, firms must be able to predict what the other will do. Thus, partners infer from a positive reputation that the target is not going to defect and lower the collective payoffs (Weigelt & Camerer, 1988).

Finally, according to theories of organizational effectiveness, corporate reputation is a measure of a company's effectiveness, and it may be a function of financial performance, product quality, management effectiveness, or some combination of factors that appeal to a firm's multiple constituencies (Tsui, 1984).

In conclusion, all this evidence confirms the relevance of corporate reputation in the decision to form a strategic alliance, with several theoretical frameworks providing a basis for this assumption.

Strategic Alliance as a Path to Acquire Corporate Reputation

Prior studies have suggested that firms are constantly seeking new sources to gain a competitive advantage (e.g. Teece et al., 1997). In this context, proponents of the resource-based view theory argue that competitive advantage arises from resources and capabilities that are rare, valuable, non-substitutable, and difficult to imitate (Barney, 1991). Traditionally, this search for advantage has focused on internal resources. However, some authors propose that critical resources may extend beyond firm boundaries and be found in partnerships or networks (Dyer & Singh, 1998). According to this perspective, strategic alliances provide a platform for firms to acquire assets, competencies, and capabilities that are not easily accessible in competitive markets, thereby generating additional value and competitive advantage (Dyer & Singh, 1998).

Specifically, strategic alliances enhance a firm's ability to create value by leveraging the complementary resources of its partners. These resources, unique to each partner, generate greater value when combined than the sum of individual resources. The value of a strategic alliance is maximized when partners bring together valuable, rare, and difficult-to-imitate resources (i.e. strategic resources), thus generating a competitive advantage.

Building on this theory, literature on strategic management recognizes strategic alliances as a key means for acquiring and enhancing corporate reputation (Kale et al., 2000; Stuart, 2000; Wassmer, 2010). This assumption has been confirmed by empirical evidence suggesting that as reputation satisfies the VRIN criteria (valuable, rare, inimitable, and non-substitutable), it represents a strategic resource that firms can acquire through strategic alliances to support their competitive advantage (Das & Teng, 2000; Olk & Ring, 1997; Oliver, 1997).

Social Capital or Social Liability in Corporate Reputation and Strategic Alliance Relationship

The core aspect of the relationship between corporate reputation and strategic alliances lies in the sharing of strategic resources between two or more firms, which enhances the value-generating capabilities of all parties involved.

However, literature also recognizes a specific form of partnership-generated value known as social capital. Social capital is defined as a set of resources rooted in relationships. It is a multidimensional concept that encompasses three interrelated dimensions: structural, relational, and cognitive (Nahapiet & Ghoshal, 1998). The structural dimension refers to the impersonal configuration of linkages between firms. The relational dimension describes the kinds of personal relationships that the firms' people have developed with each other through a history of interactions. The cognitive dimension refers to those resources that provide shared representations, interpretations, and systems of meaning among parties. Unlike other types of capital, social capital is collectively owned by the parties involved in a relationship, and no individual entity possesses, or can possess, exclusive ownership rights (Burt, 1992). Moreover, although social capital holds significant value in use, it is not easily tradable, which positions it as a potential strategic resource. Consequently, it carries important implications for competitive advantage for the firms that possess it (Wang, 2014).

Thus, engaging in strategic alliances to acquire reputation can create a dual source of competitive advantage: the acquired corporate reputation and the resulting social capital. Notably, corporate reputation acts as the primary source of competitive advantage, producing a 'halo' effect that enhances the value of social capital (Preston, 2004; Wang, 2014).

However, strategic alliances are not without risks. Notably, there are instances where strategic alliances can fail. One primary reason for such failures is a relational risk, which refers to the likelihood that a partner firm may lack commitment to the alliance or engage in opportunistic behaviour, thus jeopardizing the alliance's success. Moreover, the firms may incur risks relating to cultural clashes, lack of trust causing unsolved problems, lack of understanding, and despondent relationships, dissimilar objectives, inability to share risks, lack of coordination, differences in operating procedures, and attitudes among partners.

In these scenarios, the strategic alliance can have a detrimental effect on corporate reputation and expose firms to social liability (Elmuti & Kathawala, 2001). Specifically, if a strategic alliance proves not to be beneficial for attaining an actor's goals and turns instead into constraints that impede performance and competitive advantage, then it constitutes a social liability (Leenders & Gabbay, 1999).

In conclusion, strategic alliances are recognized as an important path to acquiring a corporate reputation and, consequently, attaining and maintaining a competitive advantage. However, this strategy is challenging and requires proactive action to mitigate potential negative impacts. To this end, Elmuti and Kathawala (2001) suggest that firms must engage in strategic alliances with a comprehensive plan outlining detailed expectations, requirements, and anticipated benefits. Strategic alliance partners should be selected based on their expertise in the operation and their cultural fit with the firm. The management of the strategic alliance project should be continuous to ensure that requirements are being met and potential problems are identified early enough to be resolved. Moreover, partners must create a management structure that supports the new organizational arrangement.

This process requires comprehensive and complex due diligence, which can be an expensive and time-consuming activity necessitating a cost-benefit analysis. If the benefits of the acquired corporate reputation are lower than the costs (both real and potential) of engaging in the strategic alliance, the firm may opt to generate it internally.

However, regardless of whether it is internally generated or acquired, reputational capital is vulnerable to negative flows that can diminish its value. The next section examines this aspect by focusing on reputational risk and crisis.

3.3 Protecting and Repairing the Reputational Capital

3.3.1 Reputation Risk Management

Prior sections have emphasized that corporate reputation is a strategic asset contributing to achieving competitive advantage. However, its value is coupled with fragility (Hall, 1993), as it can be easily eroded by destructive forces (Helm & Tolsdorf, 2013) termed reputational risks (Lamboglia & D'Onza, 2014).

Academic literature has been interestingly analysing the risks that have an impact on companies for many years (Bertini, 1987). Companies, indeed, being 'probabilistic systems' characterized by uncertainty, are required to manage a wide variety of risks that can jeopardize the achievement of their objectives and, ultimately, threaten their competitive advantage (Miller & Breton-Miller, 2005). Thus, assessing and managing them is an essential process for the survival of all organizations.

Prior studies suggest that the stronger the reputation, the stronger the risk of it being damaged (Gatzert, 2015; Ali et al., 2015; Zavyalova et al., 2016). As suggested by Eccles et al. (2007), reputation may act as a double-edged sword: on the one hand, a good reputation creates value for all stakeholders; on the other hand, it also exposes the enterprise to reputational risk. Thus, the analysis of corporate reputation is not complete without reference to the risks that can threaten it.

Eccles' seminal work (2007) identified three interconnected factors that determine a company's exposure to reputational risk. The first is whether its reputation exceeds its true character, creating a reputation-reality gap. The second is the extent to which external beliefs and expectations evolve, which can widen (or, less likely, narrow) this gap. The third is the quality of internal coordination, which can also influence the gap.

Regarding the first factor, the author suggests that effectively managing reputational risk starts with acknowledging that reputation is fundamentally a matter of perceptions. A company's reputation is shaped by how it is perceived by different stakeholders across specific categories. Importantly, reputation is distinct from the actual character or behaviour of the company and can be better or worse than reality. When a company's reputation exceeds its reality, it creates a significant risk. Over time, any failure to meet the perceived image will become evident, causing a decline in reputation until it better aligns with reality. To close reputation-reality gaps, a company must either enhance its ability to meet expectations or lower expectations by making more modest promises.

The second issue, changing beliefs and expectations, is strictly related to the first. Indeed, when expectations are shifting and the company's behaviour stays the same,

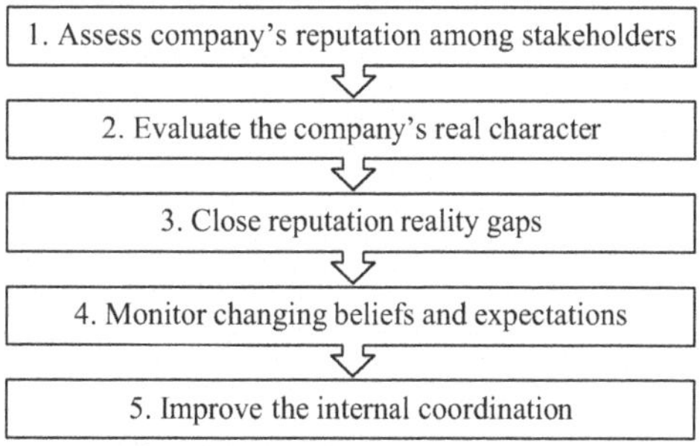

Fig. 3.8 Five-step process for managing reputational risk. Source: author's elaboration

the reputation-reality gap widens, and risks increase. These shifts can be provoked, for example, by the evolving of national norms over time (e.g. norms against the exploitation of nature and pollution) or the change in the behaviours or policies in the market.

Finally, another major source of reputational risk may be the poor coordination of the decisions made by different business units and functions. If one group creates expectations that another group fails to meet, the company's reputation can suffer. Poor internal coordination also inhibits a company's ability to identify changing beliefs and expectations.

Since companies are constantly exposed to those risks, they need to effectively manage them to preserve the value of their reputational capital. Regarding this, Eccles et al. (2007) suggests that companies should continuously implement the five-step process shown in Fig. 3.8.

Key aspects of each step are listed below:

1. *Assess reputation*—reputation is a perception and, thus, it must be measured. Various techniques exist for evaluating the company's reputation. They include media analysis, surveys of stakeholders (customers, employees, investors, NGOs) and industry executives, focus groups, and public opinion polls (see Chap. 5 for more details on corporate reputation measurement methods).
2. *Evaluate reality*—the company must objectively evaluate its ability to meet the performance expectations of stakeholders. Indeed, managers and executives generally have a natural tendency to overestimate their organizations and their capabilities, and they are prone to believe that their company has a good reputation if there is no indicator that they are wrong. Consequently, this misevaluation can generate a reputation-reality gap.
3. *Close gaps*—when the company's character exceeds its reputation, the gap should be closed by investing in building better capabilities or moderating the stakeholders' expectations.
4. *Monitor changing beliefs and expectations*—the company needs to monitor how stakeholders' beliefs and expectations are evolving. In this regard, periodic surveys, open-response questionnaires, and focus groups could be useful to develop a picture of stakeholders' expectations over time.

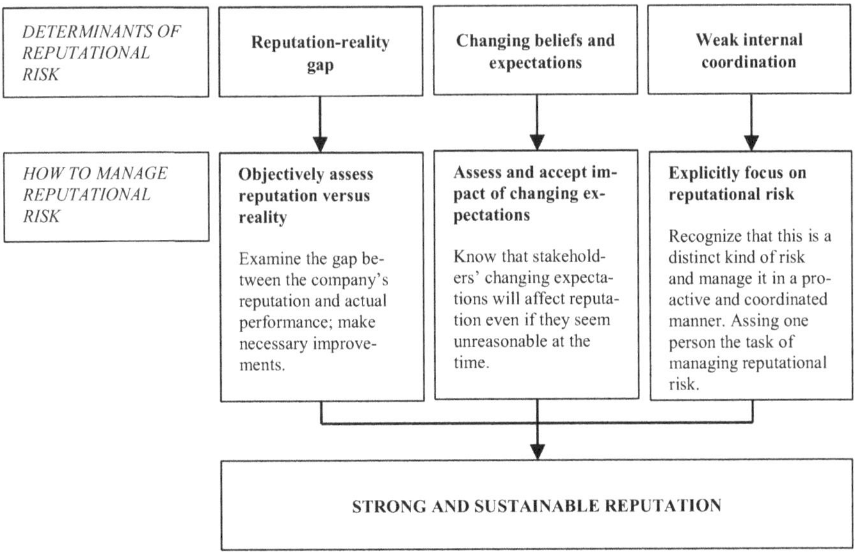

Fig. 3.9 Determinants of reputational risk and actions to manage it. Source: Eccles et al. (2007)

5. *Put one person in charge*—the company should give one person the responsibility to assess reputation, evaluate reality, identify, and close gaps and monitor changing beliefs and expectations. In general, those whose existing responsibilities pose potential conflicts probably shouldn't be chosen

By proactively implementing such a process, companies can mitigate the likelihood of negative impacts from reputational risk, thereby safeguarding the value of their reputational capital.

Figure 3.9 summarizes the determinants of reputational risk and how to manage them.

Seven years later, Lamboglia and D'Onza (2014) provide a comprehensive definition of reputational risk that aligns with the accounting and management literature. They describe reputational risk as the possibility that internal or external events within the firm's operations (primary risks) could lead to a deterioration in stakeholders' perceptions of the company, resulting in a reduction of its reputational capital and, consequently, worsening the prospective equilibrium conditions of the firm.

Building on this definition, Lavorato et al. (2021) identified four key elements that characterize the 'lifecycle' of reputational risk and its management (Fig. 3.10):

1. The occurrence of internal and external events within the company that have the potential to trigger reputational risk.
2. The deterioration of stakeholders' opinions serves as a link between operational risk and reputational risk.

Fig. 3.10 Lifecycle of reputational risk. Source: author's elaboration based on Lavorato et al. (2021) and Lamboglia and D'Onza (2014)

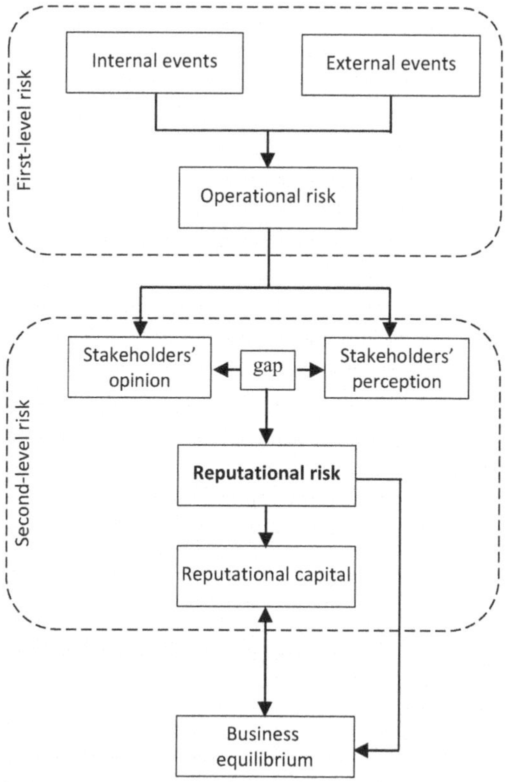

3. The impact of reputational risk on reputational capital is defined as the cumulative perception of a company based on financial, social, and environmental evaluations.
4. The effect of reputational risk on corporate performance, highlighting the cyclical relationship between reputation and organizational success

According to Lavorato et al. (2021), the first element involves primary events, whether internal (e.g. governance failures) or external (e.g. market shock), that may escalate operational risks into reputational risks. The second element focuses on stakeholders' perceptions, emphasizing how reputational risk arises when a misalignment occurs between stakeholders' expectations and the company's actual values or objectives. This misalignment often results from the materialization of operational risks.

The third element pertains to reputational capital, which Lavorato et al. (2021) describe as the aggregation of external judgements attributed to the company, reflecting its financial, social, and environmental performance. A loss of reputational capital not only affects the company's standing among stakeholders but also diminishes its ability to navigate market challenges.

Finally, the fourth element connects reputational risk to corporate performance, emphasizing a bidirectional relationship. High reputational capital often enhances corporate performance, while better performance, in turn, reinforces reputation. Conversely, when reputational risk escalates, it can undermine both reputation and financial results, creating a detrimental feedback loop (for more details on the relationship between reputational capital and performance, see Sect. 4.2 that examines in depth this topic).

By synthesizing the findings of Eccles et al. (2007) and Lavorato et al. (2021), it can be concluded that a gap between reputation and reality, shifts in stakeholders' beliefs and expectations, and weak internal coordination can lead to a misalignment between stakeholders' expectations and a company's actions ultimately weaken corporate performance through the loss of reputational capital. Within the corporate reputation management framework presented earlier in this book (Fig. 3.1), the evidence underscores that reputational risk represents a negative flow impacting the stock of reputational capital.

The next section completes the analysis of the determinants and processes influencing reputational capital by analysing crisis management.

3.3.2 Crisis Management to Safeguard Reputation Capital

Corporate reputation can be threatened also by other types of risks linked to 'low-probability, high-impact events that threaten the viability of the organization and are characterized by ambiguity of cause, effect and means of resolution, as well as by a belief that decision must be made swiftly' (Pearson & Clair, 1998). These are known as organizational crises.

A crisis leads to three main outcomes for the firm: first, it may prompt stakeholders to question the firm's legitimacy; second, the firm will be scrutinized concerning its contribution to the causes and development of the crisis; and third, the firm may be blamed and held responsible for having caused or contributed to the crisis (Dean, 2004). Thus, a corporate crisis can bring the affected firm into disrepute, which could imperil an organization's future profitability, growth, and possibly its survival (Tucker & Melewar, 2005). The survival of the firm and the safeguarding of its reputation are therefore closely tied to the goals of crisis management (Coombs, 2007; Robert & Lajtha, 2002).

Focusing on management research, crisis management can be defined as the 'systematic attempt by organizational members with external stakeholders to avert or to effectively manage those [crises] that do occur' (Pearson & Clair, 1998).

Corporate reputation is associated with crisis management and a two-sided relationship exists between those two concepts.

Figure 3.11 underscores the interplay between crisis management and corporate reputation, highlighting that both concepts influence and shape each other.

Fig. 3.11 Relationship between corporate reputation and crisis management. Source: author's elaboration

On one hand, corporate reputation defends company value by moderating the impact of crises; on the other hand, crisis management is crucial for preserving corporate reputation.

This topic holds significant relevance for companies, as they often fail to allocate adequate resources to prepare for crisis management, resulting in a negative consequence on corporate reputation (Bowers et al., 2017). It may stem from the notion that it is very difficult to anticipate a crisis. Lockwood (2005) presented five reasons why managers and organizations fail in this regard:

1. Denial of an impending threat to the organization.
2. A reluctance to make crisis preparedness a priority.
3. A lack of awareness of the risks inherent to the business.
4. Ignorance of warning signs accompanied by a failure to critically analyse the organization's history or the disaster experiences of others in the industry or country.
5. Reliance on weak, untested plans that will not effectively protect organizations in a real crisis

In this context, considering the depth and breadth of losses that typically are related to an organizational crisis, and recognizing that the response to that crisis will determine the trajectory of recovery and future organizational performance, many authors focus on identifying ways to effectively manage or avert them (Perrow, 1986; Tron et al., 2018). For example, King (2002) emphasized that effective crisis management depends upon a company's team-related factors (e.g. team composition, prior interactions, task knowledge) that may influence an organization's response and its ethical responsibility. Bowers et al. (2017) suggested that the organizations' leadership and cultural dynamics set the conditions leading up to the events that may provoke the crisis. Seeger and Ulmer (2001) highlight a critical connection between a company's core values and the resilience it exhibits in times of crisis, particularly regarding corporate social responsibility (CSR) and entrepreneurship. This resilience manifests through virtues like swift response, support for affected parties, and the ability to rebuild and renew. These values play a pivotal role in mitigating the potential damage that a crisis can inflict on an organization's values and relationships with stakeholders.

Comparing factors that prior literature associated with the effectiveness of management crisis with factors (drivers and inputs) that cause reputation according to the framework by Money et al. (2017) (for more details see Sect. 2.1.3), it's worth noting an overlap of items. This comparison indicates a potential interconnectedness or shared elements between what drives effective crisis management and what influences a company's reputation. This association implies that certain factors or inputs that impact crisis management effectiveness could also play a role in shaping or influencing a company's reputation. Understanding this overlap could be pivotal in developing a more comprehensive approach to managing crisis while simultaneously safeguarding and nurturing a positive reputation. Recognizing these commonalities presents an opportunity to streamline strategies that address both crisis response and reputation management concurrently. This approach can ultimately enhance the overall resilience of the organization. Moreover, this connection implies that the strategies a company adopts to build and maintain its reputation may also enhance the effectiveness of crisis management during times of crisis and vice versa.

The above assumptions have led the scholars' interest in analysing the role of corporate reputation in influencing crisis management effectiveness and attenuating the negative effect the crisis has on firm performance (e.g. Dwiedienawati et al., 2021; Helm & Tolsdorf, 2013; Koronis & Ponis, 2012; Jones et al., 2000). Indeed, a positive reputation can act as a buffer during crises, aiding in maintaining trust with stakeholders and mitigating the fallout. Scholars are increasingly recognizing the significance of corporate reputation and understanding its impact on how companies deal with and recover from crisis. Schnietz and Epstein (2005) analysed a sample comprising over 400 companies to investigate whether a reputation for social responsibility could shield firms from financial losses during an organizational crisis. Their findings provided robust evidence supporting the idea that such a reputation indeed acted as a protective factor. Jones et al. (2000) recognized the reputation as a source of company resilience that assists the firm in its interaction with the environment and ultimately its capacity to maintain financial performance over time. The authors referred to a 'reservoir of goodwill' when they suggested that 'firms can reduce the uncertainty associated with a competitive and hostile environment' by developing their reputation.

However, the literature also highlights an alternate impact of reputation on crisis management. It suggests that during a crisis, a pre-existing positive reputation might become a liability. This viewpoint supports the idea that violating stakeholder expectations affects highly reputable firms more severely, whereas firms with comparatively poorer reputations might have less at stake (Helm & Tolsdorf, 2013). While some studies propose that reputation serves as a protective factor, others offer a contrasting perspective.

On the other side of the relationship between corporate reputation and crisis management, prior evidence suggested that a crisis may damage corporate reputation and affect how stakeholders interact with the organization (Barton, 2001; Dowling, 2002). Even though Coombs (2007) believes the priority in any crisis is to protect stakeholders from harm, crisis managers should also turn their attention to reputational assets (Šontaitė-Petkevičienė, 2014).

The literature emphasizes three critical components in crisis management aimed at safeguarding corporate reputation: the CEO's role, organizational initiatives, and communication strategies, all of which interplay. Turk et al. (2012) highlighted that fostering positive relationships between a company and its stakeholders, coupled with an active and visible leadership stance by the CEO during a crisis, can enable the adoption of more assertive yet defensive corporate initiatives and communication strategies. This underscores the interdependence among reputation, leadership, and communication.

This evidence underscored the pivotal role of communication strategies in both repairing corporate reputation and proactively averting potential reputational harm to an organization. Consistent with this view, Coombs (2007) developed the situational crisis communication theory (SCCT), an evidence-based framework that guides organizations in optimizing crisis communication to safeguard their reputation. SCCT delineates key factors within a crisis scenario that influence the threat to reputation (Table 3.1), identifies crisis types through crisis clustering and assesses their impact on reputation (Table 3.2), and proposes crisis response strategies aiming to repair a reputation, diminish negative affect, and prevent negative behavioural intentions (Table 3.3).

Crisis response strategies have three objectives aimed at protecting reputations (Coombs, 1995):

1. Shaping the attribution of the crisis.
2. Changing the perception of the role of organization in crisis.
3. Reducing the negative effect generated by the crisis

These three objectives all support the larger goal of reputation safeguard and resolve into two principal types of strategies: the deny strategies and the bolstering strategies.

The first attempts to remove any connection between the organization and the crisis. If the organization is not involved in a crisis, it will not suffer any damage from the event.

Table 3.1 SCCT factors that shape the reputational threat

The threat is the amount of damage a crisis could inflict on the organization's reputation if no action is taken. Three factors in the crisis situation shape the reputational threat:
1. The initial attribution of crisis responsibility (how much stakeholders believe organizational actions caused the crisis)
2. The organization's crisis history (whether similar crises occurred previously)
3. The preceding relational reputation (how stakeholders perceive the organization's treatment of them in other contexts)

Source: Coombs (2007)

Table 3.2 SCCT crisis types by crisis clusters

Victim cluster: In these crisis types, the organization is also a victim of the crisis
(Weak attributions of crisis responsibility = Mild reputational threat)
Natural disaster: Acts of nature damage an organization such as an earthquake
Rumour: False and damaging information about an organization is being circulated
Workplace violence: Current or former employees attack current employees onsite
Product tampering/Malevolence: External agent causes damage to an organization
Accidental cluster: In these crisis types, the organizational actions leading to the crisis were unintentional
(Minimal attributions of crisis responsibility = Moderate reputational threat)
Challenges: Stakeholders claim an organization is operating inappropriately
Technical-error accidents: A technology or equipment failure causes an industrial accident
Technical-error product harm: A technology or equipment failure causes a product to be recalled
Preventable cluster: In these crisis types, the organization knowingly placed people at risk, took inappropriate actions, or violated a law/regulation
(Strong attributions of crisis responsibility = Severe reputational threat)
Human-error accidents: Human error causes an industrial accident
Human-error product harm: Human error causes a product to be recalled
Organizational misdeed with no injuries: Stakeholders are deceived without injury
Organizational misdeed management misconduct: Laws or regulations are violated by management
Organizational misdeed with injuries: Stakeholders are placed at risk by management and injuries occur

Source: Coombs (2007)

The second offers a minimal opportunity to develop reputational assets. Managers who have had positive relationships with stakeholders can draw upon that goodwill to help protect the organizational reputation, praise stakeholders for their efforts during the crisis as a means of improving relationships with them, or draw sympathy from being a victim of the crisis. Praising stakeholders generates some goodwill and being cast as the victim evokes sympathy for the organization (Coombs, 2007).

On the same topic, Dwiedienawati et al. (2021) have recently conducted a questionnaire to 296 participants from various organizations in Indonesia to confirm the association between corporate reputation and crisis management. Specifically, their analysis focuses on the leadership style, communication quality, and human resources involved in the crisis process as key factors influencing the effectiveness of the crisis management process. Their findings confirm that businesses need to deliver effective crisis management to safeguard the organization's reputation, thus suggesting that the occurrence of a crisis has a negative impact on the reputational capital.

Taken together, the evidence highlighted in this section enriches the corporate reputation management framework introduced earlier in this book (Fig. 3.1) by emphasizing the importance of including crises as a determinant of corporate reputation.

Table 3.3 SCCT crisis response strategies

Primary crisis response strategies
Deny crisis response strategies
Attack the accuser: A crisis manager confronts the person or group claiming something is wrong with the organization
Denial: Crisis manager asserts that there is no crisis
Scapegoat: A crisis manager blames some person or group outside of the organization for the crisis. Diminish crisis response strategies
Excuse: Crisis manager minimizes organizational responsibility by denying intent to harm and/or claiming inability to control the events that triggered the crisis
Justification: A crisis manager minimizes the perceived damage caused by the crisis. Rebuild crisis response strategies
Compensation: Crisis manager offers money or other gifts to victims
Apology: The crisis manager indicates the organization takes full responsibility for the crisis and asks stakeholders for forgiveness
Secondary crisis response strategies
Bolstering crisis response strategies
Reminder: Tell stakeholders about the past good works of the organization
Ingratiation: Crisis manager praises stakeholders and/or reminds them of past good works by the organization
Victimage: Crisis managers remind stakeholders that the organization is a victim of the crisis too

Source: Coombs (2007)

Building on the reputation management framework introduced at the beginning of this chapter (Fig. 3.1), the next section incorporates an in-depth analysis of corporate reputation outcomes, thereby presenting a more comprehensive reputation management framework.

References

Adams, C. A. (2004). The ethical, social and environmental reporting-performance portrayal gap. *Accounting, Auditing & Accountability Journal, 17*(5), 731–757. https://doi.org/10.1108/09513570410567791

Adams, C. A., & Larrinaga-González, C. (2007). Engaging with organisations in pursuit of improved sustainability accounting and performance. *Accounting, Auditing and Accountability Journal, 20*(3), 333–355. https://doi.org/10.1108/09513570710748535

Adams, C. A., & McNicholas, P. (2007). Making a difference: Sustainability reporting, accountability and organisational change. *Accounting, Auditing and Accountability Journal, 20*(3), 382–402. https://doi.org/10.1108/09513570710748553

Agrawal, A., & Jaffe, J. F. (2000). The post-merger performance puzzle. In *Advances in mergers and acquisitions* (Vol. 1, pp. 7–41). Emerald Group Publishing Limited. https://doi.org/10.1016/S1479-361X(00)01002-4

Ahuja, G., & Yayavaram, S. (2011). PERSPECTIVE—Explaining influence rents: The case for an institutions-based view of strategy. *Organization Science, 22*(6), 1631–1652. https://doi.org/10.1287/orsc.1100.0623

Ali, A., Chen, T.-Y., & Radhakrishnan, S. (2007). Corporate disclosures by family firms. *Journal of Accounting and Economics, 44*(1), 238–286. https://doi.org/10.1016/j.jacceco.2007.01.006

Ali, R., Lynch, R., Melewar, T. C., & Jin, Z. (2015). The moderating influences on the relationship of corporate reputation with its antecedents and consequences: A meta-analytic review. *Journal of Business Research, 68*(5), 1105–1117. https://doi.org/10.1016/j.jbusres.2014.10.013

Allegrini, M. (2003). *L'informativa di periodo nella comunicazione economico-finanziaria.* Principi e contenuti.

Arend, R. J. (2009). Reputation for cooperation: Contingent benefits in alliance activity. *Strategic Management Journal, 30*(4), 371–385. https://doi.org/10.1002/smj.740

Axjonow, A., Ernstberger, J., & Pott, C. (2018). The impact of corporate social responsibility disclosure on corporate reputation: A non-professional stakeholder perspective. *Journal of Business Ethics, 151*(2), 429–450. https://doi.org/10.1007/s10551-016-3225-4

Baier, C., Göttsche, M., Hellmann, A., & Schiemann, F. (2022). Too good to be true: Influencing credibility perceptions with signaling reference explicitness and assurance depth. *Journal of Business Ethics, 178*(3), 695–714. https://doi.org/10.1007/s10551-020-04719-7

Balakrishnan, S., & Koza, M. P. (1993). Information asymmetry, adverse selection and joint-ventures: Theory and evidence. *Journal of Economic Behavior and Organization, 20*(1), 99–117.

Bandettini, A. (1978). Decisioni e necessita d'informazione nelle aziende. *Cedam.*

Barney, J. (1991). Firm resources and sustained competitive advantage. *Journal of Management, 17*(1), 99–120. https://doi.org/10.1177/014920639101700108

Baron, D. P. (1995). Integrated strategy: Market and nonmarket components. *California Management Review, 37*(2), 47–65. https://doi.org/10.2307/41165788

Barton, L. (2001). *Crisis in organizations II*. South-Western College Pub.

Basdeo, D. K., Smith, K. G., Grimm, C. M., Rindova, V. P., & Derfus, P. J. (2006). The impact of market actions on firm reputation. *Strategic Management Journal, 27*(12), 1205–1219. Scopus. https://doi.org/10.1002/smj.556

Basir, N. (2020). Reputation enhancing through patent portfolios: An exploration of lapsed patents and IPOS. *Corporate Reputation Review, 23*(1), 42–56. https://doi.org/10.1057/s41299-019-00074-0

Baum, J., & Ingram, P. (2002). Interorganizational learning and network organization: Toward a behavioral theory of the interfirm (pp. 191–218). https://doi.org/10.4337/9781035335503.00020

Baumgartner, K. T., Ernst, C. A., & Fischer, T. M. (2022). How corporate reputation disclosures affect stakeholders' behavioral intentions: Mediating mechanisms of perceived organizational performance and corporate reputation. *Journal of Business Ethics, 175*(2), 361–389. https://doi.org/10.1007/s10551-020-04642-x

Beatty, R. P. (1989). Auditor reputation and the pricing of initial public offerings. *The Accounting Review, 64*(4), 693–709.

Bebbington, J., Larrinaga, C., & Moneva, J. M. (2008). Corporate social reporting and reputation risk management. *Accounting, Auditing and Accountability Journal, 21*(3), 337–361. https://doi.org/10.1108/09513570810863932

Belderbos, R., Gilsing, V., & Lokshin, B. (2012). Persistence of, and interrelation between, horizontal and vertical technology alliances. *Journal of Management, 38*(6), 1812–1834. https://doi.org/10.1177/0149206310386962

Bennett, R., & Kottasz, R. (2000). Practitioner perceptions of corporate reputation: An empirical investigation. *Corporate Communications: An International Journal, 5*(4), Articolo 4.

Bertinetti, G. (1996). *Comunicazione finanziaria aziendale e teoria della finanza*. EGEA.

Bertini, U. (1987). *Introduzione allo studio dei rischi nell'economia aziendale*. Giuffrè.

Boiral, O. (2013). Sustainability reports as simulacra? A counter-account of A and A+ GRI reports. *Accounting, Auditing & Accountability Journal, 26*(7), 1036–1071. https://doi.org/10.1108/AAAJ-04-2012-00998

Bowers, M. R., Hall, J. R., & Srinivasan, M. M. (2017). Organizational culture and leadership style: The missing combination for selecting the right leader for effective crisis management. *Business Horizons, 60*(4), 551–563. https://doi.org/10.1016/j.bushor.2017.04.001

Brivot, M., Gendron, Y., & Guénin, H. (2017). Reinventing organizational control: Meaning contest surrounding reputational risk controllability in the social media arena. *Accounting, Auditing and Accountability Journal, 30*(4), 795–820. https://doi.org/10.1108/AAAJ-06-2015-2111

Brown, D., Guidry, R., & Patten, D. (2009). Sustainability reporting and perceptions of corporate reputation: An analysis using fortune most admired scores. *Advances in Environmental Accounting and Management, 4*, 83–104. https://doi.org/10.1108/S1479-3598(2010)0000004007

Bunting, M., & Lipski, R. (2000). Drowned out? Rethinking corporate reputation management for the internet. *Journal of Communication Management, 5*(2), 170–178. https://doi.org/10.1108/13632540110806758

Burt, R. S. (1992). *Structural holes: The social structure of competition*. Harvard University Press.

Busco, C., Frigo, M. L., Quattrone, P., & Riccaboni, A. (2013). *Integrated reporting: Concepts and cases that redefine corporate accountability*. Springer International Publishing.

Cannella, B., Finkelstein, S., & Hambrick, D. C. (2009). Strategic leadership: Theory and research on executives, top management teams, and boards, *1–448*. https://doi.org/10.1093/acprof:oso/9780195162073.001.0001

Christensen, C., Alton, R., Rising, C., & Waldeck, A. (2011). The new M&APlaybook. *Harvard Business Review, 89*(3), 48–57.

Clark, B. H., & Montgomery, D. B. (1998). Deterrence, reputations, and competitive cognition. *Management Science, 44*(1), 62–82.

Coda, V. (1991). Comunicazione e immagine nella strategia dell'impresa. *Giappichelli*. https://www.libreriauniversitaria.it/comunicazione-immagine-strategia-impresa-coda/libro/9788834806258

Connelly, B. L., Certo, S. T., Ireland, R. D., & Reutzel, C. R. (2011). Signaling theory: A review and assessment. *Journal of Management, 37*(1), 39–67. https://doi.org/10.1177/0149206310388419

Conte, F. (2018). Understanding the influence of CEO tenure and CEO reputation on corporate reputation: An exploratory study in Italy. *International Journal of Business and Management, 13*(3), 54. https://doi.org/10.5539/ijbm.v13n3p54

Coombs, W. T. (1995). Choosing the right words: The development of guidelines for the selection of the "appropriate" crisis-response strategies. *Management Communication Quarterly, 8*(4), 447–476. https://doi.org/10.1177/0893318995008004003

Coombs, W. T. (2007). Protecting organization reputations during a crisis: The development and application of situational crisis communication theory. *Corporate Reputation Review, 10*(3), 163–176. https://doi.org/10.1057/palgrave.crr.1550049

Corvi, E. (1997). Economia e gestione della comunicazione economico-finanziaria d'impresa. *EGEA spa*. https://www.libreriauniversitaria.it/economia-gestione-comunicazione-economico-finanziaria/libro/9788823803916

Dameri, R. P., & Ferrando, P. M. (2021). Implementing integrated reporting to disclose intellectual capital in health organisations: A case study. *Journal of Intellectual Capital, 22*(2), 311–336. https://doi.org/10.1108/JIC-01-2020-0019

Das, T. K., & Teng, B.-S. (2000). A resource-based theory of strategic alliances. *Journal of Management, 26*(1), 31–61. https://doi.org/10.1177/014920630002600105

Dean, D. H. (2004). Consumer reaction to negative publicity: Effects of corporate reputation, response, and responsibility for a crisis event. *The Journal of Business Communication (1973), 41*(2), 192–211. https://doi.org/10.1177/0021943603261748

Deegan, C., & Unerman, J. (2006). Financial accounting theory: European edition. https://research.manchester.ac.uk/en/publications/financial-accounting-theory-european-edition

Deephouse, D. L. (1997). The effect of financial and media reputations on performance. *Corporate Reputation Review, 1*(1), 68–72. https://doi.org/10.1057/palgrave.crr.1540023

Deephouse, D. L., & Carter, S. M. (2005). An examination of differences between organizational legitimacy and organizational reputation. *Journal of Management Studies, 42*(2), 329–360. Scopus. https://doi.org/10.1111/j.1467-6486.2005.00499.x

Devos, E., Kadapakkam, P.-R., & Krishnamurthy, S. (2009). How do mergers create value? A comparison of taxes, market power, and efficiency improvements as explanations for synergies. *The Review of Financial Studies, 22*(3), 1179–1211. https://doi.org/10.1093/rfs/hhn019

Di Stefano, G. (1990). Il sistema delle comunicazioni economico-finanziarie nella realtà aziendale moderna. *Giuffrè Editore*. https://www.unilibro.it/libro/di-stefano-giancarlo/sistema-comunicazioni-economico-finanziarie-realta-aziendale-moderna/9788814025631

Dierickx, I., & Cool, K. (1989). Asset stock accumulation and sustainability of competitive advantage. *Management Science, 35*(12), 1504–1511.

DiMaggio, P. J., & Powell, W. W. (1983). The iron cage revisted: Institutional isomorphism and collective rationality in organizational fields. *American Sociological Review, 48*, 147–160. https://doi.org/10.17323/1726-3247-2010-1-34-56

Dollinger, M. J., Golden, P. A., & Saxton, T. (1997). The effect of reputation on the decision to joint venture. *Strategic Management Journal, 18*(2), 127–140. Scopus. https://doi.org/10.1002/(SICI)1097-0266(199702)18:2<127::AID-SMJ859>3.0.CO;2-H

Dowling, G. (2002). *Creating corporate reputations: Identity, image, and performance*. Oxford University Press.

Dowling, G. R. (2006). Communicating corporate reputation through stories. *California Management Review, 49*(1), 82–100. https://doi.org/10.2307/41166372

Dreher, S. (2014). Social media and the world of work: A strategic approach to employees' participation in social media. *Corporate Communications: An International Journal, 19*(4), 344–356. https://doi.org/10.1108/CCIJ-10-2013-0087

Drucker, P. F. (1996). The shape of things to come. *Leader to Leader, 1996*(1), 12–18. https://doi.org/10.1002/ltl.40619960306

Dutot, V., Lacalle Galvez, E., & Versailles, D. W. (2016). CSR communications strategies through social media and influence on e-reputation: An exploratory study. *Management Decision, 54*(2), 363–389. https://doi.org/10.1108/MD-01-2015-0015

Dwiedienawati, D., Tjahjana, D., Faisal, M., Gandasari, D., & Abdinagoro, S. B. (2021). Determinants of perceived effectiveness in crisis management and company reputation during the COVID-19 pandemic. *Cogent Business and Management, 8*(1), 1912523. https://doi.org/10.1080/23311975.2021.1912523

Dyer, J. H., & Singh, H. (1998). The relational view: Cooperative strategy and sources of Interorganizational competitive advantage. *Academy of Management Review, 23*(4), 660–679. https://doi.org/10.5465/AMR.1998.1255632

Eberle, D., Berens, G., & Li, T. (2013). The impact of interactive corporate social responsibility communication on corporate reputation. *Journal of Business Ethics, 118*(4), 731–746. https://doi.org/10.1007/s10551-013-1957-y

Eccles, R. G., & Krzus, M. P. (2010). *One report: Integrated reporting for a sustainable strategy*. John Wiley & Sons.

Eccles, R. G., Lanes, K. L., & Wilson, T. C. (1999). Are you paying too much for that acquisition? *Harvard Business Review*. https://hbr.org/1999/07/are-you-paying-too-much-for-that-acquisition, *77*, 136.

Eccles, R., Newquist, S., & Schatz, R. (2007). Reputation and its risks. *Harvard Business Review, 85*(104–114), 156.

Edi, Basri, Y. Z., & Arafah, W. (2020). Ceo characteristics, firm reputation and firm performance after merger and acquisition. *Business: Theory and Practice, 21*(2), 850–858. https://doi.org/10.3846/btp.2020.12782

Elmuti, D., & Kathawala, Y. (2001). An overview of strategic alliances. *Management Decision, 39*(3), 205–218. https://doi.org/10.1108/EUM0000000005452

Eppler, M. J., & Mengis, J. (2004). The concept of information overload: A review of literature from organization science, accounting, marketing, MIS, and related disciplines. *The Information Society, 20*(5), 325–344. https://doi.org/10.1080/01972240490507974

Etter, M., Ravasi, D., & Colleoni, E. (2019). Social media and the formation of organizational reputation. *Academy of Management Review, 44*(1), 28–52. https://doi.org/10.5465/amr.2014.0280

Feldman, E. R., & Hernandez, E. (2022). Synergy in mergers and acquisitions: Typology, life cycles, and value. *Academy of Management Review, 47*(4), 549–578. https://doi.org/10.5465/amr.2018.0345

Fombrun, C. J. (1996). *Reputation: Realizing value from the corporate image*. Harvard Business School Press.

Fombrun, C., & Shanley, M. (1990). What's in a name? Reputation building and corporate strategy. *Academy of Management Journal, 33*, 233–258. https://doi.org/10.2307/256324

Fombrun, C., & van Riel, C. (1997). The reputational landscape. *Corporate Reputation Review, 1*(2), 5–13. https://doi.org/10.1057/palgrave.crr.1540024

Fombrun, C. J., & van Riel, C. B. M. (2004). *Fame and fortune: How successful companies build winning reputations*. FT Press.

Fombrun, C. J., Gardberg, N. A., & Sever, J. M. (2000). The reputation QuotientSM: A multi-stakeholder measure of corporate reputation. *Journal of Brand Management, 7*(4), 241–255. https://doi.org/10.1057/bm.2000.10

Francesconi, A., & Dossena, C. (2009). L'IT per l'analisi e la gestione della web corporate reputation. Un caso aziendale. 10o Workshop di Organizzazione Aziendale "Per lo sviluppo, la competitività e l'innovazione del sistema economico: il contributo degli studi in organizzazione aziendale", Cagliari.

Francis, J., & Schipper, K. (1999). Have financial statements lost their relevance? *Journal of Accounting Research, 37*(2), 319–352. https://doi.org/10.2307/2491412

Franco, M., & Haase, H. (2020). The role of reputation in the business cooperation process: Multiple case studies in small and medium-sized enterprises. *Journal of Strategy and Management, 14*(1), 82–95. https://doi.org/10.1108/JSMA-01-2020-0012

Freeman, R. E., & McVea, J. (2001). A stakeholder approach to strategic management (SSRN Scholarly Paper 263511). https://doi.org/10.2139/ssrn.263511

Gabbioneta, C., Ravasi, D., & Mazzola, P. (2007). Exploring the drivers of corporate reputation: A study of Italian securities analysts. *Corporate Reputation Review, 10*(2), 99–123. https://doi.org/10.1057/palgrave.crr.1550048

Gaines-Ross, L. (2000). CEO reputation: A key factor in shareholder value. *Corporate Reputation Review, 3*(4), 366–370. Scopus. https://doi.org/10.1057/palgrave.crr.1540127

Garzella, S. (2005). *Il sistema d'azienda e la valorizzazione delle «potenzialità inespresse». Una «visione» strategica per il risanamento*. Giappichelli.

Garzella, S., & Fiorentino, R. (2017). Synergy value and strategic management. Springer International Publishing. https://doi.org/10.1007/978-3-319-40671-8

Gatzert, N. (2015). The impact of corporate reputation and reputation damaging events on financial performance: Empirical evidence from the literature. *European Management Journal, 33*(6), 485–499. Scopus. https://doi.org/10.1016/j.emj.2015.10.001

Giacosa, E. (2012). *La Comunicazione Economico-Finanziaria d'Impresa*. G. Giappichelli Editore.

Giannessi, E. (1960). Le aziende di produzione originaria: Volume primo : le aziende agricole. Colombo Cursi.

Gibbs, R., & Humphries, A. (2009). *Strategic alliances and marketing partnerships: Gaining competitive advantage through collaboration and partnering*. Kogan Page Publishers.

Gibson, C. H. (2001). *Financial reporting and analysis: Using financial accounting information*. South-Western College Pub.

Gigler, F., & Hemmer, T. (1998). On the frequency, quality, and informational role of mandatory financial reports. *Journal of Accounting Research, 36*, 117–147. https://doi.org/10.2307/2491310

Gotsi, M., & Wilson, A. M. (2001). Corporate reputation: Seeking a definition. *Corporate Communications: An International Journal, 6*(1), 24–30. Scopus. https://doi.org/10.1108/13563280110381189

Gray, R., Kouhy, R., & Lavers, S. (1995). Corporate social and environmental reporting: A review of the literature and a longitudinal study of UK disclosure. *Accounting, Auditing and Accountability Journal, 8*(2), 47–77. https://doi.org/10.1108/09513579510146996

Gray, R., Owen, D., & Adams, C. (1996). *Accounting and accountability: Changes and challenges in corporate social and environmental reporting*. Prentice Hall.

Gulati, R., & Wohlgezogen, F. (2023). Can purpose Foster stakeholder trust in corporations? *Strategy Science, 8*(2), 270–287. https://doi.org/10.1287/stsc.2023.0196

Guthrie, J., & Parker, L. D. (1989). Corporate social reporting: A rebuttal of legitimacy theory. *Accounting and Business Research, 19*(76), 343–352. https://doi.org/10.1080/00014788.1989.9728863

Hall, R. (1993). A framework linking intangible resources and capabiliites to sustainable competitive advantage. *Strategic Management Journal, 14*(8), 607–618. https://doi.org/10.1002/smj.4250140804

Hambrick, D. C., & Mason, P. A. (1984). Upper echelons: The organization as a reflection of its top managers. *The Academy of Management Review, 9*(2), 193–206. https://doi.org/10.2307/258434

Hammond, S. A., & Slocum, J. W. (1996). The impact of prior firm financial performance on subsequent corporate reputation. *Journal of Business Ethics, 15*(2), 159–165. https://doi.org/10.1007/BF00705584

Harrigan, K. R. (2017). Strategic alliances as agents of competitive change. In L. F. Mesquita, R. Ragozzino, & J. J. Reuer (Eds.), (A c. Di) *Collaborative strategy*. Edward Elgar Publishing. https://doi.org/10.4337/9781783479580.00010

Harris, F., & de Chernatony, L. (2001). Corporate branding and corporate brand performance. *European Journal of Marketing, 35*(3/4), 441–456. https://doi.org/10.1108/03090560110382101

Haspeslagh, P. C., & Jemison, D. B. (1991). The challenge of renewal through acquisitions. *Planning Review, 19*(2), 27–30. https://doi.org/10.1108/eb054320

Hasseldine, J., Salama, A. I., & Toms, J. S. (2005). Quantity versus quality: The impact of environmental disclosures on the reputations of UK Plcs. *The British Accounting Review, 37*(2), 231–248. https://doi.org/10.1016/j.bar.2004.10.003

Healy, P. M., & Palepu, K. G. (2001). Information asymmetry, corporate disclosure, and the capital markets: A review of the empirical disclosure literature. *Journal of Accounting and Economics, 31*(1), 405–440. https://doi.org/10.1016/S0165-4101(01)00018-0

Helm, S. (2011). Employees' awareness of their impact on corporate reputation. *Journal of Business Research, 64*(7), 657–663. https://doi.org/10.1016/j.jbusres.2010.09.001

Helm, S., & Tolsdorf, J. (2013). How does corporate reputation affect customer loyalty in a corporate crisis? *Journal of Contingencies and Crisis Management, 21*(3), 144–152. https://doi.org/10.1111/1468-5973.12020

Henard, D. H., & Dacin, P. A. (2010). Reputation for product innovation: Its impact on consumers*. *Journal of Product Innovation Management, 27*(3), 321–335. https://doi.org/10.1111/j.1540-5885.2010.00719.x

Hennart, J.-F. (1988). A transaction costs theory of equity joint ventures. *Strategic Management Journal, 9*(4), 361–374. https://doi.org/10.1002/smj.4250090406

Höflinger, P. J., Nagel, C., & Sandner, P. (2018). Reputation for technological innovation: Does it actually cohere with innovative activity? *Journal of Innovation and Knowledge, 3*(1), 26–39. https://doi.org/10.1016/j.jik.2017.08.002

Hogan, J., & Lodhia, S. (2011). Sustainability reporting and reputation risk management: An Australian case study. *International Journal of Accounting and Information Management, 19*, 267–287. https://doi.org/10.1108/18347641111169269

Hogner, R. H. (1982). Corporate social reporting: 8 decades of development at US Steel. *Corporate Social Performance and Policy, 4*, 243–250.

Hoque, M. E. (2017). Why company should adopt integrated reporting? *International Journal of Economics and Financial Issues, 7*(1), 241–248.

Hosmer, L. T. (1995). Trust: The connecting link between organizational theory and philosophical ethics. *Academy of Management Review, 20*(2), 379–403. https://doi.org/10.5465/amr.1995.9507312923

Ireland, R., & Hitt, M. (1999). Achieving and maintaining strategic competitiveness in the 21 st century: The role of trategic leadership. *Academy of Management Perspectives, 13*. https://doi.org/10.5465/AME.1999.1567311

Jones, G. H., Jones, B. H., & Little, P. (2000). Reputation as reservoir: Buffering against loss in times of economic crisis. *Corporate Reputation Review, 3*(1), 21–29. https://doi.org/10.1057/palgrave.crr.1540096

Kale, P., Singh, H., & Perlmutter, H. (2000). Learning and protection of proprietary assets in strategic alliances: Building relational capital. *Strategic Management Journal, 21*(3), 217–237. https://doi.org/10.1002/(SICI)1097-0266(200003)21:3<217::AID-SMJ95>3.0.CO;2-Y

Kaul, A., Chaudhri, V., Cherian, D., Freberg, K., Mishra, S., Kumar, R., Pridmore, J., Lee, S. Y., Rana, N., Majmudar, U., & Carroll, C. E. (2015). Social media: The new mantra for managing reputation. *Vikalpa, 40*(4), 455–491. https://doi.org/10.1177/0256090915618029

King, G. (2002). Crisis management and team effectiveness: A closer examination. *Journal of Business Ethics, 41*(3), 235–249. https://doi.org/10.1023/A:1021200514323

Kitchen, P. J., & Laurence, A. (2003). Corporate reputation: An eight-country analysis. *Corporate Reputation Review, 6*(2), 103–117. https://doi.org/10.1057/palgrave.crr.1540193

Koronis, E., & Ponis, S. T. (2012). Introducing corporate reputation continuity to support organizational resilience against crises. *Journal of Applied Business Research (JABR), 28*(2), Articolo 2. https://doi.org/10.19030/jabr.v28i2.6850

Krishnan, V. (2005). Transformational leadership and outcomes: Role of relationship duration. *Leadership and Organization Development Journal, 26*, 442–457. https://doi.org/10.1108/01437730510617654

Lamboglia, R. (2018). La corporate social responsibility e la reputazione aziendale: Le principali relazioni. In L'azienda e la corporate social responsibility. Approfondimenti dottrinali e riflessioni gestionali (pp. 43–64). Franco Angeli. https://ricerca.uniparthenope.it/handle/11367/71363

Lamboglia, R., & D'Onza, G. (2014). Un modello di gestione del rischio reputazionale. Dall'identificazione al fronteggiamento. MANAGEMENT CONTROL, 2013/3. https://doi.org/10.3280/MACO2013-003002

Laskin, A. V. (2013). Reputation or financial performance: Which comes first? In *The handbook of communication and corporate reputation* (pp. 376–387). John Wiley and Sons, Ltd.. https://doi.org/10.1002/9781118335529.ch31

Laud, R. L., & Schepers, D. H. (2009). Beyond transparency: Information overload and a model for intelligibility. *Business and Society Review, 114*(3), 365–391. https://doi.org/10.1111/j.1467-8594.2009.00347.x

Lavorato, D., Lamboglia, R., & Mancini, D. (2021). La relazione tra rischio reputazionale e controllo-guida: Possibili linee di ricerca. *Management Control, 2021*(suppl), 2. https://doi.org/10.3280/MACO2021-002-S1003

Leenders, R. T. A. J., & Gabbay, S. M. (1999). *Corporate social capital and liability*. Springer US. https://doi.org/10.1007/978-1-4615-5027-3. (A c. Di).

Leland, H. E. (2007). Financial synergies and the optimal scope of the firm: Implications for mergers, spinoffs, and structured finance. *The Journal of Finance, 62*(2), 765–807. https://doi.org/10.1111/j.1540-6261.2007.01223.x

Lemke, F., & Petersen, H. L. (2013). Teaching reputational risk management in the supply chain. *Supply Chain Management: An International Journal, 18*(4), 413–429. https://doi.org/10.1108/SCM-06-2012-0222

Lindblom, C. K. (1993). The implications of organisational legitimacy for corporate social performance and disclosure. Conference paper, Critical Perspectives on Accounting Conference.

Lockwood, N. R. (2005). Crisis management in today's business environment. *SHRM Research Quarterly, 4*, 1–9.

Love, E. G., & Kraatz, M. (2009). Character, conformity, or the bottom line? How and why downsizing affected corporate reputation. *Academy of Management Journal, 52*(2), 314–335. https://doi.org/10.5465/AMJ.2009.37308247

Love, E. G., Lim, J., & Bednar, M. K. (2017). The face of the firm: The influence of CEOs on corporate reputation. *Academy of Management Journal, 60*(4), 1462–1481. https://doi.org/10.5465/amj.2014.0862

Mahon, J. F., & Wartick, S. L. (2003). Dealing with stakeholders: How reputation, credibility and framing influence the game. *Corporate Reputation Review, 6*(1), 19–35. https://doi.org/10.1057/palgrave.crr.1540187

Maltese, L., Pons, F., & Prévot, F. (2017). Managing E-reputation and key stakeholders in the context of sport expressive organizations. *International Studies of Management and Organization, 47*(1), 88–105. https://doi.org/10.1080/00208825.2017.1241090

Marchi, L., & Mancini, D. (1999). Gestione informatica dei dati aziendali. *FrancoAngeli*. https://www.ibs.it/gestione-informatica-dei-dati-aziendali-libro-vari/e/9788856812893

Mariconda, S., Zamparini, A., & Lurati, F. (2023). Organizational reputation: In search of lost time. *Strategic Organization, 21*(4), 961–974. https://doi.org/10.1177/14761270211046062

McGuire, J. B., Scheeweis, T., & Branch, B. (1990). Perceptions of firm quality: A cause or result of firm performance. *Journal of Management, 16*(1), 167. https://doi.org/10.1177/014920639001600112

Michelon, G. (2011). Sustainability disclosure and reputation: A comparative study. *Corporate Reputation Review, 14*(2), 79–96. https://doi.org/10.1057/crr.2011.10

Miles, S. J., & Mangold, W. G. (2014). Employee voice: Untapped resource or social media time bomb? *Business Horizons, 57*(3), 401–411. https://doi.org/10.1016/j.bushor.2013.12.011

Miller, D., & Breton-Miller, I. L. (2005). *Managing for the long run: Lessons in competitive advantage from great family businesses*. Harvard Business Press.

Moizer, P. (1997). Auditor reputation: The international empirical evidence. *International Journal of Auditing, 1*(1), 61–74. https://doi.org/10.1111/1099-1123.00013

Money, K., Saraeva, A., Garnelo-Gomez, I., Pain, S., & Hillenbrand, C. (2017). Corporate reputation past and future: A review and integration of existing literature and a framework for future research. *Corporate Reputation Review, 20*(3/4), 193–211. https://doi.org/10.1057/s41299-017-0034-3

Nahapiet, J., & Ghoshal, S. (1998). Social capital, intellectual capital, and the organizational advantage. *Academy of Management Review, 23*(2), 242–266. https://doi.org/10.5465/AMR.1998.533225

Odriozola, M. D., & Baraibar-Diez, E. (2017). Is corporate reputation associated with quality of CSR reporting? Evidence from Spain. *Corporate Social Responsibility and Environmental Management, 24*(2), 121–132. https://doi.org/10.1002/csr.1399

Oliver, C. (1997). Sustainable competitive advantage: Combining institutional and resource-based views. *Strategic Management Journal, 18*(9), 697–713.

Olk, P., & Ring, P. S. (1997). Part V: Other consequences of corporate reputation: Strategic alliances and firm-based legitimacy. *Corporate Reputation Review, 1*(2), 109–114. https://doi.org/10.1057/palgrave.crr.1540028

Patten, D. M. (1991). Exposure, legitimacy, and social disclosure. *Journal of Accounting and Public Policy, 10*(4), 297–308. https://doi.org/10.1016/0278-4254(91)90003-3

Pearson, C. M., & Clair, J. A. (1998). Reframing crisis management. *Academy of Management Review, 23*(1), 59–76. https://doi.org/10.5465/amr.1998.192960

Perrow, C. (1986). Economic theories of organization. *Theory and Society, 15*(1/2), 11–45.

Petrick, J. A., Scherer, R. F., Brodzinski, J. D., Quinn, J. F., & Ainina, M. F. (1999). Global leadership skills and reputational capital: Intangible resources for sustainable competitive advantage. *Academy of Management Perspectives, 13*(1), 58–69. https://doi.org/10.5465/ame.1999.1567322

Pineiro-Chousa, J., Vizcaíno-González, M., López-Cabarcos, M. Á., & Romero-Castro, N. (2017). Managing reputational risk through environmental management and reporting: An options theory approach. *Sustainability, 9*(3), Articolo 3. https://doi.org/10.3390/su9030376

Podolny, J. M. (1993). A status-based model of market competition. *American Journal of Sociology, 98*(4), 829–872. https://doi.org/10.1086/230091

Preston, L. E. (2004). Reputation as a source of corporate social capital. *Journal of General Management, 30*(2), 43–50. https://doi.org/10.1177/030630700403000204
Quagli, A. (2008). Comunicare il futuro. L'informativa economico-finanziaria di tipo previsionale delle società quotate italiane. Franco Angeli. https://www.libreriauniversitaria.it/comunicare-futuro-informativa-economico-finanziaria/libro/9788846463869
Raithel, S., & Schwaiger, M. (2015). The effects of corporate reputation perceptions of the general public on shareholder value. *Strategic Management Journal, 36*(6), 945–956. https://doi.org/10.1002/smj.2248
Rao, H. (1994). The social construction of reputation: Certification contests, legitimation, and the survival of organizations in the American Automobile Industry: 1895–1912. *Strategic Management Journal, 15*(S1), 29–44. https://doi.org/10.1002/smj.4250150904
Reilly, B. J., & Di Angelo, J. A. (1990). Communication: A cultural system of meaning and value. *Human Relations, 43*(2), 129–140.
Rindova, V. P., & Fombrun, C. J. (1999). Constructing competitive advantage: The role of firm-constituent interactions. *Strategic Management Journal, 20*(8), 691–710.
Rindova, V. P., Williamson, I. O., Petkova, A. P., & Sever, J. M. (2005). Being good or being known: An empirical examination of the dimensions, antecedents, and consequences of organizational reputation. *Academy of Management Journal, 48*(6), 1033–1049. https://doi.org/10.5465/AMJ.2005.19573108
Robert, B., & Lajtha, C. (2002). A new approach to crisis management. *Journal of Contingencies and Crisis Management, 10*(4), 181–191. https://doi.org/10.1111/1468-5973.00195
Roberts, P. W., & Dowling, G. R. (2002). Corporate reputation and sustained superior financial performance. *Strategic Management Journal, 23*(12), 1077–1093. https://doi.org/10.1002/smj.274
Romenti, S. (2008). Corporate governance e reputazione: Dallo stakeholder relationship management allo stakeholder engagement. stakeholder engagement, 2.
Salvioni, D. M. (2002). Cultura della trasparenza e comunicazione economico-finanziaria d'impresa. Symphonya : Emerging issues in management. N. 2—Cultura d'impresa e complessità di mercato, 2002, 1000–1013. https://doi.org/10.1400/90602
Salvioni, D. M. (2003). La comunicazione economico-finanziaria nell'evoluzione telematica dei flussi informativi. In D. M. Salvioni & C. Teodori (Eds.), *Internet e comunicazione economico-finanziaria d'impresa*. FrancoAngeli.
Schaarschmidt, M., & Walsh, G. (2020). Social media-driven antecedents and consequences of employees' awareness of their impact on corporate reputation. *Journal of Business Research, 117*, 718–726. https://doi.org/10.1016/j.jbusres.2018.11.027
Schmitt, J. B., Debbelt, C. A., & Schneider, F. M. (2018). Too much information? Predictors of information overload in the context of online news exposure. *Information, Communication and Society, 21*(8), 1151–1167. https://doi.org/10.1080/1369118X.2017.1305427
Schnietz, K. E., & Epstein, M. J. (2005). Exploring the financial value of a reputation for corporate social responsibility during a crisis. *Corporate Reputation Review, 7*(4), 327–345. https://doi.org/10.1057/palgrave.crr.1540230
Seeger, M. W., & Ulmer, R. R. (2001). Virtuous responses to organizational crisis: Aaron Feuerstein and Milt Colt. *Journal of Business Ethics, 31*(4), 369–376. https://doi.org/10.1023/A:1010759319845
Shannon, C. E., & Weaver, W. (1971). *La teoria matematica delle comunicazioni*. Etas Compas.
Shaver, P. R., & Mikulincer, M. (2006). Attachment theory, individual psychodynamics, and relationship functioning. In *The Cambridge handbook of personal relationships* (pp. 251–271). Cambridge University Press. https://doi.org/10.1017/CBO9780511606632.015
Shi, W., Sun, J., & Prescott, J. (2012). A temporal perspective of merger and acquisition and strategic alliance initiatives: Review and Future Direction. *Journal of Management, 38*, 164–209. https://doi.org/10.1177/0149206311424942
Simnett, R., Vanstraelen, A., & Chua, W. F. (2009). Assurance on sustainability reports: An international comparison. *The Accounting Review, 84*(3), 937–967. https://doi.org/10.2308/accr.2009.84.3.937

Smith, K. G., & Grimm, C. M. (1991). A communication-information model of competitive response timing. *Journal of Management, 17*(1), 5–23. https://doi.org/10.1177/014920639101700102

Šontaitė-Petkevičienė, M. (2014). Crisis management to avoid damage for corporate reputation: The case of retail chain crisis in the baltic countries. *Procedia—Social and Behavioral Sciences, 156*, 452–457. https://doi.org/10.1016/j.sbspro.2014.11.220

Spence, M. (1973). Job market signaling. *The Quarterly Journal of Economics, 87*(3), 355–374. https://doi.org/10.2307/1882010

Spence, M. (1974). Competitive and optimal responses to signals: An analysis of efficiency and distribution. *Journal of Economic Theory, 7*(3), 296–332. https://doi.org/10.1016/0022-0531(74)90098-2

Stuart, T. E. (2000). Interorganizational alliances and the performance of firms: A study of growth and innovation rates in a high-technology industry. *Strategic Management Journal, 21*(8), 791–811.

Sundaram, D., Mitra, K., & Webster, C. M. (1998). Word-of-mouth communications: A motivational analysis. *ACR North American Advances*. https://www.semanticscholar.org/paper/Word-Of-Mouth-Communications%3A-a-Motivational-Sundaram-Mitra/92e08995653754c51d2fc9bf730ecc6a11c7ffb5

Teece, D. J., Pisano, G., & Shuen, A. (1997). Dynamic capabilities and strategic management. *Strategic Management Journal, 18*(7), 509–533. https://doi.org/10.1002/(SICI)1097-0266(199708)18:7<509::AID-SMJ882>3.0.CO;2-Z

Todeva, E., & Knoke, D. (2005). Strategic alliances and models of collaboration. *Management Decision, 43*(1), 123–148. https://doi.org/10.1108/00251740510572533

Toms, J. S. (2002). Firm resources, quality signals and the determinants of corporate environmental reputation: Some UK Evidence. *The British Accounting Review, 34*(3), 257–282. https://doi.org/10.1006/bare.2002.0211

Torelli, R., Balluchi, F., & Lazzini, A. (2020). Greenwashing and environmental communication: Effects on stakeholders' perceptions. *Business Strategy and the Environment, 29*(2), 407–421. https://doi.org/10.1002/bse.2373

Tron, A., Valenza, G., & Caputo, A. (2018). Corporate crisis management in Italy: Execution, monitoring and performance analysis of recovery business and financial plans. *International Journal of Foresight and Innovation Policy, 13*. https://doi.org/10.1504/IJFIP.2018.095861

Tsui, A. S. (1984). A role set analysis of managerial reputation. *Organizational Behavior and Human Performance, 34*(1), 64–96. https://doi.org/10.1016/0030-5073(84)90037-0

Tucker, L., & Melewar, T. C. (2005). Corporate reputation and crisis management: The threat and manageability of anti-corporatism. *Corporate Reputation Review, 7*(4), 377–387. https://doi.org/10.1057/palgrave.crr.1540233

Turk, J. V., Jin, Y., Stewart, S., Kim, J., & Hipple, J. R. (2012). Examining the interplay of an organization's prior reputation, CEO's visibility, and immediate response to a crisis. *Public Relations Review, 4*(38), 574–583. https://doi.org/10.1016/j.pubrev.2012.06.012

van Riel, C. B. M., & Fombrun, C. J. (2007). *Essentials of corporate communication: Implementing practices for effective reputation management*. Routledge. https://doi.org/10.4324/9780203390931

von Alberti-Alhtaybat, L., Hutaibat, K., & Al-Htaybat, K. (2012). Mapping corporate disclosure theories. *Journal of Financial Reporting and Accounting, 10*(1), 73–94. https://doi.org/10.1108/19852511211237453

Walsh, G., Mitchell, V.-W., Jackson, P. R., & Beatty, S. E. (2009). Examining the antecedents and consequences of corporate reputation: A customer perspective. *British Journal of Management, 20*(2), 187–203. https://doi.org/10.1111/j.1467-8551.2007.00557.x

Wang, C.-H. (2014). How relational capital mediates the effect of corporate reputation on competitive advantage: Evidence from Taiwan high-tech industry. *Technological Forecasting and Social Change, 82*, 167–176. https://doi.org/10.1016/j.techfore.2013.06.009

Wang, L., & Zajac, E. J. (2007). Alliance or acquisition? A dyadic perspective on interfirm resource combinations. *Strategic Management Journal, 28*(13), 1291–1317. https://doi.org/10.1002/smj.638

Wassmer, U. (2010). Alliance portfolios: A review and research agenda. *Journal of Management, 36*(1), 141–171. https://doi.org/10.1177/0149206308328484

Weigelt, K., & Camerer, C. (1988). Reputation and corporate strategy: A review of recent theory and applications. *Strategic Management Journal, 9*(5), 443–454.

Weiss, A. M., Anderson, E., & MacInnis, D. J. (1999). Reputation management as a motivation for sales structure decisions. *Journal of Marketing, 63*(4), 74–89. https://doi.org/10.2307/1251975

Weng, P.-S., & Chen, W.-Y. (2017). Doing good or choosing well? Corporate reputation, CEO reputation, and corporate financial performance. *The North American Journal of Economics and Finance, 39*, 223–240. https://doi.org/10.1016/j.najef.2016.10.008

Williamson, O. E. (1975). *Markets and hierarchies, analysis and antitrust implications: A study in the economics of internal organization*. Free Press.

Xiao, S. (2020). In L. Yang & Z. Xu (Eds.), *Environmental information disclosure and auditing of listed companies in heavy pollution industries*. Beijing Jiaotong University. https://doi.org/10.1051/e3sconf/202018502018. (WOS:000625412200109; Vol. 185). (A c. Di).

Zavyalova, A., Pfarrer, M. D., Reger, R. K., & Hubbard, T. D. (2016). Reputation as a benefit and a burden? How stakeholders' organizational identification affects the role of reputation following a negative event. *Academy of Management Journal, 59*(1), 253–276. https://doi.org/10.5465/amj.2013.0611

Zeithaml, V. A., Berry, L. L., & Parasuraman, A. (1996). The behavioral consequences of service quality. *Journal of Marketing, 60*(2), 31–46. https://doi.org/10.2307/1251929

Chapter 4
Corporate Reputation Outcomes

Kindly words do not enter so deeply into men as a reputation for kindness.

[Mencius, ancient Chinese Confucian philosopher]

4.1 Corporate Reputation Outcomes Through Two Perspectives

Prior sections analysed in depth the determinants of corporate reputation that can be defined as factors that enable positive or negative processes impacting the value of corporate reputation. However, the management and accounting literature (Marchi, 2014) posits that each business process, thus also those generating corporate reputation and corporate reputation itself, must be analysed under three key dimensions:

1. The prerequisites of the process.
2. The elements of the process.
3. The outcomes of the process.

The prerequisites are the factors that initiate the process (e.g. management decisions). The elements are the resources that enable the process (e.g. resources and assets). The outcomes are the results of that process (e.g. financial and non-financial results).

While Chap. 3 focuses on Point 1 (the prerequisites of the process) and Point 2 (the elements of the process), this chapter extends the analysis by examining Point 3 (outcomes of the process).

Before delving into this latter dimension, it could be useful to the understanding of the framework, summarizing what a business process is and why corporate reputation can be considered a business process influenced by other sub-processes (i.e. corporate reputation building, corporate reputation acquiring, reputational risk management, and crisis management).

D. Vito, *Corporate Reputation as Strategic Intangible Asset*, SIDREA Series in Accounting and Business Administration,
https://doi.org/10.1007/978-3-031-93331-8_4

All firms operate based on their business processes, which are sets of interdependent activities performed using various inputs (ideas, materials, information, facilities, documents) that are processed to obtain a specific output by engaging human resources, top management, and stakeholders. This output can be an object of exchange with the market or an internal realization necessary for management. In both cases, the activities forming a process are all directed toward achieving the same goal. In other words, a process is a set of connected activities with the same aim (Ferrero, 1968).

Traditional business processes include the financial process, the marketing process, the procurement process, the production process, and the monetary process. Nowadays, the landscape of business processes is expanding to include new emerging processes, such as the corporate reputation process that has been an increasingly important consideration by companies (Gotsi & Wilson, 2001; Helm, 2011; Shamma, 2012). Since 2001, corporate reputation has started to be considered a process. In that year, Pruzan (2001) predicted that 'the management of reputation will become a key business process like quality management, financial management or customer service'. More than 20 years later, companies and practitioners seem to be aware of the relevance of this critical business process (e.g. IPSOS, 2023).

Building on literature that considers corporate reputation as a process, and including the three key dimensions of business processes suggested by Marchi (2014), this chapter extends the framework proposed earlier in this book by including also the prerequisites and the outcomes of the corporate reputation process. Consequently, Fig. 4.1 provides a more comprehensive view of the corporate reputation management process.

Specifically, while the relevance of the prerequisites (management decisions) was highlighted in the previous chapter through an analysis of corporate reputation determinants (e.g. management decisions are the basis of communication strategies, M&A strategies, risk and crisis management), the analysis of outcomes must still be addressed. Thus, this chapter delves into the corporate reputation outcomes from an organization-oriented perspective (in terms of impact on performance) as well as from a stakeholder-oriented perspective (in terms of impact on decision-making), following prior studies (Money et al., 2017).

Similarly to Money et al. (2017), in this framework, the perspectives of the organization and its stakeholders are deeply interconnected, reflecting two sides of the same coin. These perspectives are mutually reinforcing and should be viewed as equally significant.

The difference between organization- and stakeholder-oriented perspectives lies in the focal point of analysis. The organization-oriented perspective is primarily concerned with how corporate reputation impacts the internal functioning and strategic outcomes of the organization itself. Specifically, it concentrates on internal processes and, thus, performance metrics, highlighting the outcomes of the strategic advantage gained through a strong reputation. Contrarily, the stakeholder-oriented perspective centres on the interests, expectations, and influences of various stakeholders, including customers, employees, suppliers, investors, regulators, and the community. It emphasizes understanding and managing relationships with external entities.

Although the organization and stakeholder perspectives reflect one another, distinguishing between them facilitates a more comprehensive analysis. This approach

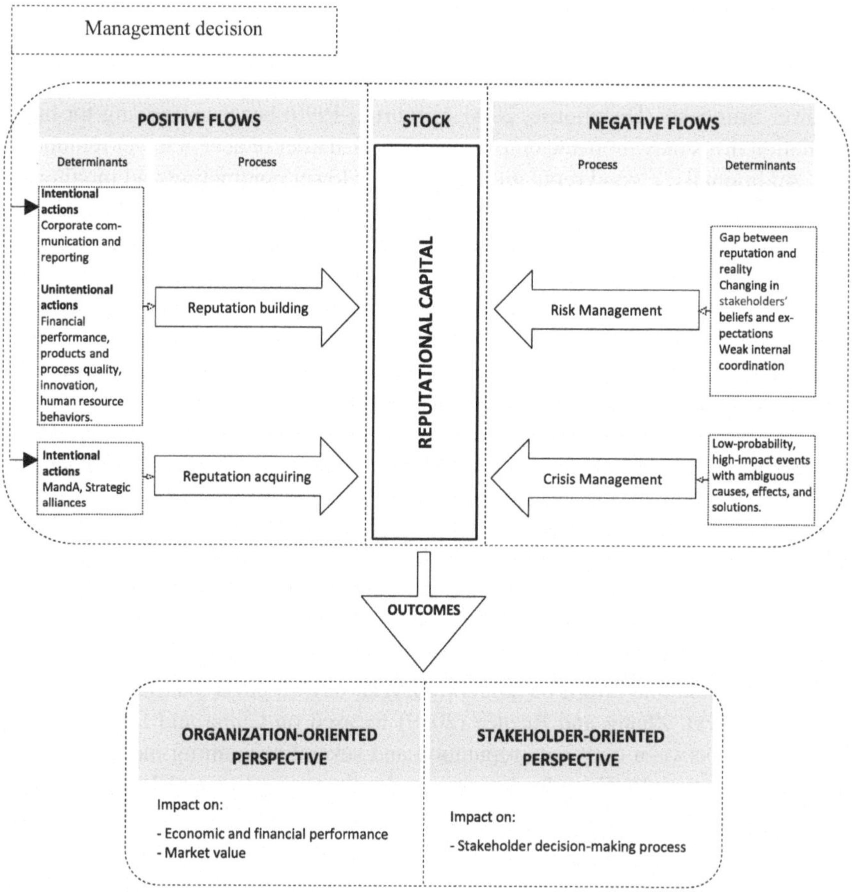

Fig. 4.1 The comprehensive corporate reputation management framework. (Source: author's elaboration)

ensures that both external influences and internal impacts are considered, offering a balanced view. The following sections delve into each perspective in detail.

4.2 Corporate Reputation Outcomes in the Organization-Oriented Perspective

4.2.1 Economic and Financial Performance

Since the emergence of corporate reputation literature, a wide range of research has focused on investigating the relationship between corporate reputation and economic and financial performance (Herremans et al., 1993; McGuire et al., 1990;

Preston & Sapienza, 1990; Sabate & Puente, 2003). Improved economic and financial performance can be seen as the outcome of effective reputation management, achieved through various ancillary benefits. For example, a good reputation can lead to lower firm costs (Deephouse, 2000; Fombrun, 1996) because working for high-reputation firms may motivate employees to work harder or accept lower remuneration. Additionally, a good reputation may favour lower contracting and monitoring costs as suppliers may be less concerned about contractual hazards when dealing with high-reputation firms (Roberts & Dowling, 2002). A good reputation can also increase profitability by enabling firms to charge premium prices (Deephouse, 2000; Fombrun & Shanley, 1990). Serving as a signal of the underlying quality of a firm's products and services, a good reputation encourages consumers to pay a premium for offerings from high-reputation firms (Roberts & Dowling, 2002). Furthermore, a good reputation creates competitive barriers (Fombrun, 1996), thus lowering the competitive intensity and favouring the competitive advantage (Eberl & Schwaiger, 2005). Moreover, a well-known firm can easily attract applicants (Fombrun, 1996), investors (Srivastava et al., 1997), and customers (Fombrun, 1996).

Specific accounting metrics have been used to empirically demonstrate the positive relationship between corporate reputation and financial performance. For instance, Roberts and Dowling (2002) analysed 540 firms in the US context and found a positive relation between corporate reputation and return on equity (ROE). Similarly, Sánchez and Sotorrío (2007) showed a positive association between corporate reputation and return on assets (ROA) as well as gross margin profit, in the Spanish context. Zhang and Rezaee (2009) focused on China and found positive associations between corporate reputation and several accounting metrics, including profit margins, ROE, and sales growth. Furthermore, Lee and Jungbae (2012) confirmed the positive results obtained by Roberts and Dowling (2002) after 10 years, analysing the association between corporate reputation and ROE, ROA, and sales growth. Blajer-Gołębiewska (2014) also provided confirming evidence, albeit with a weaker association, between corporate reputation and financial metrics (ROA, ROE, net profit) in the Polish context.

Moreover, Roberts and Dowling (2002) emphasize that reputation plays a crucial role in influencing a firm's economic and financial performance, especially under conditions of uncertainty about the quality of a firm's offerings. They also examined the persistence of the positive relationship between reputation and financial performance over time. Using autoregressive profit models and proportional hazards regression models, they demonstrated that superior-performing firms have a greater chance of sustaining superior performance over time if they also possess relatively good reputations.

Earlier, Podolny (1993) argued for a positive relationship between corporate reputation and a firm's economic and financial performance, suggesting the existence of a 'virtuous cycle.' In his view, firms with strong reputations are more motivated to undertake actions that further bolster their reputations, creating a reinforcing feedback loop. This perspective underscores the strategic value of corporate reputation, highlighting how it not only reflects past performance but also influences future strategic decisions and outcomes.

However, it is worth noting that the results on the positive relationship between corporate reputation and economic and financial performance are not consistent throughout the literature. For example, Rose and Thomsen (2004), analysing a sample of Danish companies, did not find evidence that reputation impacts financial performance. Similarly, findings from Martínez-León et al. (2023) did not convincingly support the hypothesis that reputation influences economic and financial performance in the Spanish context. Additionally, Tomak (2023) suggests that a good reputation does not necessarily equate to higher business performance in developing countries like Turkey. In this regard, she explains that emerging markets have certain characteristics that restrain firms aiming to build a good reputation, such as a lack of engagement with sociohistorical specificities, corruption and instability, strict authoritarianism, and unique cultural customs. Thus, she underscores the necessity of considering the context when analysing this association, as it may impact the validity of the relationship.

Moreover, Martínez-León et al. (2023) introduce a compelling perspective by suggesting that the relationship between corporate reputation and economic and financial performance may be mediated by the specific stakeholder group considered, thereby adding a crucial layer of complexity to our understanding. They argue that corporate reputation, as a socio-cognitive construct influenced by individuals' experiences, beliefs, knowledge, and impressions of the organization, can significantly vary across different stakeholder groups. This view is consistent with evidence suggesting that the impact of corporate reputation on financial performance is not uniform but depends on the perceptions of distinct stakeholder groups (Helm, 2013).

Therefore, scholars need to consider these specific groups when analysing the link between corporate reputation and financial performance. Doing so will enable a more accurate capture of the nuanced and potentially varying impacts that reputation can have on financial outcomes in different contexts. Ignoring this variability could lead to incomplete or misleading conclusions.

Despite the importance of this perspective, empirical evidence on this aspect is still lacking, highlighting a critical area for future research. Addressing this gap will enhance our understanding of the reputation-performance link and provide more targeted insights for organizations aiming to leverage their reputation effectively.

The necessity for more research has also been advocated by Kaur and Singh (2020), who highlight the need for further investigation into the reputation-performance link due to ongoing concerns regarding both the nature of the relationship and the direction of causation. While many studies indicate a strong relationship between corporate reputation and financial performance, the direction of this relationship remains debated (Roberts & Dowling, 2002; Eberl & Schwaiger, 2005) as it is like the 'chicken and egg' riddle, and it remains unclear whether corporate reputation affects economic and financial performance or *vice versa*, or if both factors influence each other.

This work sheds light on both sides of the link, drawing from literature suggesting a bidirectional relationship between corporate reputation and economic and financial performance (e.g. Martínez-León et al., 2023). While this section explores how corporate reputation influences economic and financial performance, Sect. 3.2.2 delves into the reverse: how economic and financial performance impacts corporate reputation. Both sections cite literature that supports the existence of these reciprocal effects. Chap. 6 also addresses this topic with empirical analyses, responding to the suggestion by Martínez-León et al. (2023) to focus on specific stakeholder groups to gain valuable insights into the relationship between corporate reputation and firm performance.

4.2.2 Market Performance

The assumption that reputation may influence equity market evaluation has substantial theoretical support. According to Fombrun and Shanley (1990), reputation results from a firm actively signalling 'key characteristics to constituents to maximize (the firm's) social status'. The information stored in the reputation may influence evaluations by the public, allow the firm to attain privileged positions with its stakeholders (Hall, 1993), and, potentially, influence evaluations of investors.

Having established the significance of corporate reputation in influencing equity market valuation, it is now pertinent to delve into empirical evidence supporting this assertion. Research in this area provides valuable insights into how corporate reputation translates into tangible effects on market performance.

In 1997, Srivastava et al. offered one of the first empirical evidence that firm reputation can be linked with greater market valuation and illustrated that the potential payoff associated with reputation may be very substantial. The authors based their study on the clear distinction between objective risk and perceived risk. Equity markets commonly express the objective risk associated with an investment in terms of Beta, the measure related to the historical volatility of returns from that investment. According to the capital asset pricing model (CAPM),[1] the required rate of return (ROR) for a particular investment would be completely determined by the objective risk characteristics of the investment portfolio (Beta).

However, if investors consider a firm's reputation in assessing the risk of investing (i.e. they are investing based on perceived risk), then the required ROR that a firm must offer will not be completely predictable from Beta. If a strong reputation causes an investor to perceive the firm as being less risky, the investor may be willing to accept a lower ROR than the objective risk (Beta) alone would indicate. Equivalently, holding ROR constant, firms with more positive reputations might be able to sustain higher Betas. Firms that could operate at much higher risk/return

[1]According to the capital asset pricing model (CAPM), the return required from an investment (consisting of a diversified portfolio) with a given level of objective risk is defined as follows: $R_p = R_f + \beta_p (R_m - R_f)$, where R_m is the return on the market portfolio, R_f is the risk-free rate, R_p is the return required for the investment (rate of return or ROR), and β_p is the Beta associated with the portfolio.

ratios would benefit from a lower cost of capital and, as we show later, a potentially higher market valuation.

This positive association between reputation and market value is confirmed also in times of uncertainty and economic turmoil that can provoke market decline (Jones et al., 2000). In this case, corporate reputation can be considered a 'reservoir of goodwill' and can serve to buffer a corporation from economic loss in specific types of crises. More generally, Jones et al. (2000) suggest that 'corporations can reduce the uncertainty associated with a competitive and potentially hostile environment by cultivating a reservoir of goodwill, and reputation is the vessel in which goodwill accumulates'.

The benefits of corporate reputation on market value are clear focusing also on extraordinary finance operations like merger and acquisition transactions (M&A). In this context, literature discusses the reputational spillover effects that occur when making investment decisions (Boone & Uysal, 2020). Reputational spillovers in M&A could be negative or positive. Negative spillovers occur when one partner's reputational capital decreases the ability of the combined firm to engage in implicit contracts (Klein & Leffler, 1981). Thus, firms with lower reputations would exhibit a lower propensity to engage in takeovers relative to other reputations because they have the highest potential for negative spillover effects for the other party. Positive spillovers occur when pairing a lower reputation firm with a higher one allows for new transactions or enables the entities to extract more of the future surplus from ongoing contracts. This suggests that firms with a positive reputation would be more desirable partners both as an acquirer and a target. Boone and Uysal (2020) produced empirical evidence on this topic suggesting that firms with good reputations are more selective in their acquisition choices. In this case, results suggest that firms tend to acquire targets within their reputational category (high, medium, low, or negative reputation). Therefore, corporate reputation appears to hold value in enhancing market value, as well as in M&A operations.

Just as a positive reputation can bolster a company's market value, a lower or negative reputation may have the opposite effect. To empirically test this assumption, many scholars concentrate on corporate scandals, which demonstrate a company's misconduct or violation of laws or good governance principles. Unlike minor corporate misdeeds that may go unnoticed and result in negligible harm, corporate scandals are especially damaging because they occur in full public view, attracting widespread attention and scrutiny. For instance, in 2010, Hewlett-Packard Co.'s share price dropped by 8.30% during trading immediately after news broke that its CEO was resigning due to revelations of misconduct (Worthen & Tam, 2010).

As expected, the literature indicates that the market reaction to corporate scandals is negative. However, this negative impact seems to be confined to the short term. In this regard, Jory et al. (2015) analysed major corporate scandals that affected US publicly listed firms between 1993 and 2011 and observed an increase in the stock price volatility of scandal-affected firms in the days following the announcement. However, their results suggest that the value damage is limited to the short run. The stock price performance of the firms affected by the scandals matches that of scandal-free firms in the long run post-announcement. Moreover, the operating performance of those firms is better than that of their matched counterparts in the years after the scandal. Therefore, these empirical results suggest that the corrective actions taken by scandal-hit firms bring valuable benefits to market value in the long term, confirming the positive relationship between activities aimed at building a good reputation and market performance.

Another strand of academic literature in this field focuses on corporate crises[2] suggesting that reputation can function as either a value-preserving asset or a liability, amplifying the adverse effects of a crisis on a company's value. For example, Jones et al. (2000) and Pfarrer et al. (2010) offer evidence that reputation can mitigate the negative consequences of a crisis, preserving firm value. Conversely, Rhee and Haunschild (2006) argue that reputation can also act as a liability, exacerbating the detrimental impacts of a crisis on a firm's value.

Wei et al. (2017) build on this dualistic view, analysing how two dimensions of reputation (i.e. generalized favourability and being known)[3] affect firm value during the onset of a crisis, providing nuanced insights into this complex relationship. Their study's results point out that generalized favourability serves as a buffer, while being known can be a burden, in influencing firm value in times of corporate crisis. These findings suggest that well-considered firms can leverage their generalized favourability among stakeholders to mitigate the loss of firm value during a crisis, as they benefit from a pre-established trust and positive sentiment. In contrast, well-known firms may need to focus more on effective communication strategies with stakeholders, as their heightened visibility and the scrutiny they face can amplify the negative impact on firm value. To better deal with a crisis, firms should therefore enhance their generalized favorability and simultaneously mitigate stakeholders' excessive attention. In addition, well-considered firms can further buffer against the loss in firm value by reducing the perceived intentionality of a crisis.

Taken together, prior evidence suggests that a good corporate reputation may generate long-term value for firms with a positive reputation and that actions aimed at building (or rebuilding) a good reputation may counteract losses from negative events such as scandals or corporate crises.

The impact of reputation on market value is often mediated by its influence on financial performance. In other words, by improving economic and financial results, corporate reputation can enhance the company's overall value. Economic and financial performance metrics such as revenue, operating margins, and cost of capital are recognized as key drivers of shareholder value (Rappaport, 1998). However, the enhancement of these metrics due to reputation may take some time to manifest in improvements in shareholder value. This delay occurs because capital markets tend to discount the value of intangible assets until their benefits are realized in earnings (Aksoy et al., 2008; Gu & Wang, 2005; Laamanen, 2007). Consequently, analysing

[2] In this context, corporate crisis is a situation in which 'stakeholders believe that the default social codes of the stricken organization are violated' (Yu et al., 2008).

[3] See Sect. 2.1 for more details on dimension of corporate reputation.

financial performance becomes crucial in capturing the diverse effects through which a superior reputation may benefit firms, both in the short and long term.

The following section completes the analysis of the comprehensive corporate reputation management framework (Fig. 4.1) by exploring the outcomes of corporate reputation from a stakeholder-oriented perspective.

4.3 Corporate Reputation Outcomes in the Stakeholder-Oriented Perspective

4.3.1 The Influence on Stakeholders' Decision-Making

Prior sections point out that corporate reputation is a perception-based construct as it directly depends on stakeholder perceptions (see Sect. 2.4 for more details).

These perceptions, in turn, may translate into judgements and subsequent actions that impact the organization's results and value (Beretta Zanoni, 2005). By translating perception into actions, stakeholders decide to interact with a firm. Prior studies indicate that the long-term success of business organizations is closely tied to their relationships with other organizations and key actors, commonly referred to as stakeholders (Oliver, 1990; Pfeffer & Salancik, 1978; Pajunen, 2006).

This assumption can be grounded in the seminal concepts of the field of *Economia Aziendale,*[4] which explores the purpose and management of business organizations.

In this regard, Zappa (1927, 1956) points out that the ontological aim of companies is to meet human needs. He does not explain what needs he refers to, but it seems clear that they represent something greater than just simple economic needs. Onida (1954) underlines the need to consider both ethical and economic aspects in any judgement. In its concrete ethical qualification, an economic problem is not a matter of the conservation of wealth or a growth problem, but it seems to be a matter of the conservation or growth of human well-being. Moreover, he suggests that all the legal or ethical restrictions necessary to reconcile the company's interests (or utility) with those of society at large are not detrimental to the purposes of the organization, but rather they are factors favouring consolidation and lasting prosperity (Onida, 1954). In these views, the stakeholder is considered not for his/her power to affect the organization or as an opportunity to increase the profit, but as the 'aim' of the economic activity. Masini (1964) underlines that companies may last in time

[4] *Economia Aziendale* is the unitary approach to the analysis of the *azienda* (company), for which all different aspects, elements, and phenomena are considered in their systemic relationships. This theoretical approach was proposed by the Italian scholar Zappa and studied by many other Italina authors (Aldo Amaduzzi, Carlo Masini, and Pietro Onida). The core of this science is the *azienda*, defined as an economic institution intended to last for an indefinite length of time and that, with the aim of meeting human needs, manages the production, procurement, or consumption of resources in continuous coordination (Zappa, 1956).

only using a dynamic reconciliation of different interests. Thus, the harmonic conciliation of different interests seems to be not only the most convenient way to run a company, to ensure its persistence, but also the right thing to do (Masini, 1964). This Italian scholar's perspective on economic success is very important because it highlights the critical role of interacting with stakeholders.

This assumption is also supported by theories in the academic literature, such as legitimacy theory, which agree on the relevance of introducing the analysis of corporate reputation when investigating organization-stakeholder interactions (Carnevale, 2014; Gazzola, 2012; Signori & Rusconi, 2009; Rusconi, 2014). Furthermore, in situations where stakeholders lack direct experience with a firm, the literature suggests that assessing corporate reputation becomes crucial, as reputation serves as a key indicator for stakeholders to evaluate a company's trustworthiness and credibility (Puncheva, 2008).

Studies on legitimacy theory suggest that companies must gain the support and acceptance of stakeholders to sustain operations and create long-term value. This support is typically achieved by meeting or exceeding stakeholder expectations, which can be done through organizational legitimacy (Puncheva, 2008; Suchman, 1995). Essentially, legitimacy serves as a means to earn the trust and approval of key stakeholders, ensuring continued business success.

Indeed, organizational legitimacy can be defined as the generalized perception or assumption that the actions of an entity are desirable, proper, or appropriate within a social system in terms of rules, values, norms, and definitions (Deephouse et al., 2017; Powell, 1991; Suchman, 1995). Ashforth and Gibbs, in their seminal work of 1990, state that 'legitimacy resides in the eye of the beholder' and, thus, organizational legitimacy is not universally defined. It depends on the individual's expectations. When these expectations are met, the organization is judged as legitimate, which corresponds to a stakeholder's favourable attitude towards the organization-stakeholder interaction.

Scholarly discussions in management literature have compared the concept of corporate reputation to that of organizational legitimacy because they have similar definitions[5] (Bitektine, 2011; Puncheva, 2008), often partially overlap (Bitektine, 2011) and both are critically important for organizations' long-term business value (Fombrun, 1996; Podolny, 2005). Specifically, corporate reputation and organizational legitimacy result from similar social construction processes as stakeholders evaluate an organization (Ashforth & Gibbs, 1990; Fombrun & Shanley, 1990), they have similar antecedents (Fombrun & Shanley, 1990; Oliver, 1990), and they improve the company's ability to acquire resources (Hall, 1993; Suchman, 1995).

While legitimacy and corporate reputation share common ground, key differences between these two concepts arise, particularly in the dimensions used to assess them. Legitimacy assessment is primarily confined to regulative, normative, or cognitive dimensions, which focus on the alignment of organizational actions with societal expectations (e.g. Suchman, 1995). In contrast, corporate reputation

[5] See Sect. 2.1 for more details on the definition of corporate reputation.

can be evaluated across a broader range of attributes, not only along the same dimensions but also across other factors that can serve as sources of status comparisons, such as innovation, leadership, or corporate social responsibility (e.g. Fombrun, 1996). As a result, there may be certain attributes that can be assessed as part of corporate reputation, but not as components of legitimacy, highlighting the broader scope of reputation as a concept. This relationship between corporate reputation and organizational legitimacy highlights that, just as legitimacy is crucial for fostering organization-stakeholder interaction, corporate reputation plays a similarly vital role (Bebbington et al., 2014).

Puncheva (2008) addresses this issue by proposing a theoretical model (Fig. 4.2) pointing out the role of corporate reputation in the decision-making process of stakeholders. She builds on the assumption that the stakeholder decision-making process for exchange with a company is based on several exchange rules, and one of these is corporate reputation.

By deciding to interact with an organization, stakeholders ask companies to figurately sign a social contract, which is a theoretical construct that encompasses the stakeholders' expectations of the company's behaviour (Deegan, 2002).

To decide to 'sign' the social contract, the stakeholders make a process that involves four consecutive steps with corporate reputation serving as the starting point (Fig. 4.2). First, stakeholders assess the corporate reputation. If a company is

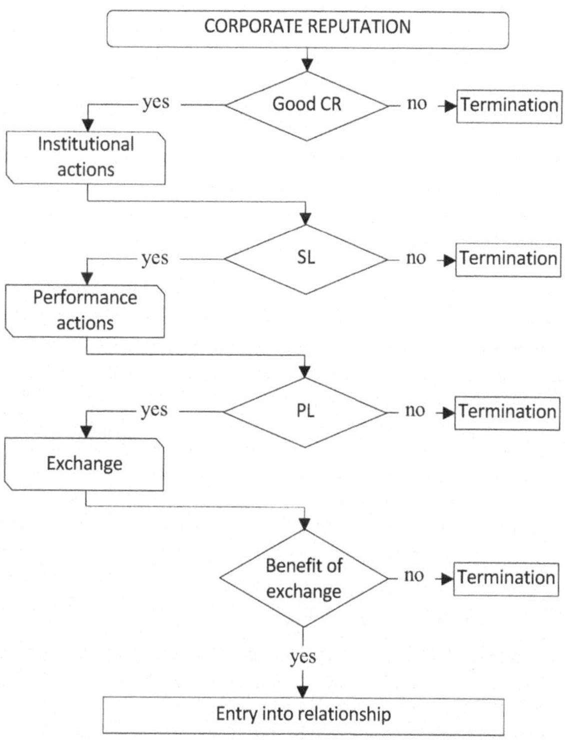

Fig. 4.2 Stakeholders' decision-making process. (Source: Puncheva, 2008)

assessed as having a poor reputation, stakeholders decide not to enter into an exchange relationship with it. Alternatively, when that firm is believed to have a good reputation, stakeholders continue the decision process and look for information regarding the firm's actions (Puncheva, 2008). Second, stakeholders try to verify the company's social legitimacy[6] (SL) by analysing its institutional actions. Third, they look for the organization's pragmatic legitimacy[7] (PL) by examining the company's performative actions. Finally, they evaluate the benefit of the exchange by relying on criteria that they set according to personal expectations and interests.

If the benefits satisfy their expectations, the stakeholders decide to start a relationship with a company. When stakeholders are not satisfied that the organization is operating in an acceptable, or legitimate manner, then they will effectively revoke the organization's contract to continue its operations. This might be evident through, for example, consumers reducing or eliminating the demand for the products of the business, factor suppliers eliminating the supply of labour and financial capital to the business, or constituents lobbying the government for increased taxes, fines, or laws to prohibit those actions that do not conform with the expectations of the community (Deegan, 2002). Consequently, the organization-stakeholder interaction will stop causing losses to the organization.

A second theory in the academic literature that underscores the necessity for companies to establish positive interactions with their stakeholders is stakeholder theory.

Freeman's (1984) initial formulation of stakeholder theory highlights the relevance of aligning corporate strategies with the diverse needs and interests of stakeholders. Building on Freeman's (1984) foundational formulation of stakeholder theory, Donaldson and Preston (1995) expand its scope by identifying three key approaches to its study: descriptive, normative, and instrumental. The descriptive approach seeks to determine whether and how firms consider the needs of their stakeholders (Brenner & Cochran, 1991). Conversely, the normative approach prioritizes ethical and moral principles within stakeholder theory, disregarding instrumentality towards financial goals (Vitolla et al., 2019). Lastly, the instrumental approach posits that firms acknowledge the requests and needs of stakeholders for strategic advantage and long-term competitiveness (Deegan & Blomquist, 2006; Vitolla et al., 2019). Therefore, the prerequisite of the instrumental approach is the recognition of stakeholder consensus as critical, given that their contributions are essential for achieving financial goals and ensuring the firm's survival (Freeman, 1984). This assumption rests on the understanding that stakeholders provide

[6] Social legitimacy suggests that companies have satisfied minimum requirements for ethical behaviour (Handelman & Arnold, 1999). It means that the actions that organizations take to achieve their objectives and the outcomes of their actions are accepted as proper by the society in which they operate (Suchman, 1995).

[7] Pragmatic legitimacy is related to the economic performance of companies (Handelman & Arnold, 1999). and depends on the organization's conformity to the relevant institutionally legitimate definitions of effectiveness and efficiency (Greenwood & Hinings, 1988). It refers to whether companies meet their economic and legal responsibilities (Puncheva, 2008).

essential resources (financial and non-financial), shape industry structures (including supply chain associates and strategic alliances), and influence the sociopolitical landscape (e.g. communities and governments) (Freeman et al., 2010). Within this perspective, corporate reputation reflects the extent to which a company meets the needs and expectations of its stakeholders (Helm, 2005).

The strategic management literature describes this dynamic as 'strategic complementarity' between companies and their stakeholders (Brandenburger & Nalebuff, 1996). This complementarity is crucial for improving organizational interactions with stakeholders, ensuring that a company's policies and activities deliver benefits to them (Post et al., 2002). Bundy et al. (2018) renewed the concept of 'strategic complementarity' more than 20 years later by confirming that an organization should fulfil stakeholders' expectations to gain personal benefits from the interaction with the organization. In doing so, companies can obtain needed resources and/or capabilities from stakeholders to achieve their strategic goals. The authors identify four relational factors associated with strategic complementarity that contribute to fostering extrinsically motivated cooperation: the establishment of competence-based trust, increased environmental predictability, the encouragement of material exchange and reciprocity, and enhanced instrumental communication. Corporate reputation plays a significant role in defining the first factor, aiding the organization in developing strategic complementarity with its stakeholders. Expanding on reputation research (McKnight et al., 1998), Bundy et al. (2018) suggest that when firms become 'known for something' (e.g. quality products, knowledge resources, etc.), their reputation influences the categorization process, which fosters further stakeholder trust and cooperation. Thus, corporate reputation enhances the partner's efficacy, which is a function of competence-based trust, motivating exchange, and facilitating positive relational outcomes.

In summary, academic literature theoretically highlights that corporate reputation is a critical component of the relationship between stakeholders and companies. As stated above, before deciding to interact with an organization, the stakeholder assesses the personal benefit of the exchange. For stakeholders, the benefits of interacting with the company may range from tangible to intangible and monetary to psychological effects. It is also important to note that what constitutes a benefit to one stakeholder may hold little value to another, and in some cases, rewards to one stakeholder may conflict with the interests of another stakeholder (Bhattacharya et al., 2009). However, this interaction constitutes a bidirectional relationship because it brings benefits to stakeholders and simultaneously to companies.

The impact of corporate reputation on stakeholders' decisions to interact with a company has attracted the interest of scholars who empirically test these relations. Specifically, research studies have demonstrated the positive impact that holding a favourable reputation has on customers' decisions. Burlea-Schiopoiu and Balan (2021) indicate that, among all stakeholders, customers are arguably viewed as one of the most important target groups. Central to this debate is the increasingly pivotal role of end-use customers in securing the company's top-line performance. They conducted a study in the Romanian context to investigate if corporate reputation can modify customers' normal behaviour. Their findings suggest that it has a medium-to-high impact on customers' decisions to interact with a firm and, specifically, to be favourable to buying new products or services. Prior studies also suggest that corporate reputation significantly influences customer loyalty (e.g. de Leaniz & del Bosque Rodríguez, 2016), which refers to a deeply held commitment to repurchase or consistently patronize a preferred product or service in the future, even in the face of situational influences and competing marketing efforts that might otherwise prompt switching behaviour (Oliver, 1997). A different strand of literature focuses on employees. Prior studies show that corporate reputation affects job seekers' decisions to apply for employment (Gatewood et al., 1993) and lowers employees' intentions to leave the organization (Riordan et al., 1997). Finally, other empirical studies focus on shareholders by examining whether corporate reputation influences their intention to buy or increase holdings in the firm's shares (Caruana et al., 2006).

However, the literature analysis conducted as the basis of this book (see Sect. 2.1 for details on the literature review process) reveals scant empirical evidence on the impact of corporate reputation on the decision-making of specific stakeholder groups, particularly banks and auditors. In line with Helm's (2013) suggestion to study corporate reputation with a focus on specific stakeholder groups, given that its impact on a firm's outcomes can vary, Chap. 6 addresses these gaps by empirically examining how corporate reputation influences the decisions of banks and auditors to engage with an organization.

Prior sections have highlighted the relevance of measuring corporate reputation while also acknowledging the challenges involved (e.g. Sects. 3.2.3 and 3.3.1). Before delving into the empirical section of this book, it is important to address the issue of corporate reputation measurement to provide a more comprehensive understanding of the concept and set the stage for the empirical analysis presented in Chap. 6. Therefore, the next section examines the measurement methods used in the literature, highlighting their strengths and weaknesses.

References

Aksoy, L., Cooil, B., Groening, C., Keiningham, T. L., & Yalçın, A. (2008). The long-term stock market valuation of customer satisfaction. *Journal of Marketing, 72*(4), 105–122. https://doi.org/10.1509/jmkg.72.4.105

Ashforth, B. E., & Gibbs, B. W. (1990). The double-edge of organizational legitimation. *Organization Science, 1*(2), 177–194.

Bebbington, J., Unerman, J., & O'Dwyer, B. (2014). *Sustainability accounting and accountability*. Routledge.

Beretta Zanoni, A. (2005). Il governo delle relazioni con gli stakeholder nella prospettiva del valore. In B. Campedelli (Ed.), *Reporting aziendale e sostenibilità: I nuovi orizzonti del bilancio sostenibile*. FrancoAngeli.

Bhattacharya, C. B., Korschun, D., & Sen, S. (2009). Strengthening stakeholder–company relationships through mutually beneficial corporate social responsibility initiatives. *Journal of Business Ethics, 85*(2), 257–272. https://doi.org/10.1007/s10551-008-9730-3

Bitektine, A. (2011). Toward a theory of social judgments of organizations: The case of legitimacy, reputation, and status. *Academy of Management Review, 36*(1), 151–179. https://doi.org/10.5465/amr.2009.0382

Blajer-Gołębiewska, A. (2014). Corporate Reputation and Economic Performance: The Evidence from Poland. *ECONOMICS & SOCIOLOGY, 7*, 194–207. https://doi.org/10.14254/2071-789X.2014/7-3/15

Boone, A., & Uysal, V. B. (2020). Reputational concerns in the market for corporate control. *Journal of Corporate Finance, 61*, 101399. https://doi.org/10.1016/j.jcorpfin.2018.08.010

Brandenburger, A., & Nalebuff, B. (1996). *Co-opetition*. Doubleday. ISBN: 9781861975072.

Brenner, S. N., & Cochran, P. L. (1991). The stakeholder theory of the firm: Implications for business and society theory and research. In J. F. Mahon (Ed.), *Proceedings of the Second Annual Meeting of the International Association for Business and Society* (pp. 449–467). UT.

Bundy, J., Vogel, R. M., & Zachary, M. A. (2018). Organization–stakeholder fit: A dynamic theory of cooperation, compromise, and conflict between an organization and its stakeholders. *Strategic Management Journal, 39*(2), 476–501. https://doi.org/10.1002/smj.2736

Burlea-Schiopoiu, A., & Balan, D. A. (2021). Modelling the impact of corporate reputation on customers' behaviour. *Corporate Social Responsibility and Environmental Management, 28*(3), 1142–1156. https://doi.org/10.1002/csr.2113

Carnevale, C. (2014). *Stakeholder, Csr ed economie di mercato. La complementarietà delle sfere economico-istituzionali: La complementarietà delle sfere economico-istituzionali*. FrancoAngeli.

Caruana, A., Cohen, C., & Krentler, K. A. (2006). Corporate reputation and shareholders' intentions: An attitudinal perspective. *Journal of Brand Management, 13*(6), 429–440. https://doi.org/10.1057/palgrave.bm.2540284

de Leaniz, P. M. G., & del Bosque Rodríguez, I. R. (2016). Corporate image and reputation as drivers of customer loyalty. *Corporate Reputation Review, 19*(2), 166–178. https://doi.org/10.1057/crr.2016.2

Deegan, C. (2002). The legitimising effect of social and environmental disclosures – A theoretical foundation. *Accounting, Auditing & Accountability Journal, 15*, 282–311. https://doi.org/10.1108/09513570210435852

Deegan, C., & Blomquist, C. (2006). Stakeholder influence on corporate reporting: An exploration of the interaction between WWF-Australia and the Australian Minerals Industry. *Accounting, Organizations and Society, 31*, 343–372. https://doi.org/10.1016/j.aos.2005.04.001

Deephouse, D. L. (2000). Media reputation as a strategic resource: An integration of mass communication and resource-based theories. *Journal of Management, 26*(6), 1091–1112. https://doi.org/10.1177/014920630002600602

Deephouse, D. L., Bundy, J., Tost, L. P., & Suchman, M. C. (2017). *Organizational legitimacy: Six key questions* (SSRN Scholarly Paper 2849636). https://papers.ssrn.com/abstract=2849636.

Donaldson, T., & Preston, L. E. (1995). The Stakeholder Theory of the Corporation: Concepts, Evidence, and Implications. *The Academy of Management Review, 20*(1), 65–91. https://doi.org/10.2307/258887

Eberl, M., & Schwaiger, M. (2005). Corporate reputation: Disentangling the effects on financial performance. *European Journal of Marketing, 39*(7/8), 838–854. https://doi.org/10.1108/03090560510601798

Ferrero, G. (1968). *Istituzioni di economia d'azienda*. A. Giuffrè.

Fombrun, C. J. (1996). *Reputation: Realizing value from the corporate image*. Harvard Business School Press.

Fombrun, C., & Shanley, M. (1990). What's in a name? Reputation building and corporate strategy. *Academy of Management Journal, 33*, 233–258. https://doi.org/10.2307/256324

Freeman, R. E. (1984). *Strategic management: A stakeholder approach*. Pitman.

Freeman, R. E., Harrison, J. S., Wicks, A. C., Parmar, B. L., & de Colle, S. (2010). *Stakeholder theory: The state of the art*. Cambridge University Press.

Gatewood, R. D., Gowan, M. A., & Lautenschlager, G. J. (1993). Corporate image, recruitment image and initial job choice decisions. *Academy of Management Journal, 36*(2), 414–427. https://doi.org/10.5465/256530

Gazzola, P. (2012). CSR e reputazione nella creazione di valore sostenibile. Economia Aziendale Online, 2, Articolo 2. https://doi.org/10.13132/2038-5498/2006.2.27-45

Gotsi, M., & Wilson, A. M. (2001). Corporate reputation: Seeking a definition. *Corporate Communications: An International Journal, 6*(1), 24–30. Scopus. https://doi.org/10.1108/13563280110381189

Greenwood, R., & Hinings, C. R. (1988). Organizational design types, tracks and the dynamics of strategic change. *Organization Studies, 9*(3), 293–316. https://doi.org/10.1177/017084068800900301

Gu, F., & Wang, W. (2005). Intangible Assets, Information Complexity, and Analysts' Earnings Forecasts. *Journal of Business Finance & Accounting, 32*(9–10), 1673–1702. https://doi.org/10.1111/j.0306-686X.2005.00644.x

Handelman, J. M., & Arnold, S. J. (1999). The role of marketing actions with a social dimension: Appeals to the institutional environment. *Journal of Marketing, 63*(3), 33–48. https://doi.org/10.1177/002224299906300303

Hall, R. (1993). A framework linking intangible resources and capabiliites to sustainable competitive advantage. *Strategic Management Journal, 14*(8), 607–618. https://doi.org/10.1002/smj.4250140804

Helm, S. (2005). Designing a formative measure for corporate reputation. *Corporate Reputation Review, 8*(2), 95–109. https://doi.org/10.1057/palgrave.crr.1540242

Helm, S. (2011). Employees' awareness of their impact on corporate reputation. *Journal of Business Research, 64*(7), 657–663. https://doi.org/10.1016/j.jbusres.2010.09.001

Helm, S. (2013). A matter of reputation and pride: Associations between perceived external reputation, pride in membership, job satisfaction and turnover intentions. *British Journal of Management, 24*(4), 542–556. https://doi.org/10.1111/j.1467-8551.2012.00827.x

Herremans, I. M., Akathaporn, P., & McInnes, M. (1993). An investigation of corporate social responsibility reputation and economic performance. *Accounting, Organizations and Society, 18*(7), 587–604. https://doi.org/10.1016/0361-3682(93)90044-7

IPSOS (2023), Unlocking the value of reputation, IPSOS Views. Available at: https://www.ipsos.com/sites/default/files/ct/publication/documents/2023-09/IpsosViews_UnlockingTheValueOfReputation_WEB.pdf

Jones, G. H., Jones, B. H., & Little, P. (2000). Reputation as reservoir: Buffering against loss in times of economic crisis. *Corporate Reputation Review, 3*(1), 21–29. https://doi.org/10.1057/palgrave.crr.1540096

Jory, S. R., Ngo, T. N., Wang, D., & Saha, A. (2015). The market response to corporate scandals involving CEOs. *Applied Economics, 47*(17), 1723–1738. https://doi.org/10.1080/00036846.2014.995361

Kaur, A., & Singh, B. (2020). Disentangling the reputation—Performance paradox: Indian evidence. *Journal of Indian Business Research, 12*(2), 153–167. https://doi.org/10.1108/JIBR-02-2018-0081

Klein, B., & Leffler, K. B. (1981). The role of market forces in assuring contractual performance. *Journal of Political Economy, 89*(4), 615–641.

Laamanen, T. (2007). On the role of acquisition premium in acquisition research. *Strategic Management Journal, 28*(13), 1359–1369.

Lee, J., & Jungbae Roh, J. (2012). Revisiting corporate reputation and firm performance link. *Benchmarking: An International Journal, 19*(4/5), 649–664. https://doi.org/10.1108/14635771211258061

Marchi, L. (2014). *Introduzione all'economia aziendale: Il sistema delle operazioni e le condizioni di equilibrio aziendale* (Nona edizione). G Giappichelli Editore.

Martínez-León, I. M., Olmedo-Cifuentes, I., & Davies, G. (2023). The virtuous circle of internal corporate reputation and financial performance. *Corporate Reputation Review, 26*(2), 97–110. https://doi.org/10.1057/s41299-022-00140-0

Masini, C. (1964). *La struttura dell'impresa*. Giuffrè Editore.

McGuire, J. B., Scheeweis, T., & Branch, B. (1990). Perceptions of firm quality: A cause or result of firm performance. *Journal of Management, 16*(1), 167. https://doi.org/10.1177/014920639001600112

McKnight, D. H., Cummings, L. L., & Chervany, N. L. (1998). Initial trust formation in new organizational relationships. *The Academy of Management Review, 23*(3), 473–490. https://doi.org/10.2307/259290

Money, K., Saraeva, A., Garnelo-Gomez, I., Pain, S., & Hillenbrand, C. (2017). Corporate reputation past and future: A review and integration of existing literature and a framework for future research. *Corporate Reputation Review, 20*(3/4), 193–211. https://doi.org/10.1057/s41299-017-0034-3

Oliver, C. (1990). Determinants of interorganizational relation ships: Integration and future directions. *Academy of Management Review, 15*, 241–265.

Oliver, C. (1997). Sustainable competitive advantage: Combining institutional and resource-based views. *Strategic Management Journal, 18*(9), 697–713.

Onida, P. (1954). *L'azienda: Primi principi di gestione e di organizzazione*. Giuffrè Editore.

Pajunen, K. (2006). Stakeholder influences in organizational survival. *Journal of Management Studies, 43*(6), 1261–1288. https://doi.org/10.1111/j.1467-6486.2006.00624.x

Pfarrer, M. D., Pollock, T. G., & Rindova, V. P. (2010). A tale of two assets: The effects of firm reputation and celebrity on earnings surprises and investors' reactions. *Academy of Management Journal, 53*(5), 1131–1152. https://doi.org/10.5465/amj.2010.54533222

Pfeffer, J., & Salancik, G. R. (1978). *The external control of organizations: A resource dependence perspective* (SSRN Scholarly Paper 1496213). https://papers.ssrn.com/abstract=1496213.

Podolny, J. M. (1993). A status-based model of market competition. *American Journal of Sociology, 98*(4), 829–872. https://doi.org/10.1086/230091

Podolny, J. M. (2005). *Status signals: A sociological study of market competition*. Princeton University Press. https://www.jstor.org/stable/j.ctt7sbsh

Post, J. E., Preston, L. E., & Sachs, S. (2002). Managing the extended enterprise: The new stakeholder view. *California Management Review, 45*(1), 6–28. https://doi.org/10.2307/41166151

Powell, W. W. (1991). Expanding the scope of institutional analysis. In *The new institutionalism in organizational analysis*. University of Chicago Press.

Preston, L. E., & Sapienza, H. J. (1990). Stakeholder management and corporate performance. *Journal of Behavioral Economics, 19*(4), 361–375.

Pruzan, P. (2001). Corporate reputation: Image and identity. *Corporate Reputation Review, 4*(1), 50–64. https://doi.org/10.1057/palgrave.crr.1540132

Puncheva, P. (2008). The role of corporate reputation in the stakeholder decision-making process. *Business and Society, 47*(3), 272–290. https://doi.org/10.1177/0007650306297946

Rappaport, A. (1998). *Creating shareholder value: A guide for managers and investors*. Free Press.

Rhee, M., & Haunschild, P. R. (2006). The liability of good reputation: A study of product recalls in the U.S. automobile industry. *Organization Science, 17*(1), 101–117. https://doi.org/10.1287/orsc.1050.0175

Riordan, C. M., Gatewood, R. D., & Bill, J. B. (1997). Corporate image: Employee reactions and implications for managing corporate social performance. *Journal of Business Ethics, 16*(4), 401–412. https://doi.org/10.1023/A:1017989205184

Roberts, P. W., & Dowling, G. R. (2002). Corporate reputation and sustained superior financial performance. *Strategic Management Journal, 23*(12), 1077–1093. https://doi.org/10.1002/smj.274

Rose, C., & Thomsen, S. (2004). The impact of corporate reputation on performance: Some Danish evidence. *European Management Journal, 22*, 201–210. https://doi.org/10.1016/j.emj.2004.01.012

Rusconi, G. (2014). La teoria degli stakeholder come legame tra etica e business. Impresa Progetto - Electronic. *Journal of Management, 3*.

Sabate, J. M. de la F., & Puente, E. de Q. (2003). Empirical analysis of the relationship between corporate reputation and financial performance: A survey of the literature. *Corporate Reputation Review, 6*(2), 161–177. https://doi.org/10.1057/palgrave.crr.1540197

Sánchez, J. L. F., & Sotorrío, L. L. (2007). The creation of value through corporate reputation. *Journal of Business Ethics, 76*(3), 335–346. https://doi.org/10.1007/s10551-006-9285-0

Shamma, H. M. (2012). Toward a comprehensive understanding of corporate reputation: Concept, measurement and implications. *International Journal of Business and Management, 7*(16), 151. https://doi.org/10.5539/ijbm.v7n16p151

Signori, S., & Rusconi, G. (2009). Ethical thinking in traditional italian economia Aziendale and the stakeholder management theory: The search for possible interactions. *Journal of Business Ethics, 89*(S3), 303–318. https://doi.org/10.1007/s10551-010-0391-7

Srivastava, R. K., McInish, T. H., Wood, R. A., & Capraro, A. J. (1997). Part IV: How do reputations affect corporate performance?: The value of corporate reputation: Evidence from the equity markets. *Corporate Reputation Review, 1*(1), 61–68. https://doi.org/10.1057/palgrave.crr.1540018

Suchman, M. C. (1995). Managing legitimacy: Strategic and institutional approaches. *Academy of Management Review, 20*(3), 571–610. https://doi.org/10.5465/amr.1995.9508080331

Tomak, S. (2023). Corporate reputation and financial performance of firms in Turkey Serpil Tomak. *Ömer Halisdemir Üniversitesi İktisadi ve İdari Bilimler Fakültesi Dergisi, 7*, 289–303.

Vitolla, F., Raimo, N., & Rubino, M. (2019). Appreciations, criticisms, determinants, and effects of integrated reporting: A systematic literature review. *Corporate Social Responsibility and Environmental Management, 26*(2), 518–528. https://doi.org/10.1002/csr.1734

Wei, J., Ouyang, Z., & (Allan) Chen, H. (2017). Well known or well liked? The effects of corporate reputation on firm value at the onset of a corporate crisis. Strategic Management Journal, 38(10), 2103–2120. https://doi.org/10.1002/smj.2639.

Worthen, B., & Tam, A. P.-W. (2010). Hewlett-Packard CEO Mark Hurd Resigns After Sexual Harassment Probe. *Wall Street Journal*. https://www.wsj.com/articles/SB10001424052748703309704575413663370670900

Yu, T., Sengul, M., & Lester, R. H. (2008). Misery loves company: The spread of negative impacts resulting from an organizational crisis. *The Academy of Management Review, 33*(2), 452–472.

Zappa, G. (1927). *Le valutazioni di bilancio con particolare riguardo ai bilanci delle società per azioni*. Istituto editoriale scientifico.

Zappa, G. (1956). *Le produzioni nell'economia delle imprese*. Giuffrè.

Zhang, R., & Rezaee, Z. (2009). Do credible firms perform better in emerging markets? Evidence from China. *Journal of Business Ethics, 90*(2), 221–237. https://doi.org/10.1007/s10551-009-0038-8

Chapter 5
Measuring Corporate Reputation

A good reputation is more valuable than money.
[Publilius Syrus, ancient Latin writer]

The development of this book was driven by the goal of highlighting the importance of effectively managing corporate reputation, as its relevance to a company's growth has reached unprecedented levels and continues to increase. Prior sections have extensively reviewed the literature to provide a comprehensive overview of corporate reputation's definition, determinants, and outcomes. This in-depth analysis has culminated in the creation of a corporate reputation management framework that identifies the key elements involved and their interconnections under a stock and flow perspective.

However, to complete this analysis, it is crucial to address an additional issue: the measurement of corporate reputation. As one of the most well-known quotes in management literature states, 'You can't manage what you can't measure' (Peter Drucker). This underscores the necessity of establishing reliable and valid methods for measuring corporate reputation, which is a prerequisite for developing effective management strategies.

Measuring a concept that is perception-based and intangible, however, is not without its challenges. The subjective nature of corporate reputation makes it difficult to capture with absolute precision, as it can vary across different stakeholder groups and evolve over time (Mitchell et al., 1997; Zyglidopoulos, 2001; Wartick, 2002; Hillenbrand & Money, 2007).

In response to this issue, the literature adopts various measurement methods, each with its strengths and weaknesses.

In 2021, Vito conducted a systematic literature review to investigate whether these methods are used interchangeably or if there is an identifiable association between the chosen method and the specific stakeholder group considered in the analyses. While no dominant method emerges when research typically treats

D. Vito, *Corporate Reputation as Strategic Intangible Asset*, SIDREA Series in Accounting and Business Administration,
https://doi.org/10.1007/978-3-031-93331-8_5

stakeholders as a whole, the literature review uncovers an association between specific stakeholder groups and the chosen measurement methods.

Specifically, the study identifies four different methods commonly adopted in the literature to measure corporate reputation:

- Ranking/rating of corporate reputation.
- Structured questionnaires.
- Indices from third parties.
- Media coverage.

According to the study by Vito (2021), which analysed 97 empirical studies published between 1997 and 2020 in the 10 major academic journals in the fields of management, accounting, and organization theory, the distribution of methods is approximately uniform (Table 5.1).

In Table 5.1, it is noted that structured questionnaires are the most commonly adopted method, utilized in 33% of cases. Ranking or rating by business journals follows closely behind at 29%. Indices provided by third parties account for 28% of the total usage, with media coverage analyses making up the remaining 10%.

However, when differentiated by stakeholder groups, this distribution changes significantly, with one method consistently preferred in each case. Table 5.2 shows the distribution of measurement methods of corporate reputation by stakeholder groups.

The findings presented in Table 5.2 suggest that studies examining corporate reputation in relation to stakeholders such as clients, employees, or the community predominantly employ structured questionnaires. In contrast, rankings and ratings published by business journals are frequently utilized in research involving investors or competitors. Studies focusing on shareholders commonly rely on indices provided by independent entities. Lastly, the use of media coverage as a method for measuring corporate reputation appears to be relatively underexplored in the literature.

The following sections provide a detailed examination of each measurement method, highlighting their strengths and weaknesses.

Table 5.1 Distribution of measurement methods of corporate reputation in empirical studies

Measurement method	Frequency
Structured questionnaires	33%
Ranking/rating	29%
Indices from third parties	28%
Media coverage	10%
Total	100%

Source: adapted from Vito 2021

Table 5.2 Distribution of measurement methods of corporate reputation in empirical studies by stakeholder groups

Stakeholder group	Measurement method	Frequency
Clients	Structured questionnaires	64%
	Ranking/rating	5%
	Indices from third parties	23%
	Media coverage	9%
	Total	100%
Competitors	Structured questionnaires	10%
	Ranking/rating	70%
	Indices from third parties	0%
	Media coverage	20%
	Total	100%
Community	Structured questionnaires	67%
	Ranking/rating	0%
	Indices from third parties	33%
	Media coverage	0%
	Total	100%
Employees	Structured questionnaires	50%
	Ranking/rating	31%
	Indices from third parties	12%
	Media coverage	6%
	Total	100%
Investors	Structured questionnaires	6%
	Ranking/rating	56%
	Indices from third parties	28%
	Media coverage	11%
	Total	100%
Shareholders	Structured questionnaires	17%
	Ranking/rating	33%
	Indices from third parties	50%
	Media coverage	0%
	Total	100%

Source: adapted from Vito (2021)

5.1 Structured Questionnaires

Structured questionnaires are among the methods most adopted in corporate reputation literature. They are widely used in the study of corporate reputation and recognized as a useful method for providing a systematic and quantitative approach to assess stakeholders' perceptions of a firm's reputation. These questionnaires enable researchers to collect data from a broad audience, ensuring consistency in responses and facilitating comparative analysis across different studies. By using predetermined questions and standardized response options, structured questionnaires help minimize bias and enhance the reliability of the results. They are particularly effective in capturing the multifaceted nature of corporate reputation, as they can encompass its various dimensions, including trustworthiness, social responsibility, quality perception, and financial performance. Moreover, the data collected through structured questionnaires can be easily analysed using statistical tools, offering insights into the factors that drive reputation and how they vary across different contexts and demographic groups.

Typically, researchers employ a 5-point Likert scale, offering five alternative responses for each item in the questionnaire. In addition, these questionnaires often feature closed-ended questions, which facilitate the collection of structured responses, supporting quantitative data analysis and enabling robust generalizations. The questionnaires are usually divided into sections: one for general information, aimed at capturing the biographical characteristics of respondents, and another for specific information, designed to gather data directly related to the study's objectives (e.g. Almeida & Coelho, 2019; Conte, 2018; Martínez & Rodríguez del Bosque, 2014; Muthoni & Kinyua, 2020).

The item generation approach is the major method used by researchers to build questionnaires. It is a deductive method that ensures adequate representation of the domains of interest within a construct (Jian et al., 2014). These items are generally selected from existing literature. Key scales frequently referenced include those developed by Fombrun (1996), Helm (2007), Walsh et al. (2009), and Arikan et al. (2016). Despite these notable contributions, literature encompasses a wide array of scales. More than 10 years ago, Bennett and Gabriel (2003) notably identified over 54 potential scales of items, underscoring the diversity and depth of measurement approaches available in this field. It is reasonable to assume that nowadays this number is even greater, even though the literature lacks recent studies providing a comprehensive overview of all validated scales and items.

This variety enables researchers to tailor reputation measures according to the specific stakeholder group or the context under study. However, the abundance of available items presents challenges in questionnaire design, especially for busy respondents like top managers or investors in time-constrained situations, necessitating careful selection of items for inclusion.

Fombrun et al. (2000) and Caruana and Chircop (2000) propose a four-phase process that may support researchers in developing a reputational measure through structured questionnaires (Fig. 5.1).

Researchers aiming to generate a reputational measure should begin by considering the theoretical perspective as the first step. Although theoretical underpinning is somewhat less emphasized, its effectiveness has a pivotal impact on subsequent research success. The next step involves generating a list of items to be used in the subsequent scale development. When defining items to test, researchers should include both positive and negative items to control for the possibility of acquiescence (Cronbach, 1951). They should then test the selected items through a preliminary survey to ensure that the measurement can be developed. Specifically, researchers should ask each respondent to indicate their degree of agreement or disagreement with these items using a five-point Likert scale ranging from 1 = 'I disagree strongly' to 5 = 'I agree strongly'. Researchers may then adopt the Cronbach alpha (Cronbach, 1951) and perform an exploratory factor analysis.

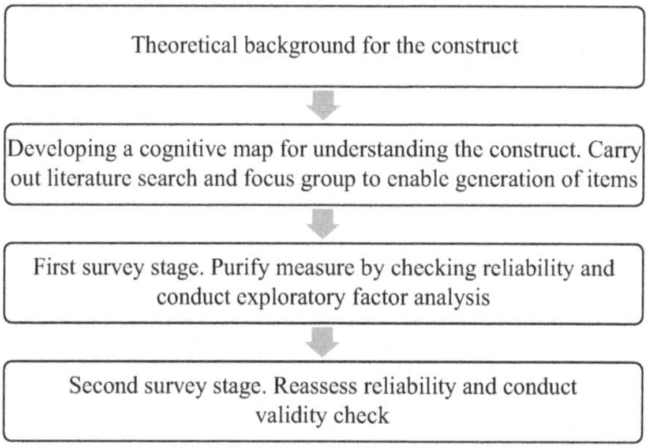

Fig. 5.1 Phases in the development of a reputation instrument. Source: Caruana and Chircop (2000)

Finally, they should conduct a second survey to verify the reliability and validity of the revised instrument.

5.2 Rankings and Ratings of Corporate Reputation

The second method used to measure reputation was relying on the ranking or rating of companies that are regularly reported by media around the world. In a study published in 2007, Fombrun identified and catalogued the number of rankings that evaluate companies based on clearly defined criteria related to reputation. His findings revealed more than 160 such rankings, distributed across 38 countries. Specifically, he found that:

- Sixty-one rankings provide an overall evaluation of companies based on a general measure of reputation.
- Seventy-three of them focus on evaluating the quality of the company's workplace.
- Fifteen rankings assess various aspects of corporate citizenship.
- The other 11 rate companies based on subjective evaluations of their financial performance and future prospects.

Thus, all these rankings are constructed using identifiable criteria that are associated with the perceptions of specific stakeholder groups, such as employees, managers, CEOs, and analysts.

Consequently, one of the major weaknesses of using ranking to measure reputation is comparability. Since each ranking has determinants that are often very different from one another, comparability makes sense only when conducted using the same ranking. It becomes meaningless when conducted across different rankings.

Ranking or rating also has benefits, especially for firms included in the list. As rankings are often created by well-known magazines like BusinessWeek and Fortune, and newspapers like Financial Times and The Wall Street Journal, they increase the visibility and legitimacy of firms, thereby contributing to improving their reputation. Rindova et al. (2006) suggest that they can turn ordinary companies into celebrity firms. However, they can also topple the famous into infamy. Moreover, it is important to note that none of the lists are comprehensive, and various filters are applied by the rating agents that naturally influence who gets on the list, and so how well a company appears. Some rankings are inclusive of all types of companies, while others examine only the largest companies or those in a particular industry, region, or country. Even in this case, comparability is lacking.

A further weakness of this method of reputation measurement relies on the usefulness of rating or ranking for management decisions (Fombrun, 2007). Given the high number of lists available, managers must develop a thorough understanding of the relative importance of these different reputation ratings and rankings. This requires a thorough familiarity with the quality of those lists, the criteria being used to evaluate the companies, the audience likely to be influenced by the list, and the visibility conferred upon the list by the media that is publicizing it.

For research purposes, rankings and ratings are readily accessible to scholars. Furthermore, these lists are typically published periodically, enabling longitudinal analysis. They provide readily accessible aggregate data and allow researchers to analyse companies that might otherwise be inaccessible.

Some of the most famous and widely adopted rankings in academic literature include America's Most Admired Companies by Fortune, the Survey of Corporate Reputation by the Financial Times for the American context, MERCO ranking for the Spanish context, and Britain's Most Admired Companies for the UK context. In the Italian context, one of the prominent rankings referenced in academic literature is the Best Workplaces in Italy published by Il Sole 24 Ore newspaper. This ranking assesses and identifies companies that are considered the best workplaces in Italy based on various criteria such as workplace culture, employee satisfaction, benefits, and overall workplace environment. Thus, it primarily focuses on employees as stakeholders.[1]

5.3 Indices from Third Parties

The third of the most widely adopted methods for measuring corporate reputation is the use of indices provided by third-party organizations. Some of the most popular are the Reputation Quotient (RQ), RepRisk (RRI), and RepTrak (Gardberg, 2006; Aaron et al., 2012; Deephouse & Jaskiewicz, 2013; Burke et al., 2019). The Reputation Quotient (RQ), originally developed by Harris and Fombrun and now published by The Harris Poll, is a comprehensive measure of corporate reputation. As Fig. 5.2 shows, RQ evaluates companies across seven key dimensions (citizenship, ethics, culture, trust, vision, growth, and products and services),

[1] For a comprehensive list of rankings and ratings available worldwide, see Fombrun (2007).

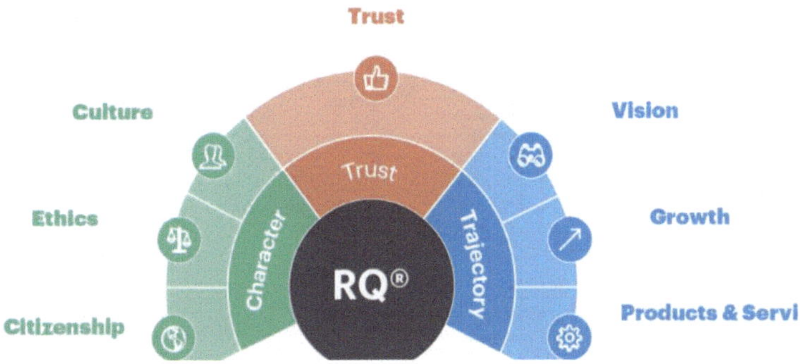

Fig. 5.2 RQ framework. Source: https://theharrispoll.com/

grouped into three clusters (character, trust, and trajectory). Data for the RQ is collected from a broad spectrum of American stakeholders, including the public, employees, suppliers, opinion elites, financial communities, NGOs, media, business partners, policy-makers, and customers, providing a holistic view of a company's reputational standing.

RepRisk, offered by RepRisk AG, is one of the world's largest and most comprehensive databases on corporate reputation, with a focus on ESG (environmental, social, and governance) risks associated with companies. It counts 264,216 companies, across 34 sectors with a global focus. RepRisk screens, daily, over 100,000 public sources and stakeholders in 23 languages. These include print media, online media, social media, blogs, government bodies, regulators, think tanks, newsletters, and other online sources. These sources range from the international to the regional, national, and local levels. This list of sources is reviewed regularly and extended according to daily searches, RepRisk's research, and client feedback. RepRisk uses an outside-in approach to ESG risks, by analysing information from public sources and stakeholders and excluding company self-disclosures. This approach is based on the assumption that self-reported information could be not reliable data, thus invalidating the reliability of the index.

RepRisk covers 28 ESG issues translating into 102 ESG risk factors (Fig. 5.3).

Finally, RepTrak is a robust database with a storied history spanning more than 20 years provided by The RepTrak Company (formerly Reputation Institute). RepTrak specializes in the analysis of stakeholder perceptions and offers insights into how companies are viewed by their stakeholders. The RepTrak database synthesizes millions of perceptions and sentiment data points sourced from online surveys, media outlets, and third-party sources. Covering over 1000 companies across 60 countries and 20 industries, RepTrak provides a comprehensive representation of corporate reputation by integrating factors such as workplace environment, citizenship, performance, leadership, innovation, conduct, and products and services (Fig. 5.4). Notably, similar to RepRisk, RepTrak adopts an outside-in approach, excluding self-reported information from companies.

Fig. 5.3 Reprisk framework. Source: https://www.reprisk.com/

Fig. 5.4 Reptrak framework. Source: https://www.reptrak.com/

In contrast to RQ and RepRisk, which rely on proprietary data that is not publicly accessible, RepTrak offers an open access rating known as 'Global RepTrak® 100'.

In conclusion, leveraging indices provided by third parties allows researchers to capture a comprehensive measure of corporate reputation by drawing on a wide range of sources and stakeholders in their analysis. These indices typically cover a substantial number of companies, making them well-suited for quantitative analysis and providing robust insights into industry-wide reputational trends. However, due to their proprietary nature, utilizing these datasets often comes with associated costs that can limit access to these indices.

5.4 Media Coverage

Media coverage is another method used to measure reputation, even if it has limited adoption (e.g. Brown, 1997; Deephouse, 2000; Fombrun & Shanley, 1990; Vecchio et al., 2011; Agnihotri, 2014).

The fundamental premise is that the media serves as both a mirror and a shaper of public opinion. It encompasses the frequency, tone, and context of media reports related to an organization. The frequency refers to how often an organization is mentioned in the media, which can indicate its prominence and relevance in the public sphere. Tone analysis assesses whether the media coverage is positive, negative, or neutral, providing insight into the public sentiment towards the organization. Context analysis examines the circumstances or issues being discussed concerning the organization, helping to understand the specific areas influencing its reputation.

Researchers utilize various methodologies to analyse media content such as content analysis, sentiment analysis, media framing analysis, and keyword frequency analysis.

Content analysis is one of the most common methods used in this realm. It involves systematically coding and categorizing media content to quantify the presence of certain words, themes, or concepts. For instance, Carroll (2015) employed content analysis to study and analyse media articles regarded a company, finding that positive media coverage was associated with a favourable corporate reputation. Similarly, Geppert and Lawrence (2008) predict firm reputation through content analysis of shareholders' letters. Given that the content of these letters is neither mandated nor strictly regulated, the authors argue that management uses them strategically to influence both asset valuation and perceived corporate reputation. This influence is exerted through mechanisms such as symbolic management, perceived credibility, and transparency.

To analyse the letters, Geppert and Lawrence adopted a structured coding scheme, allowing them to categorize the content into thematic scores. They employed DICTION 5.0 Text-Analysis software, which classifies the words in each letter into thematic categories and sub-categories. These classifications were then used to calculate thematic and sub-feature differences among firms, enabling the authors to assign a reputation score (high or low) using a logit regression model.

To validate their approach, they compared these scores with established rankings, such as Fortune Magazine's Most Admired Companies. Their findings demonstrated a significant alignment between the reputation scores derived through content analysis and these widely recognized rankings, confirming the validity and robustness of their method.

A second method in this domain is sentiment analysis. Grounded in media system dependency theory (Ball-Rokeach and DeFleur, 1976) and the need for an orientation framework (Weaver, 1980), sentiment analysis suggests that stakeholders rely on news media to obtain information about firm reputation attributes they consider important. This method assesses the tone of news media coverage, often leveraging natural language processing (NLP) techniques to automatically evaluate the emotional tone of media articles. These NLP techniques utilize validated lexical resources, such as WordNet v.2, which categorize thousands of lexical entries by their positive, negative, or neutral polarity.

Einwiller et al. (2010) demonstrated the relevance of sentiment analysis by showing that the sentiment expressed in media coverage—whether positive, negative, or neutral—significantly influences public perception and, by extension, a company's reputation. In their study, the authors manually coded articles from major newspapers and online portals to classify overall sentiment. To ensure the reliability and validity of these sentiment scores, they applied statistical methods such as partial least squares (PLS) analysis. Their results confirmed the robustness of sentiment analysis as a tool for understanding and quantifying the impact of media coverage on corporate reputation.

Finally, media framing analysis is a research method developed specifically for psychological research and aimed at enabling a better understanding of the influence of news media in contemporary culture (Giles & Shaw, 2009). This method investigates how media shapes public perception by highlighting certain aspects of a story while downplaying others (e.g. Mahon & Wartick, 2003). Specifically, media framing refers to the process by which media stories are structured through patterns of selection, emphasis, interpretation, and exclusion (Carragee & Roefs, 2004). Journalists 'frame' stories by highlighting specific aspects of perceived reality concerning social or political issues, thereby increasing their significance within a given context (Entman, 1993). Frames provide sociopolitical issues with meaning, promote interpretations and definitions, make moral assessments, propose solutions, and reinforce power dynamics while upholding the existing order (Entman, 1993). Media frames are endowed with symbolic power, utilizing myths, narratives, and metaphors that resonate within the culture, and are recognized as cultural rather than purely cognitive phenomena (Hertog & McLeod, 2001). Therefore, media framing can shape stakeholders' perceptions, thereby defining corporate reputation. The media framing analysis consists of seven stages (Giles & Shaw, 2009):

1. *Initial data collection*. Initial data collection involves systematically gathering media content relevant to a specific issue or event. This is generally done through databases like Nexis Uni, covering newspapers, online sources, and TV news.
2. *Screening*. The screening process filters collected material to ensure relevance to the research question. It avoids including irrelevant content that does not contribute to the analysis of media frames.
3. *Identifying story*. Each unit of analysis (e.g. news articles, TV segments) is linked to a specific event or news point that initiated the story. This step resembles Entman's concept of problem definition,[2] focusing on identifying the central event or trigger for media coverage.

[2]According to Entman (1993), problem definition involves highlighting certain aspects of a perceived reality while downplaying or excluding others. This process influences which aspects of an issue or event are considered important, newsworthy, and worthy of public attention.

4. *Identifying character.* This includes identifying key figures who frequently appear and influence the narrative. For example, in studies on company fraud, recurring characters can include executives accused of misconduct, whistleblowers providing insider information, regulatory officials commenting on investigations, or analysts offering interpretations of financial implications.
5. *Reader identification.* This stage explores whom the media invites its audience to identify with. It considers elements like headlines, quoted individuals, and visual representations that guide audience empathy or alignment.
6. *Narrative form.* This stage examines how stories are structured and presented narratively in media content. It involves analysing narrative conventions such as dramatic structures or thematic storytelling methods used in feature articles or longer news items. This aspect helps in understanding how media frames events to convey meaning and evoke emotional responses.
7. *Analysis of language categories.* This stage involves a detailed analysis of language use and discourse within media texts. This can include examining linguistic constructions, discourse patterns, or rhetorical strategies employed to frame issues and influence audience interpretation.
8. *Generalization.* This step involves identifying overarching themes or recurring narratives (e.g. 'Watergate' as media templates) that shape public understanding and influence reputation over time.

Despite the chosen technique, using media coverage to measure reputation offers several strengths. It provides real-time feedback on public perception, captures a broad range of stakeholders' viewpoints, and offers qualitative insights into brand visibility and public sentiment. However, it has also some weaknesses. The susceptibility to bias and sensationalism in media coverage can distort the accuracy of reputation measurement. Quantifying qualitative data into meaningful metrics poses a significant challenge, often requiring sophisticated analytical methods. Moreover, the potential for inconsistency in coverage across different media channels and platforms underscores the need for robust triangulation and analysis techniques to improve reliability in reputation assessment.

5.5 Other Measurement Methods

In recent years, using CEO reputation as a proxy for measuring a company's reputation has gained traction in both academic and practical fields (e.g. Sun et al., 2024). CEO reputation often embodies perceptions of leadership, vision, and ethical standards that stakeholders attribute not only to the CEO personally but also to the company they represent. This approach is grounded in stakeholder theory, which suggests that stakeholders view the CEO as the face of the company, thus aligning their perception of the CEO with the company's reputation (Love et al., 2017; Fombrun & Shanley, 1990). Moreover, CEOs often serve as symbolic representations of their firms, making their personal reputation critical in shaping stakeholders' perceptions (Petkova et al., 2008; Sun et al., 2024).

Various methods are commonly employed to measure CEO reputation, serving as proxies for corporate reputation. *Media coverage* of the CEO, for example, captures both the frequency and tone of mentions, which can signal the CEO's prominence and public sentiment towards their leadership. Studies like those by Deephouse (2000) and Bednar et al. (2013) have shown that positive media coverage of a CEO can boost perceptions of the company's reputation. Another related approach is analysing *media prominence* (also referred to as *celebrity*), which involves counting the CEO's appearances in high-profile publications, further amplifying their visibility as a corporate representative (Chen & Meindl, 1991).

Notoriety and *awards* won by the CEO are also indicators used in studies to evaluate CEO reputation, which indirectly impacts the company's reputation. Notoriety can highlight a CEO's influence and recognizability, while industry awards can enhance credibility and signal trustworthiness and leadership capabilities (Fombrun, 2007). *CEO-specific rankings*, such as inclusion in top CEOs' lists or leadership awards from reputable institutions, also are used as proxies to measure corporate reputation as they influence investors, customers, and other stakeholders' perceptions (Carter and Deephouse, 1999).

The rationale behind using CEO reputation as a measure of company reputation is threefold. Firstly, symbolic leadership suggests that CEOs are seen as a reflection of corporate values and identity, meaning their reputation directly influences public perceptions of the company (Rindova et al., 2006). Secondly, attribution theory posits that stakeholders attribute company success or failure to CEOs, leading to a strong association between the CEO's image and the company's reputation (Hayward et al., 2004). Finally, social identity theory implies that stakeholders often personify the company through its CEO, thereby merging the CEO's reputation with the corporate image (Ashforth & Mael, 1989).

This approach, while effective, is not without its limitations. Solely relying on CEO reputation can sometimes overemphasize individual actions and characteristics, potentially overlooking the broader organizational factors that contribute to corporate reputation. However, despite this limitation, the association between CEO reputation and corporate reputation remains widely validated in the literature, providing a solid foundation for empirical studies exploring the reputational impacts of leadership on organizational outcomes.

In conclusion, the literature reveals a diverse range of methods for measuring corporate reputation, though no single approach has been universally validated. Each method, however, serves specific objectives and is suited to particular contexts or stakeholder groups.

The next chapter presents empirical evidence to corroborate the key features of corporate reputation outlined in Chap. 2 and to validate the assumptions discussed in the preceding chapters, which form the foundation of the corporate reputation management framework presented in Chaps. 3 and 4.

Specifically, the next chapter aims to validate the stakeholder sensitivity of corporate reputation, acknowledging that its impact may vary depending on the specific stakeholder groups involved in the analysis. It further examines the influence of corporate reputation on firm outcomes, considering both organizational and stakeholder perspectives. Finally, it underscores that the use of different measurement methods leads to varying results, reinforcing the idea that there is no singular, universally applicable method for measuring corporate reputation. Given its intangible and perception-based nature, capturing a universally valid value is inherently complex, thus confirming the context-sensitive characteristics of corporate reputation.

References

Aaron, J. R., McMillan, A., & Cline, B. N. (2012). Investor reaction to firm environmental management reputation. *Corporate Reputation Review, 15*(4), 304–318. Scopus. https://doi.org/10.1057/crr.2012.15

Agnihotri, A. (2014). Mass-media-based corporate reputation and firms' market valuation—Evidence from emerging markets. *Corporate Reputation Review, 17*(3), 206–218. https://doi.org/10.1057/crr.2014.10

Almeida, M. D. G. M. C., & Coelho, A. F. M. (2019). The antecedents of corporate reputation and image and their impacts on employee commitment and performance: The moderating role of CSR. *Corporate Reputation Review, 22*(1), 10–25. https://doi.org/10.1057/s41299-018-0053-8

Arikan, E., Kantur, D., Maden, C., & Telci, E. (2016). Investigating the mediating role of corporate reputation on the relationship between corporate social responsibility and multiple stakeholder outcomes. *Quality and Quantity: International Journal of Methodology, 50*(1), 129–149.

Ashforth, B. E., & Mael, F. (1989). Social identity theory and the organization. *The Academy of Management Review, 14*(1), 20–39. https://doi.org/10.2307/258189

Ball-Rokeach, S. J., & DeFleur, M. L. (1976). A Dependency Model of Mass-Media Effects. *Communication Research, 3*(1), 3–21. https://doi.org/10.1177/009365027600300101

Bednar, M. K., Boivie, S., & Prince, N. R. (2013). Burr Under the Saddle: How Media Coverage Influences Strategic Change. *Organization Science, 24*(3), 910–925. https://doi.org/10.1287/orsc.1120.0770

Bennett, R., & Gabriel, H. (2003). Image and reputational characteristics of UK charitable organizations: An empirical study. *Corporate Reputation Review, 6*(3), 276–289. https://doi.org/10.1057/palgrave.crr.1540206

Brown, B. (1997). Part IV: How do reputations affect corporate performance?: Stock market valuation of reputation for corporate social performance. *Corporate Reputation Review, 1*(1), 76–80. https://doi.org/10.1057/palgrave.crr.1540021

Burke, J. J., Hoitash, R., & Hoitash, U. (2019). Auditor response to negative media coverage of client environmental, social, and governance practices. *Accounting Horizons, 33*(3), 1–23. https://doi.org/10.2308/acch-52450

Carragee, K., & Roefs, W. (2004). The neglect of power in recent framing research. *Journal of Communication, 54*, 214–233. https://doi.org/10.1111/j.1460-2466.2004.tb02625.x

Carroll, C. E. (2015). *The handbook of communication and corporate reputation*. John Wiley and Sons.

Carter, S. M., & Deephouse, D. L. (1999). 'Tough Talk' and 'Soothing Speech': Managing Reputations for Being Tough and for Being Good. *Corporate Reputation Review, 2*(4), 308–332. https://doi.org/10.1057/palgrave.crr.1540089

Caruana, A., & Chircop, S. (2000). Measuring corporate reputation: A case example. *Corporate Reputation Review, 3*(1), 43–57. https://doi.org/10.1057/palgrave.crr.1540098

Chen, C. C., & Meindl, J. R. (1991). The construction of leadership images in the popular press: The case of Donald Burr and People express. *Administrative Science Quarterly, 36*(4), 521–551. https://doi.org/10.2307/2393273

Conte, F. (2018). Understanding the influence of CEO tenure and CEO reputation on corporate reputation: An exploratory study in Italy. *International Journal of Business and Management, 13*(3), 54. https://doi.org/10.5539/ijbm.v13n3p54

Cronbach, L. J. (1951). Coefficient alpha and the internal structure of tests. *Psychometrika, 16*(3), 297–334. https://doi.org/10.1007/BF02310555

Deephouse, D. L. (2000). Media reputation as a strategic resource: An integration of mass communication and resource-based theories. *Journal of Management, 26*(6), 1091–1112. https://doi.org/10.1177/014920630002600602

Deephouse, D. L., & Jaskiewicz, P. (2013). Do family firms have better reputations than non-family firms? An integration of socioemotional wealth and social identity theories. *Journal of Management Studies, 50*(3), 337–360. https://doi.org/10.1111/joms.12015

Einwiller, S. A., Carroll, C. E., & Korn, K. (2010). Under what conditions do the news media influence corporate reputation? The roles of media dependency and need for orientation. *Corporate Reputation Review, 12*(4), 299–315. https://doi.org/10.1057/crr.2009.28

Entman, R. M. (1993). Framing: Toward clarification of a fractured paradigm. *Journal of Communication, 43*(4), 51–58. https://doi.org/10.1111/j.1460-2466.1993.tb01304.x

Fombrun, C. J. (1996). *Reputation: Realizing value from the corporate image*. Harvard Business School Press.

Fombrun, C. J. (2007). List of lists: A compilation of international corporate reputation ratings. *Corporate Reputation Review, 10*(2), 144–153. https://doi.org/10.1057/palgrave.crr.1550047

Fombrun, C., & Shanley, M. (1990). What's in a name? Reputation building and corporate strategy. *Academy of Management Journal, 33*, 233–258. https://doi.org/10.2307/256324

Fombrun, C. J., Gardberg, N. A., & Sever, J. M. (2000). The reputation QuotientSM: A multi-stakeholder measure of corporate reputation. *Journal of Brand Management, 7*(4), 241–255. https://doi.org/10.1057/bm.2000.10

Gardberg, N. A. (2006). Reputatie, reputation, réputation, reputazione, Ruf: A cross-cultural qualitative analysis of construct and instrument equivalence. *Corporate Reputation Review, 9*(1), 39–61. https://doi.org/10.1057/palgrave.crr.1550009

Geppert, J., & Lawrence, J. E. (2008). Predicting firm reputation through content analysis of shareholders' letter. *Corporate Reputation Review, 11*(4), 285–307. Scopus. https://doi.org/10.1057/crr.2008.32

Giles, D., & Shaw, R. L. (2009). The psychology of news influence and the development of media framing analysis. *Social and Personality Psychology Compass, 3*(4), 375–393. https://doi.org/10.1111/j.1751-9004.2009.00180.x

Hayward, M. L. A., Rindova, V. P., & Pollock, T. G. (2004). Believing one's own press: The causes and consequences of CEO celebrity. *Strategic Management Journal, 25*(7), 637–653. https://doi.org/10.1002/smj.405

Helm, S. (2007). The role of corporate reputation in determining investor satisfaction and loyalty. *Corporate Reputation Review, 10*(1), 22–37. https://doi.org/10.1057/palgrave.crr.1550036

Hertog, J. K., & McLeod, D. M. (2001). A multiperspectival approach to framing analysis: A field guide. In Framing public life. Routledge.

Hillenbrand, C., & Money, K. (2007). Corporate responsibility and corporate reputation: Two separate concepts or two sides of the same coin? *Corporate Reputation Review, 10*(4), 261–277. https://doi.org/10.1057/palgrave.crr.1550057

Jian, G., Shi, X., & Dalisay, F. (2014). Leader–member conversational quality: Scale development and validation through three studies. *Management Communication Quarterly, 28*(3), 375–403. https://doi.org/10.1177/0893318914533201

Love, E. G., Lim, J., & Bednar, M. K. (2017). The face of the firm: The influence of CEOs on corporate reputation. *Academy of Management Journal, 60*(4), 1462–1481. https://doi.org/10.5465/amj.2014.0862

Mahon, J. F., & Wartick, S. L. (2003). Dealing with stakeholders: How reputation, credibility and framing influence the game. *Corporate Reputation Review, 6*(1), 19–35. https://doi.org/10.1057/palgrave.crr.1540187

Martínez, P., & Rodríguez del Bosque, I. (2014). Sustainability dimensions: A source to enhance corporate reputation. *Corporate Reputation Review, 17*(4), 239–253. https://doi.org/10.1057/crr.2014.13

Mitchell, R. K., Agle, B. R., & Wood, D. J. (1997). Toward a theory of stakeholder identification and salience: Defining the principle of who and what really counts. *The Academy of Management Review, 22*(4), 853–886. https://doi.org/10.2307/259247

Muthoni, D., & Kinyua, G. (2020). Corporate reputation and firm performance: An empirical analysis of motor vehicle assemblers in Nairobi City County, Kenya. *Journal of Business and Economic Development, 5*, 73. https://doi.org/10.11648/j.jbed.20200502.13

Petkova, A. P., Rindova, V. P., & Gupta, A. K. (2008). How can new ventures build reputation? An exploratory study. *Corporate Reputation Review, 11*(4), 320–334. https://doi.org/10.1057/crr.2008.27

Rindova, V. P., Pollock, T. G., & Hayward, M. L. A. (2006). Celebrity firms: The social construction of market popularity. *Academy of Management Review, 31*(1), 50–71. https://doi.org/10.5465/amr.2006.19379624

Sun, X., Cifuentes-Faura, J., Xiao, Y., & Liu, X. (2024). A good name is rather to be chosen: The impact of CEO reputation incentives on corporate green innovation. *Business Strategy and the Environment, 33*(3), 2413–2431. https://doi.org/10.1002/bse.3607

Vecchio, P. D., Laubacher, R., Ndou, V., & Passiante, G. (2011). Managing corporate reputation in the blogosphere: The case of Dell Computer. *Corporate Reputation Review, 14*(2), 133–144. https://doi.org/10.1057/crr.2011.7

Vito, D. (2021). The measurement of corporate reputation: a systematic literature review. In Ferretti, P. (Ed.), Corporate reputation: some drivers of development (pp. 1–38). G. Giappichelli Editore. ISBN/EAN 978-88-921-3970-1

Walsh, G., Mitchell, V.-W., Jackson, P. R., & Beatty, S. E. (2009). Examining the antecedents and consequences of corporate reputation: A customer perspective. *British Journal of Management, 20*(2), 187–203. https://doi.org/10.1111/j.1467-8551.2007.00557.x

Wartick, S. L. (2002). Measuring corporate reputation: Definition and data. *Business and Society, 41*(4), 371–392. https://doi.org/10.1177/0007650302238774

Weaver, D. H. (1980). Audience Need for Orientation and Media Effects. *Communication Research, 7*(3), 361–373. https://doi.org/10.1177/009365028000700305

Zyglidopoulos, S. C. (2001). The impact of accidents on firms' reputation for social performance. *Business and Society, 40*(4), 416–441. https://doi.org/10.1177/000765030104000404

Chapter 6
Empirical Evidence on the Impact of Corporate Reputation and Banks and Auditors' Decisions

> *Reputation is only a candle, of wavering and uncertain flame, and easily blown out, but it is the light by which the world looks for and finds merit.*
>
> *[James Russell Lowell, ancient American poet and critic]*

The prior chapters of this book introduced several assumptions about the concept of corporate reputation, one of which emerges as particularly significant: corporate reputation is a stakeholder-sensitive concept. This characteristic underscores that corporate reputation is deeply responsive to the diverse expectations, interests, and values of various stakeholder groups. These differences lead to varying perceptions and judgements, resulting in distinct valuations of corporate reputation and, consequently, different impacts on organizational outcomes (see Sect. 2.4 for further details on the key characteristics of corporate reputation).

As Helm (2013) emphasizes, scholars must consider this stakeholder-sensitive nature when analysing the relationship between corporate reputation and its outcomes. Doing so enables a more precise understanding of the nuanced and potentially diverse impacts of corporate reputation on organizational outcomes across different stakeholder groups. Neglecting these variations risks yielding incomplete or misleading conclusions. Despite the importance of this perspective, empirical research has predominantly examined corporate reputation in relation to stakeholders as a homogeneous entity or has mostly focused on a few specific groups such as employees, supply chain, or customers (e.g. Ali et al., 2020; von Berlepsch et al., 2024; Parray et al., 2023). This trend has created a significant gap in the literature regarding the relationship between reputation and other, less-studied stakeholder groups. Addressing this gap is crucial to advancing our understanding of how reputation influences organizational outcomes and providing actionable insights for organizations aiming to leverage their reputation effectively.

Corporate reputation is also a context-sensitive construct. This characteristic implies that the same actions, policies, or attributes of an organization may be perceived and evaluated differently across diverse cultural, economic, legal, and

D. Vito, *Corporate Reputation as Strategic Intangible Asset*, SIDREA Series in Accounting and Business Administration,
https://doi.org/10.1007/978-3-031-93331-8_6

institutional settings (e.g. Jackson & Apostolakou, 2010; Rindova et al., 2005). These contextual factors not only influence how stakeholders interpret and judge corporate behaviour but also shape the behaviour itself (La Porta et al., 1998), thereby impacting both reputation management strategies and stakeholders' perceptions. Consequently, empirical studies adopting quantitative methods generally focus on many firms in one country to enhance the validity of their evidence (e.g. Khalid et al., 2024; Liu et al., 2024; Singh, 2024; Gabbioneta et al., 2007), while empirical studies adopting qualitative methods often focus on few firms operating in one or multiple countries (e.g. Swoboda et al., 2016).

Finally, corporate reputation is also measurement-sensitive, meaning that the method used to assess it can significantly influence the value of the outcomes. Prior studies indicate that defining a unique and rigorous measurement of corporate reputation can be a challenging task (Agarwal et al., 2015) due to the key characteristics of the concept, such as its intangibility, multidimensionality, and dynamic nature. Each measurement method can have a varying impact on the results of an analysis, as each often emphasizes one dimension or stakeholder group while leaving others underexplored. Consequently, prior research suggests employing multiple measurement methods to enhance the validity and comprehensiveness of empirical findings (Rindova et al., 2005).

Building on these assumptions, the empirical analysis in this book examines the impact of corporate reputation on organizational outcomes from both an organizational and stakeholder-oriented perspective. It focuses on two specific underexplored stakeholder groups (banks and auditors), considers a single context (Italy), and employs several measurement methods (ratings, media coverage, and notoriety). In doing so, the analysis aims to validate the key characteristics of corporate reputation (especially its stakeholder sensitiveness), confirm its influence on firm outcomes, and reinforce the assumption that different measurement methods lead to varying results.

The following sections outline the motivations for the analysis, the theoretical framework underpinning it, and the hypotheses to be tested.

6.1 Theoretical Framework and Hypotheses Development

6.1.1 Motivations of the Analyses

Firstly, the empirical analysis explores the role of corporate reputation in firm-bank relationships. It examines this relationship from two perspectives: a stakeholder-oriented perspective, which investigates whether corporate reputation influences a bank's decision to grant loans to a firm, and an organizational-oriented perspective, which assesses the impact of corporate reputation on economic-financial performance through reduced cost of debt.

Several motivations underpin this analysis. Firstly, the pivotal role of banks in providing companies with essential financial resources for their operations and growth is widely recognized (e.g. Berger et al., 2014; Garzella, 2005; Song et al., 2018). This role is particularly significant in Italy, where the predominantly bank-centric financial system leads companies to rely heavily on bank loans as their primary source of financing (Bancha d'Italia, 2020).

Secondly, the literature highlights the pivotal role of corporate reputation as a mechanism for mitigating uncertainty in contexts characterized by information asymmetries (Camerer, 1988), such as those inherent in the bank-firm relationship. Indeed, this relationship is profoundly shaped by both ex ante and ex post information asymmetries, which play a critical role in the financing process (Stiglitz & Weiss, 1981). In the ex ante phase, banks face challenges in obtaining comprehensive and reliable information to accurately assess credit risk, making corporate reputation an essential tool for mitigating adverse selection. In the ex post phase, banks confront persistent uncertainties regarding firms' use of borrowed funds and their ability to generate adequate cash flows for repayment, further underscoring the importance of reputation in reducing the risk of moral hazard.

Moreover, the relevance of corporate reputation in bank-firm relationships lies also with the literature on signalling theory (Myers & Majluf, 1984; Stigler, 1962). This theoretical framework highlights how corporate reputation functions as a signal of reliability and competence to external stakeholders, particularly in contexts characterized by pronounced information asymmetries. In these cases, managers may invest in reputation-building as a strategic tool to reduce stakeholders' uncertainty, fostering trust in the firm's ability to meet its financial and operational obligations and, thus, increasing the likelihood of a firm securing loans and improving the terms of those loans. As a result, corporate reputation may mitigate the bank's adverse selection in the ex ante phase and the firm's moral hazard in the ex post phase, serving as a proxy for reduced credit risk (Stiglitz & Weiss, 1981).

The second empirical analysis focuses on the role of corporate reputation in client-auditor relationships. Consistent with the analysis of the firm-bank relationship, this study adopts a twofold perspective: the stakeholder-oriented perspective, which examines whether corporate reputation influences the auditor's decision to offer services (both auditing and consulting) to the firm, and the organizational-oriented perspective, which assesses the impact of corporate reputation on a firm's economic and financial performance through reduced audit and non-audit fees.

This analysis is significant for several reasons. First, despite often being under-examined in relation to corporate reputation, auditors are critical stakeholders due to the influence their decisions have on those of other stakeholders (Newman et al., 2005). For example, by providing independent assurance of the accuracy and reliability of financial statements, auditors help shape stakeholder confidence (Cohen et al., 2000). Moreover, auditors protect and enhance the interests of shareholders (Richard Baker & Owsen, 2002) and, more broadly, help safeguard the community by combating corruption through both prevention and detection (Jeppesen, 2019).

Second, the International Standard on Auditing (ISA) No. 220 requires audit firms to gather necessary information before initiating or continuing an engagement with a client, specifically assessing the client's audit risk, with a focus on the integrity of the entity and its management. While the standard emphasizes integrity, the International Standards on Quality Control (ISQC) further clarifies that this concept is closely linked to reputation. ISQC 1, for instance, outlines that integrity encompasses aspects such as the client's identity and business reputation, as well as any evidence suggesting the client may be involved in illicit activities, such as money laundering. Collectively, the ISA and ISQC underscore the importance of corporate reputation in auditor risk assessments (Ethridge et al., 2007) and pricing decisions (Blaskovich & Mintchik, 2007). Given that auditors shape their decisions in relation to client risk (Houston et al., 1999), corporate reputation can be seen as a signal to auditors regarding the firm's low-risk profile.

Additionally, previous studies in auditing literature (Asare et al., 1994; Adams et al., 2005) highlight the necessity of addressing information asymmetries in the auditor-client relationship. In this context, auditors face significant challenges in assessing a client's risk due to limited access to private information, which often results in an inherent information gap (De Meza & Webb, 1987; Narayanan, 1988; Noe, 1988; Myers & Majluf, 1984). As auditors are tasked with independently evaluating the client's risk profile, corporate reputation becomes an essential tool for bridging this information asymmetry. Reputation provides critical external data about the client's past and present activities (Deephouse, 2000), including actions that may otherwise go undetected or be deemed inconsequential (Bednar et al., 2013; Miller, 2006; Rogers et al., 2016; Burke et al., 2019), thus supporting the auditors' decision-making process.

Finally, the empirical analysis in this book focuses on the Italian context, which provides an appropriate and valuable setting for examining the impact of corporate reputation on banks and auditors for several reasons. The first concerns firms' ownership and governance structure, which is crucial for studying the relationship between corporate reputation and the selected categories of stakeholders.

Specifically, the Italian entrepreneurial landscape is dominated by family firms, which account for approximately 90% of businesses in the country, contributing to 75% of employment and 80% of GDP (Amato et al., 2024). Family firms also represent a significant portion of Italian-listed companies, with estimates indicating that more than 60% of these firms are family-controlled. This figure is notably higher than the European average, which stands at approximately 44% for listed companies across Western Europe (CONSOB, 2020; Pierni et al., 2022).

Unlike in economies where managerial control is widespread, in Italy, key figures such as CEOs are often members of the owning family (Corbetta & Salvato, 2012). This characteristic of the ownership and governance structure may influence both the CEO's and the firm's reputation, as these variables can be deeply intertwined with family ownership. Prior studies suggest that a family CEO can be a double-edged sword, as it may create an unwarranted association between the CEO and the firm's reputation, making the latter more susceptible to the family CEO's potentially harmful actions and decisions (Benedetti et al., 2025).

Furthermore, this ownership and governance structure is often characterized by long CEO tenures (Conte, 2018). Prior research suggests that in markets where

CEOs frequently change, the overlap between CEO reputation and firm reputation tends to be weaker than in contexts where CEOs remain in their roles for extended periods (Conte, 2018). Thus, this increased managerial stability reinforces the bidirectional connection between the CEO's and the firm's reputation.

Moreover, this ownership and governance structure influences information asymmetry dynamics. While traditional agency theory (Jensen & Meckling, 1976) suggests that family firms mitigate agency problems arising from the separation of ownership and management, research in the Italian context indicates that information asymmetry in those ownership and governance structures can be exacerbated between controlling and minority shareholders or external stakeholders (e.g. Minichilli et al., 2016; Peruffo et al., 2014). According to the resource-based view (Barney, 1991), information asymmetry can be reduced by leveraging firm resources that provide credible signals about a company's intentions. Consequently, corporate reputation, widely recognized as one such resource (e.g. Fombrun, 1996; Stevens & Makarius, 2015), becomes particularly relevant in contexts characterized by heightened information asymmetry.

The second aspect that makes the Italian context an appropriate and valuable setting for examining the impact of corporate reputation on banks and auditors is related to the long-term interactions between firms and stakeholders, built on a strong foundation of relational trust (Boesso & Kumar, 2009). This aspect involves both the firm and the stakeholder. On one hand, companies place considerable efforts on developing communication strategies and engagement initiatives aimed at strengthening and maintaining relationships with their stakeholders (Romenti, 2010; Saviano et al., 2018). On the other hand, stakeholders conduct a more thorough evaluation before engaging with a firm by considering not only the financial and operational metrics but also 'soft' information, such as corporate reputation (D'Aurizio et al., 2015).

Lastly, the third reason for interest in the Italian context concerns the specific legal framework. Unlike Anglo-Saxon countries, particularly the USA, Italy operates under a civil law system characterized by weaker investor protections (La Porta et al., 2000; Lepore et al., 2018). As indicated by La Porta et al. (2000, p. 6), «*at the extreme of no investor protection,* [...] *without a strong reputation, no rational outsider would finance a firm*». In such an environment, corporate reputation becomes even more crucial for firms seeking to attract external financing, as investors and creditors cannot rely solely on legal protections and formal contracts. Instead, they place significant emphasis on informal mechanisms such as trust, past behaviours, and the firm's reputation.

Focusing on auditing, the Italian setting is highly regulated (Cameran, 2007). In response to the financial scandals of the early 2000s, the Italian government strengthened auditor independence requirements (such as restrictions and caps on non-audit services), which are among the most stringent in the international context (Kend et al., 2021; Ratzinger-Sakel & Schönberger, 2015). According to auditing literature, these strict measures limit auditors' knowledge spillover (e.g. Sun & Habib, 2021), thereby reducing their access to insider information about the firms they audit. As a result, auditors face greater challenges in risk assessment, which, in turn, increases their litigation risk (Allen et al., 2006; Johnstone, 2000). To mitigate these risks, auditors could rely more heavily on external sources of information, such as corporate reputation when evaluating the firm risk.

Taken together, the factors highlighted above indicate that the Italian context provides a highly appropriate setting for the empirical analyses presented in the following section.

6.1.2 Theoretical Framework and Hypotheses Development

Legitimacy theory offers a powerful framework for understanding how corporate reputation influences firm-stakeholder interactions in contexts marked by trust, risk, and information asymmetry (Bitektine, 2011; Cohen & Dean, 2005). The theory posits that organizations strive to align their activities, behaviours, and disclosures with societal norms, values, and expectations to gain, maintain, and restore legitimacy in the eyes of their stakeholders (Zimmerman & Zeitz, 2002; Suchman, 1995).

In the context of this study, legitimacy theory elucidates how corporate reputation serves as a strategic asset, allowing firms to signal their adherence to ethical, professional, and societal standards. This reduces stakeholder uncertainties and risks, thereby fostering trust and promoting more favourable interactions with stakeholders, such as banks and auditors.

Corporate Reputation and Banks

Banks, as critical financial intermediaries, operate in environments where trust and risk management are paramount. Firms with strong corporate reputations signal legitimacy by demonstrating their commitment to ethical behaviour, financial stability, and compliance with societal and regulatory expectations (Patten, 1991; Hogner, 1982; Lindblom, 1993). This legitimacy addresses two core challenges in the firm-bank relationship (Mishkin, 1996; Igawa & Kanatas, 1990):

1. *Adverse selection in the ex ante phase*: Banks often face difficulties in assessing creditworthiness due to incomplete or asymmetric information (Dell'Ariccia, 2001). Firms with strong reputations reduce these uncertainties by signalling financial discipline, governance quality, and transparency, thereby increasing banks' willingness to provide loans.
2. *Moral hazard in the ex post phase*: Even after loans are granted, banks face risks related to the firm's use of borrowed funds and repayment capacity (Atkeson, 1991). A strong reputation serves as a proxy for accountability and ethical behaviour, mitigating concerns about moral hazard.

Building on these assumptions, the first empirical analysis posits the following hypotheses:

Hp1a: Corporate reputation positively influences the firm-bank relationship by facilitating the loan process.
Hp1b: Corporate reputation positively influences the firm-bank relationship by lowering the cost of debt.

Legitimacy theory reinforces these hypotheses by explaining how firms that achieve legitimacy through reputation are more likely to secure favourable financial terms. By reducing perceived credit risk, these firms strengthen their access to financial resources and improve the conditions under which these resources are obtained.

Corporate Reputation and Auditors

The legitimacy of a firm can influence the auditor-client relationship by demonstrating a commitment to transparency, ethical governance, and compliance with professional standards, which in turn can lower audit risk (Rostami OstadKelayeh et al., 2024). Furthermore, the role of legitimacy theory extends seamlessly to the auditor-client relationship, as auditors function as external validators of financial integrity and public trust, thereby shaping the perceptions of other stakeholders regarding the firm (Holm & Zaman, 2012; Power, 2003). In other words, a firm's legitimacy can strengthen the auditor-client relationship by reducing the reputational and litigation risks auditors face, which can be understood through two main perspectives:

1. *Auditors' risk appetite*: Reputable firms are perceived as lower-risk clients, reducing the likelihood of financial misstatements or unethical practices that could expose auditors to legal or reputational harm (Burke et al., 2019). Consequently, auditors may prefer to engage with reputable firms, as doing so reduces their exposure to risks.
2. *Certification of legitimacy*: By certifying financial reports or providing services to reputable firms, auditors play a pivotal role in shaping stakeholders' perceptions of a firm's legitimacy (Holm & Zaman, 2012; Power, 2003). This responsibility is particularly significant in the eyes of investors, regulators, and other relevant parties. In light of this critical role, auditors may prefer to engage with reputable firms to enhance their own credibility and reputation while also mitigating the risk of potential litigation costs (Donelson et al., 2019).

Building on these dynamics, the second empirical analysis examines the following hypotheses:

Hp2a: Corporate reputation positively influences the firm-auditor relationship by favouring the supply of services.
Hp2b: Corporate reputation positively influences the firm-auditor relationship by lowering audit fees.

Legitimacy theory supports these hypotheses by elucidating the strategic interplay between reputation and auditor engagement. Reputable firms are not only more attractive to auditors but also benefit from reduced costs due to their alignment with professional norms and reduced risks. Additionally, firms with strong reputations may negotiate favourable terms for audit and non-audit services, reflecting auditors' confidence in the firm's legitimacy.

In both firm-bank and auditor-client relationships, legitimacy theory highlights the critical role of corporate reputation as a mechanism for bridging gaps of trust and addressing information asymmetry. Firms with strong reputations benefit from improved stakeholder relationships, access to resources, and enhanced credibility. These benefits underscore the strategic value of maintaining legitimacy as a foundation for long-term success in stakeholder interactions.

Thus, legitimacy theory provides a cohesive and compelling framework for understanding the empirical relationships between corporate reputation and those groups of stakeholder dynamics, underpinning the hypotheses and reinforcing the relevance of this study.

6.2 Research Design

6.2.1 Sample Selection

The empirical analysis in this book utilizes a panel dataset comprising non-financial Italian-listed firms over 10 years (2014–2023), with a total of 910 firm-year observations.

The analysis specifically focuses on non-financial listed firms, excluding financial entities such as banks, insurance companies, and holding companies. This selection was made to ensure greater homogeneity within the sample, as financial firms differ significantly from non-financial firms in terms of financial regulations and business models. These differences could introduce heterogeneity, potentially affecting the validity of the results.

Initially, the sample included active Italian-listed companies whose data were available on the AIDA database (Bureau van Dijk) as of October 28, 2024, totalling 396 firms. After data cleaning, 305 firms were excluded: 25 firms fell under NAICS code 52 (Finance and Insurance), 97 firms were removed due to listing or delisting operations during the analysed period (2014–2023), and the remaining 183 firms were excluded due to missing data on corporate reputation. As a result, the final sample consists of 91 firms (Table 6.1).

The panel dataset has been hand-collected, incorporating data from several sources. Specifically, economic and financial data were obtained from the AIDA database (Bureau van Dijk), auditing data from AuditAnalytics Europe, and corporate reputation data from the Reputation Institute's RRR rating and the LexisNexis database.

Table 6.1 Sample selection

	Firm-year obs
Italian-listed companies	3960
Less: company in the financial sector (NAICS code 52)	250
Less: listed, delisted, IPO, M&A in the period 2014–2023	970
Less: missing corporate reputation data	1830
Final firm-year observations	910

Source: author's elaboration

6.2.2 *Model Specifications and Variable Descriptions*

Model Specifications

The empirical analyses in this book employ a quantitative research methodology based on linear regressions. Specifically, I developed four econometric models: Model 1 tests hypothesis Hp1a, Model 2 tests hypothesis Hp1b, Model 3 tests hypothesis 2a, and Model 4 tests hypothesis 2b.

Model 1

$$\begin{aligned}\text{Leverage} = \alpha + \beta 1\text{Corporate\_Reputation} + \beta 2\,\text{Profitability} + \beta 3\,\text{Rigidity} \\ + \beta 4\,\text{Turnover} + \beta 5\,\text{Volatility} + \beta 6\,\text{Liquidity} + \beta 7\,\text{Size} \\ - \sum \text{IndustryFixedEffects} + \varepsilon i\end{aligned}$$

Model 2

$$\begin{aligned}\text{Cost\_Debt} = \alpha + \beta 1\text{Corporate\_Reputation} + \beta 2\,\text{Profitability} + \beta 3\,\text{Rigidity} \\ + \beta 4\,\text{Turnover} + \beta 5\,\text{Volatility} + \beta 6\,\text{Liquidity} + \beta 7\,\text{Size} \\ + \sum \text{IndustryFixedEffects} + \varepsilon i\end{aligned}$$

Model 3

$$\begin{aligned}\text{NAS} = \alpha + \beta 1\text{Corporate\_Reputation} + \beta 2\,\text{Big4} + \beta 3\,\text{Auditor\_change} \\ + \beta 4\,\text{Profitability} + \beta 5\,\text{Rigidity} + \beta 6\,\text{Turnover} + \beta 7\,\text{Volatility} \\ + \beta 8\,\text{Liquidity} + \beta 9\,\text{Size} + \sum \text{IndustryFixedEffects} + \varepsilon i\end{aligned}$$

Model 4

$$\begin{aligned} \text{Audit\_Fees} = {} & \alpha + \beta 1\,\text{Corporate\_Reputation} + \beta 2\,\text{Big4} + \beta 3\,\text{Auditor\_change} \\ & + \beta 4\,\text{Profitability} + \beta 5\,\text{Rigidity} + \beta 6\,\text{Turnover} + \beta 7\,\text{Volatility} \\ & + \beta 8\,\text{Liquidity} + \beta 9\,\text{Size} + \sum \text{IndustryFixedEffects} + \varepsilon i \end{aligned}$$

I included industry-fixed effects to account for industry-specific characteristics. All models were estimated using ordinary least squares (OLS) regression. To mitigate the influence of outliers, all variables in the models were winsorized at the 1% level.

Variable Descriptions

Dependent Variables

The dependent variable for Model 1 is the company's leverage (*Leverage*). Following prior research on leverage (e.g. Axelson et al., 2013; Ben-Zion & Shalit, 1975; Bharath et al., 2009; Cronqvist et al., 2012; Gungoraydinoglu & Öztekin, 2011; Hovakimian et al., 2004; Rajan & Zingales, 1995), leverage is measured as the ratio of total financial debt to equity.

For Model 2, the dependent variable is the cost of debt (*Cost_Debt*), calculated as the interest expense-to-debt ratio.

The dependent variable for Model 3 is non-audit services fees (*NAS*), measured as the natural logarithm of non-audit fees charged by the auditor to the firm during the financial year. Based on prior research on auditor client-acceptance decisions (e.g. Laux & Newman, 2010; Johnstone & Bedard, 2003), non-audit fees are used as proxies for the auditor's propensity to provide services to a client.

Finally, the dependent variable for Model 4 is audit fees (*Audit_Fees*), measured as the natural logarithm of the audit fees charged by the auditor to the firm for the respective financial year, consistent with prior studies on audit fees (e.g. Abbott et al., 2003; Hay et al., 2006; Carcello et al., 2011; Lafuente & Desender, 2012).

Explanatory Variables

The explanatory variable, *Corporate_Reputation*, is measured using three distinct approaches (see Chap. 5 for a detailed discussion of the most commonly used methods for measuring corporate reputation in the literature).

First, corporate reputation is assessed using the RepRisk Rating (RRR) (*Corporate_Reputation(1)*). This rating, widely applied in prior studies on corporate reputation (e.g. Burke et al., 2019; Hummel & Schlick, 2016; Kölbel et al., 2017), categorizes firms into ten risk classes, ranked in ascending order of risk: AAA, AA, A, BBB, BB, B, CCC, CC, C, and D. For regression analysis, I converted these classes into numerical values ranging from 0 to 9, with 0 representing low reputational risk (AAA) and 9 representing high reputational risk (D).

Second, corporate reputation is measured through the negative CEO's media coverage (*Corporate_Reputation(2)*). Consistent with prior research (e.g. Love et al., 2017), this variable is based on a content analysis of articles in Italian newspapers that mention CEOs. To collect these articles, I used the Nexis Uni database and conducted searches for each CEO in the sample. These searches employed the CEOs' last names, abbreviated names, and common nicknames as keywords, and the search was restricted to Italian articles published each year. This process resulted in the identification of 7430 valid news articles. The content analysis was performed using T-Lab Plus 2020 software, a tool known for producing results comparable to those achieved through human thematic analysis (Lancia, 2012). The software satisfies the 'Turing-like' criterion for validity, as established by Salvatore et al. (2012). Text preparation involves lemmatization, which is a process that reorganizes the T-Lab database by grouping words with similar roots (e.g. 'crime' and 'criminal') into cohesive analytical categories. This step allowed for a more structured analysis of word occurrences and co-occurrences, as well as their syntactic relationships. The analysis specifically highlighted the negative tone of the articles, focusing on the co-occurrence of negatively connoted words. These words were identified using The Italian Sentiment Lexicon, developed by the Istituto di Linguistica Computazionale 'A. Zampolli' - Consiglio Nazionale delle Ricerche (ILC-CNR). This lexicon comprises 6457 Italian words classified as negative (e.g. misconduct, deception, fraud, fault, ineffectiveness, unethical). It was created by manually classifying a list of seed keywords and extending them based on ItalWordNet v.2, encompassing 24,293 lexical entries annotated with positive, negative, or neutral polarity. To construct the variable, I calculated a score for each article based on the number of negative co-occurrences it contained. The final score for each firm-year observation was obtained by aggregating the scores of all news articles related to the company's CEO for that specific year. Consistent with studies suggesting that the CEO's reputation reflects the corporate reputation (Love et al., 2017), the variable *Corporate_Reputation(2)* captures the extent of negative corporate reputation, with higher values indicating a more unfavourable perception.

Third, corporate reputation is operationalized through the CEO's notoriety (*Corporate_Reputation(3)*). In line with prior studies by Kim and Liang (2023), Hayward et al. (2004), and Love et al. (2017), CEO notoriety is measured by the frequency of mentions in news articles, utilizing data from the Nexis Uni database. For each firm-year observation, I counted the number of articles mentioning the CEO in a given year, without considering the sentiment or tone of the articles. As for the *Corporate_Reputation(2)*, I conducted searches using the CEOs' last names, abbreviated names, and common nicknames, with the search restricted to Italian articles published each year. To avoid overestimating the frequency of CEOs with common names, the count was limited to articles specifically related to the companies they lead.

Control Variables

The regression analysis incorporated control variables based on the literature addressing factors that influence a firm's financial structure (Axelson et al., 2013; Ben-Zion & Shalit, 1975; Bharath et al., 2009; Cronqvist et al., 2012; Gungoraydinoglu & Öztekin, 2011; Hovakimian et al., 2004; Rajan & Zingales, 1995) and audit pricing (e.g. Jones & Raghunandan, 1998; Choi et al., 2004; Khalil et al., 2011). Specifically, the control variables common to all models are:

- Profitability (*Profitability*), calculated as the ratio of operating income to sales revenue (return on sales). A higher return on sales may impact the bank's decision to finance due to a reduced credit risk associated with higher profitability. Conversely, higher profitability may enable the company to secure lower interest rates in the financial market. Therefore, leverage is expected to be positively associated with return on sales, while the cost of debt is expected to be negatively associated. Moreover, a higher return on sales may influence non-audit services (NAS) and audit fees through audit risk. Auditors may view more profitable firms as lower risk, potentially leading to lower audit fees. However, higher profitability might also create opportunities for auditors to offer additional non-audit services. A financially stable firm with higher profitability may be more likely to seek advisory services, creating a demand for NAS. Auditors may be more willing to provide these services, as the firm's financial health could reduce the perceived risk of potential litigation costs or reputational damage associated with offering NAS.
- Fixed asset rigidity (*Rigidity*), calculated as the ratio of fixed assets to total assets, reflects the inflexibility of the company's asset base. Greater rigidity could increase the insolvency risk for the company, as it might have a limited ability to adapt to changes in the business environment. Therefore, leverage is expected to be negatively associated with fixed asset rigidity, while the cost of debt is expected to be positively associated. As for audit fees and non-audit services (NAS), greater asset rigidity may lead to lower inclination to provide non-audit services and higher audit fees. Auditors may perceive firms with more rigid asset structures as riskier due to their limited ability to adapt to economic fluctuations or liquidity crises. As a result, these firms may require more detailed and comprehensive audit procedures, which in turn increases the complexity and cost of the audit engagement. Moreover, the perceived higher risk could expose auditors to greater litigation and reputational costs, leading them to be more cautious in offering additional non-audit services.
- Asset turnover (*Turnover*), calculated as the ratio of sales revenue to total assets, reflects the company's ability to liquidate investments through product sales. A higher asset turnover suggests that the company is more efficient in utilizing its assets to generate revenue, which may positively influence its leverage. In contrast, a higher asset turnover could be associated with a lower cost of debt due to reduced risk for lenders. As for non-audit services (NAS) and audit fees, from an auditor's perspective, a higher asset turnover could signal a lower risk profile, as

the company is better positioned to generate cash flows and meet financial obligations. This may reduce the auditor's perceived risk, potentially lowering the audit fees. However, the relatively lower perceived risk may make auditors more willing to offer non-audit services, as they are less concerned with the potential exposure to litigation or reputational damage.

- EBITDA variability (*Volatility*), used as a proxy for operational risk, reflects the volatility in a company's earnings before interest, taxes, depreciation, and amortization (EBITDA). An increase in EBITDA variability signals higher operational risk, which may make it more difficult for companies to secure credit in the market and could lead to higher borrowing costs. Consequently, leverage is expected to be negatively associated with EBITDA volatility, while the cost of debt is expected to be positively associated due to the increased perceived risk by lenders. Furthermore, higher EBITDA volatility indicates greater operational risk and financial uncertainty. Auditors may view companies with higher volatility as riskier clients, as the fluctuation in earnings could increase the likelihood of misstatements or require more intensive audit procedures to ensure the accuracy of financial reporting. This increased audit effort may drive up audit fees. Moreover, given the heightened operational risk, auditors may be more cautious about offering non-audit services, as such companies could be perceived as riskier and more likely to face financial difficulties, increasing the risk of litigation or reputational damage for the auditor.
- Current liquidity (*Liquidity*), calculated as the ratio of current assets to short-term liabilities, reflects the company's ability to meet short-term obligations through liquid assets within a timeframe compatible with the maturity of its debts. As liquidity improves, companies are seen as less risky to banks, leading to a positive association with leverage and a negative association with the cost of debt. From an auditor's perspective, companies with higher liquidity are perceived as less financially risky, as they are better equipped to meet their short-term obligations. This may reduce the auditor's perceived risk, as the firm is less likely to face liquidity crises or insolvency. Consequently, auditors may feel more comfortable offering non-audit services (NAS) to such companies, as the likelihood of financial distress or litigation risks is lower.
- Firm's dimension (*Size),* calculated as the natural logarithm of sales, controls for company size. Larger firms typically exhibit higher leverage due to their financial stability and market presence, as well as higher audit fees due to the increased audit effort required. The impact of size on the cost of debt and the auditor's willingness to offer non-audit services (NAS) can vary, as it depends on the perceived riskiness of the companies.

In addition to the control variables listed above, Models 3 and 4 also include the following variables, which are relevant for understanding auditor's pricing and decisions (Bharath et al., 2009; Leary & Roberts, 2014; Simunic, 1980; Hay et al., 2006):

- The auditor identity (*Big4*), taking value 1 if the audit firm is one of the Big 4 (KPMG, Deloitte, Ernst & Young, PwC) and 0 otherwise.

- The auditor change (*Auditor_chage*), taking value 1 if the firm experienced an auditor change during the period of analysis and 0 otherwise.

6.3 Results

6.3.1 Results on the Impact of Corporate Reputation on Banks' Decisions: Model 1 and Model 2

The results presented in Table 6.2 provide a comprehensive overview of descriptive statistics across the sample.

The *Leverage* variable has a mean value of 2.772 and a median of 2.650, suggesting a relatively symmetric distribution. The interquartile range (IQR), from 1.840 (25th percentile) to 3.300 (75th percentile), indicates that most firms exhibit moderate leverage levels. The standard deviation of 2.088 reflects some variability, though extreme outliers appear minimal. The mean *Cost_Debt* is 5.846, with a median of 4.310, showing a positively skewed distribution where a few firms incur significantly higher costs. The IQR ranges from 2.260 to 8.090, and the high standard deviation of 4.681 underscores substantial variation among firms in their borrowing costs. *Corporate_Reputation(1)* has a mean value of 3.805 and a median of 3.891. The relatively small standard deviation of 0.626 suggests consistency in this measure across firms. *Corporate_Reputation(2)* exhibits a mean of 1944.874 and a median of 2013.153. The IQR spans from 1480.573 to 2368.207, with a standard deviation of 497.973, showing moderate variability. The mean of *Corporate_Reputation(3)* is 146.962, and the median is 140.386, with an IQR from 116.425 to 176.328. A relatively high standard deviation of 89.509 indicates notable dispersion in this measure. *Profitability* has a mean value of −2.866, with a median of 0.420. The negative mean highlights that some firms in the sample face financial difficulties, dragging the average downward. The IQR ranges from −7.960 to 5.720, and

Table 6.2 Descriptive statistics (a)

Variable	Mean	Median	p25	p75	SD	*N*
Leverage	2.772	2.650	1.840	3.300	2.088	910
Cost_Debt	5.846	4.310	2.260	8.090	4.681	910
Corporate_Reputation(1)	3.805	3.891	3.221	4.337	0.626	910
Corporate_Reputation(2)	1944.874	2013.153	1480.573	2368.207	497.973	910
Corporate_Reputation(3)	146.962	140.386	116.425	176.328	89.509	910
Profitability	−2.866	0.420	−7.960	5.720	14.277	910
Rigidity	0.600	0.616	0.484	0.734	0.192	910
Turnover	0.530	0.498	0.146	0.726	0.451	910
Volatility	20,355	6022	−421	22,586	149,598	910
Liquidity	1.324	1.230	0.830	1.740	0.681	910
Size (millions)	756.276	106.908	52.212	233.881	3653.052	910

the standard deviation of 14.277 reflects significant heterogeneity in firm performance. *Rigidity* shows a mean of 0.600 and a median of 0.616, with an IQR of 0.484–0.734. The standard deviation of 0.192 indicates limited variability, suggesting that most firms exhibit similar levels of rigidity. The *Turnover* variable has a mean of 0.530 and a median of 0.498, pointing to a balanced distribution. The IQR spans from 0.146 to 0.726, with a standard deviation of 0.451, indicating moderate variability. *Volatility* has a mean of 20,355 and a median of 6022, suggesting a highly skewed distribution. The wide IQR (−421 to 22,586) and an exceptionally high standard deviation of 149,598 highlight substantial differences in firm risk profiles. The *Liquidity* measure exhibits a mean of 1.324 and a median of 1.230, indicating that most firms maintain adequate liquidity. The IQR ranges from 0.830 to 1.740, and the standard deviation of 0.681 suggests moderate variation across firms. Finally, *Size*, measured in millions, has a mean value of 756.276 and a median of 106.908. The IQR spans from 52.212 to 233.881, and the high standard deviation of 3653.052 underscores extreme variability.

Table 6.3 shows the bivariate correlations between the dependent variables, the explanatory variables, and the regression models' control variables. Even though Table 6.3 highlights some statistically significant relationships, the analysis of variance inflation factor (VIF) values confirms that multicollinearity is not a concern.[1]

Table 6.4 presents the results of the linear regression analysis for Model 1, specifically addressing the influence of corporate reputation on firm-bank relationships by facilitating the loan process. The regression results demonstrate that *Corporate_Reputation(1)*, reflecting reputational risk, is significantly and negatively associated with financial leverage (p-value <0.01). This finding suggests that firms with lower reputational risk are favouring accessing the bank loan. *Corporate_Reputation(2)*, which captures a negative reputation, also shows a significant negative relationship with leverage (p-value <0.01). Interestingly, *Corporate_Reputation(3)*, representing an alternative measure of corporate reputation named notoriety, does not exhibit a significant association with leverage.

The analysis further reveals interesting patterns among control variables. Firm size exhibits a significant and positive relationship with leverage (p-value <0.05), suggesting that larger firms, often perceived as more stable, attract debt financing more easily. Turnover demonstrates an inverse relationship with leverage (p-value <0.10), indicating that operational efficiency reduces debt dependency.

Table 6.5 presents the results of the linear regression analysis for Model 2, specifically examining the influence of corporate reputation on the cost of debt. The regression results demonstrate that *Corporate_Reputation(1)*, reflecting reputational risk, is significantly and positively associated with *Cost_Debt* (p-value <0.10). This suggests that firms with lower reputational risk are perceived as more trustworthy by banks and, consequently, secure loans at a lower cost.

[1] VIF values are not tabulated but are available from the authors.

Table 6.3 Correlation matrix (a)

Variable	1	2	3	4	5	6	7	8	9	10	11
1. Leverage	1										
2. Cost_Debt	0.367***	1									
3. Corporate_Reputation(1)	−0.0841	0.119**	1								
4. Corporate_Reputation(2)	−0.0841	0.119**	1.000***	1							
5. Corporate_Reputation(3)	−0.00578	0.0608	0.650***	0.650***	1						
6. Profitability	−0.100*	−0.104*	0.0450	0.0450	0.0513	1					
7. Rigidity	−0.0857	0.0964*	−0.00860	−0.00860	0.0576	−0.281***	1				
8. Turnover	0.0591	−0.0827	0.0828	0.0828	0.0336	0.359***	−0.712***	1			
9. Volatility	0.0803	0.260***	−0.111*	−0.111*	−0.0626	0.361***	0.0418	0.101*	1		
10. Liquidity	−0.273***	−0.142**	−0.0403	−0.0403	0.000499	0.181***	−0.331***	0.0488	−0.0405	1	
11. Size	0.269***	0.304***	−0.0228	−0.0228	0.0268	0.323***	−0.236***	0.397***	0.552***	0.0276	1

***p value <0.01; **p value <0.05; *p value <0.10

Table 6.4 Regression analysis model 1

Variables	(1) Leverage	(2) Leverage	(3) Leverage
Corporate_Reputation(1)	−0.464***		
	(0.120)		
Corporate_Reputation(2)		−0.000506***	
		(0.000156)	
Corporate_Reputation(3)			−0.00205
			(0.00153)
Profitability	−0.0184**	−0.0207**	−0.0243***
	(0.00819)	(0.00932)	(0.00938)
Rigidity	1.033	0.165	0.109
	(1.000)	(1.270)	(1.290)
Turnover	0.949*	−2.054***	−2.467***
	(0.537)	(0.748)	(0.753)
Volatility	−1.60e−06	−5.85e−07	6.75e−07
	(2.07e−06)	(2.09e−06)	(2.08e−06)
Liquidity	0.0645	0.165	0.139
	(0.144)	(0.173)	(0.176)
Size	0.364**	0.820***	0.890***
	(0.158)	(0.190)	(0.192)
Constant	−1.419	−4.542*	−5.694**
	(2.325)	(2.744)	(2.756)
Industry FE	Yes	Yes	Yes
Observations	910	910	910
R-squared (overall)	0.560	0.537	0.524
p-value	0.000	0.000	0.000

****p* value <0.01; ***p* value <0.05; **p* value <0.10

Corporate_Reputation(2), which captures a negative reputation, shows a stronger significant positive relationship with the dependent variable (*p*-value <0.01), suggesting that the negative reputation brings substantial penalties in the form of higher interest rates. Consistent with the results of Model 1, *Corporate_Reputation(3)*, representing the notoriety of the firm, does not exhibit a significant association with *Cost_Debt*.

The analysis further reveals that firm size exhibits a significant and positive relationship with leverage (*p*-value <0.01), suggesting that larger firms, potentially due to their extensive financing needs, face higher interest costs despite their reduced default risks. Finally, rigidity displays a consistently strong and positive association with *Cost_Debt* (*p*-value <0.01), highlighting that less flexible firms incur higher borrowing costs due to perceived risk.

Table 6.5 Regression analysis model 2

	(1)	(2)	(3)
Variables	Cost_Debt	Cost_Debt	Cost_Debt
Corporate_Reputation(1)	0.506*		
	(0.289)		
Corporate_Reputation(2)		0.00110***	
		(0.000397)	
Corporate_Reputation(3)			0.00341
			(0.00382)
Profitability	0.0115	0.00929	0.0157
	(0.0204)	(0.0234)	(0.0236)
Rigidity	11.28***	11.61***	12.46***
	(2.620)	(3.635)	(3.684)
Turnover	2.124*	−2.763	−1.809
	(1.289)	(1.887)	(1.897)
Volatility	−2.84e−07	2.27e−06	2.09e−08
	(6.13e−06)	(6.47e−06)	(6.53e−06)
Liquidity	1.037**	1.104**	1.202**
	(0.409)	(0.481)	(0.490)
Size	1.248***	1.858***	1.780***
	(0.395)	(0.500)	(0.506)
Constant	−23.89***	−27.43***	−26.23***
	(5.925)	(7.516)	(7.611)
Industry FE	Yes	Yes	Yes
Observations	910	910	910
R-squared (Overall)	0.569	0.618	0.608
p-value	0.000	0.000	0.000

****p* value <0.01; ***p* value <0.05; **p* value <0.10

6.3.2 Results on the Impact of Corporate Reputation on Auditors' Decisions: Model 3 and Model 4

Table 6.6 presents descriptive statistics for the key variables analysed in the study. Panel A provides a summary of continuous variables, including *Audit_Fees*, *NAS*, corporate reputation measures, and control variables.

Audit_Fees (ln) have a mean of 13.021, with a median value of 12.853. The interquartile range (IQR) is 12.170–13.764, with a standard deviation of 1.167, suggesting moderate variability in audit fees across firms. *NAS* (ln) shows a mean of 11.342 and a median of 11.314, with an IQR spanning from 10.373 to 12.301. The standard deviation is 1.421, indicating slightly higher variability compared to audit fees.

Panel B summarizes the categorical variables. Big4 audit firms are engaged by 89.52% of the sample firms, reflecting the dominance of these firms in the audit market. Meanwhile, auditor changes are less common, occurring in only 20.99% of the sample firms, highlighting the stability in auditor-client relationships.

Table 6.6 Descriptive statistics (b)

Panel A						
Variable	**Mean**	**Median**	**p25**	**p75**	**SD**	*N*
Audit_Fees (ln)	13.021	12.853	12.170	13.764	1.167	910
NAS (ln)	11.342	11.314	10.373	12.301	1.421	910
Corporate_Reputation(1)	3.805	3.891	3.221	4.337	0.626	910
Corporate_Reputation(2)	1944.874	2013.153	1480.573	2368.207	497.973	910
Corporate_Reputation(3)	146.962	140.386	116.425	176.328	89.509	910
Profitability	−2.866	0.420	−7.960	5.720	14.277	910
Rigidity	0.600	0.616	0.484	0.734	0.192	910
Turnover	0.530	0.498	0.146	0.726	0.451	910
Volatility	20,355	6022	−421	22,586	149,598	910
Liquidity	1.324	1.230	0.830	1.740	0.681	910
Size (millions)	756.276	106.908	52.212	233.881	3653.052	910
Panel B						
Variable	**0**	**1**	*N*			
Big4	10.48%	89.52%	910			
Auditor_change	79.01%	20.99%	910			

For a detailed description of variables such as *Corporate_Reputation(1)*, *Corporate_Reputation(2)*, *Corporate_Reputation(3)*, *Profitability*, *Rigidity*, *Turnover*, *Volatility*, *Liquidity*, *and Size*, see Sect. 6.3.2.

Table 6.7 shows the bivariate correlations between the dependent variables, the explanatory variables, and the regression models' control variables. Even though Table 6.7 highlights some statistically significant relationships, the analysis of variance inflation factor (VIF) values confirms that multicollinearity is not a concern (see Footnote 1).

Table 6.8 shows the results of the regression analysis for Model 3 analysing the impact of corporate reputation on favouring the provision of non-audit services.

Specifically, results show that *Corporate_Reputation(1)*, which reflects reputational risk, demonstrates a significant negative relationship with NAS (p-value <0.05). This indicates that auditors tend to offer more non-audit services to firms with lower reputational risk, confirming Hp2a. Conversely, *Corporate_Reputation(2)*, capturing negative reputation, and *Corporate_Reputation(3)*, representing firm notoriety, do not exhibit significant relationships with *NAS*.

Among the control variables, Big4 and Auditor_change do not significantly influence *NAS*, whereas *Size* shows a significant positive association (p-value <0.01) across all models, implying that larger firms are more likely to engage in non-audit services. *Rigidity* exhibits a positive and marginally significant association with *NAS* in Model 1 (p-value <0.10) but loses significance in subsequent models, indicating potential variability in this relationship.

Table 6.9 shows the results of the regression analysis for Model 4 analysing the impact of corporate reputation on auditing pricing.

Table 6.7 Correlation matrix (b)

Variable	1	2	3	4	5	6	7	8	9	10	11	12	13
1. Audit_Fees	1												
2. NAS	0.744***	1											
3. Corporate_ Reputation(1)	0.0158	−0.00667	1										
4. Corporate_ Reputation(2)	−0.0158	0.00667	−1.000***	1									
5. Corporate_ Reputation(3)	0.0679	0.0766	−0.663***	0.663***	1								
6. Big4	0.112*	0.0794	−0.104*	0.104*	0.122**	1							
7. Auditor_change	−0.0619	−0.0430	0.0505	−0.0505	−0.0664	−0.482***	1						
8. Profitability	−0.148**	−0.157**	−0.0427	0.0427	0.0341	−0.0830	0.122**	1					
9. Rigidity	0.212***	0.336***	−0.0229	0.0229	0.0913	0.0297	0.0251	−0.224***	1				
10. Turnover	−0.205***	−0.253***	−0.0177	0.0177	−0.0213	−0.0551	−0.0161	0.256***	−0.739***	1			
11. Volatility	0.387***	0.312***	0.160***	−0.160***	−0.0450	−0.105*	0.167***	0.337***	0.00897	0.105*	1		
12. Liquidity	0.117*	−0.0254	−0.0566	0.0566	0.0659	−0.0741	0.0991	0.241***	−0.307***	0.0522	−0.0106	1	
13. Size	0.639***	0.472***	0.0236	−0.0236	0.0310	−0.0148	0.0474	0.190***	−0.244***	0.399***	0.583***	0.0327	1

***p value <0.01; **p value <0.05; *p value <0.10

Table 6.8 Regression analysis model 3

Variables	(1) NAS	(2) NAS	(3) NAS
Corporate_Reputation(1)	−0.356**		
	(0.146)		
Corporate_Reputation(2)		9.76e−05	
		(0.000117)	
Corporate_Reputation(3)			−0.000566
			(0.00113)
Big4	0.188	0.145	0.168
	(0.268)	(0.288)	(0.289)
Auditor_change	−0.111	−0.129	−0.115
	(0.154)	(0.162)	(0.162)
Profitability	−0.00808	−0.0102	−0.00874
	(0.00643)	(0.00693)	(0.00687)
Rigidity	1.496*	1.019	1.038
	(0.805)	(0.904)	(0.905)
Turnover	−0.130	−0.624	−0.435
	(0.442)	(0.542)	(0.533)
Volatility	5.19e−07	2.94e−07	−1.35e−07
	(1.39e−06)	(1.40e−06)	(1.36e−06)
Liquidity	0.0866	0.0613	0.0807
	(0.109)	(0.117)	(0.118)
Size	0.411***	0.462***	0.434***
	(0.124)	(0.131)	(0.130)
Constant	4.717**	3.440*	3.873*
	(1.898)	(2.012)	(1.994)
Industry FE	Yes	Yes	Yes
Observations	910	910	910
R-squared (Overall)	0.656	0.713	0.713
p-value	0.000	0.000	0.000

***p value <0.01; **p value <0.05; *p value <0.10

Specifically, *Corporate_Reputation(1)* shows a strong positive relationship with audit fees (p-value <0.01), suggesting that firms with lower reputational risk obtain lower audit costs. Interestingly, *Corporate_Reputation(3)* demonstrates a marginally significant negative association with audit fees in Model 4 (p-value <0.10), indicating that firms with greater notoriety are perceived as less risky, thus having lower audit pricing. *Corporate_Reputation(2)*, however, does not significantly influence audit fees.

Control variables for audit fees reveal additional insights. *Big4* is positively associated with audit fees (p-value <0.10), reflecting the premium charged by large audit firms. *Auditor_change* shows a significant negative relationship (p-value <0.05), suggesting that fee reductions may occur during initial engagements to establish a long-term relationship. *Profitability* exhibits a significant negative association with

Table 6.9 Regression analysis model 4

	(1)	(2)	(3)
Variables	Audit_Fees	Audit_Fees	Audit_Fees
Corporate_Reputation(1)	0.128***		
	(0.0476)		
Corporate_Reputation(2)		−6.07e−05	
		(3.81e−05)	
Corporate_Reputation(3)			−0.000711*
			(0.000369)
Big4	0.141*	0.156*	0.156*
	(0.0752)	(0.0838)	(0.0836)
Auditor_change	−0.121**	−0.125**	−0.122**
	(0.0494)	(0.0512)	(0.0512)
Profitability	−0.00477**	−0.00415*	−0.00429*
	(0.00205)	(0.00229)	(0.00226)
Rigidity	0.898***	0.515*	0.529*
	(0.250)	(0.310)	(0.310)
Turnover	−0.723***	−0.429**	−0.425**
	(0.135)	(0.183)	(0.181)
Volatility	−2.11e−07	−3.92e−07	−3.33e−07
	(5.20e−07)	(5.17e−07)	(5.05e−07)
Liquidity	0.0885**	0.0544	0.0587
	(0.0361)	(0.0423)	(0.0423)
Size	0.425***	0.311***	0.313***
	(0.0401)	(0.0467)	(0.0463)
Constant	5.839***	7.771***	7.703***
	(0.569)	(0.676)	(0.668)
Industry FE	Yes	Yes	Yes
Observations	910	910	910
R-squared (Overall)	0.924	0.939	0.940
p-value	0.000	0.000	0.000

***p value <0.01; **p value <0.05; *p value <0.10

audit fees (p-value <0.05), indicating that auditors judge financially stable firms as less risky. Finally, *Size* and *Rigidity* show significant positive relationships with audit fees (p-value <0.01 and p-value <0.10, respectively), indicating that larger and less flexible firms require more comprehensive audits.

6.4 Discussion of Findings

This study empirically examines the impact of corporate reputation on firm-bank and firm-auditor relationships, revealing its critical role in mitigating information asymmetry and shaping stakeholder decisions. By drawing from legitimacy theory, the findings illustrate how reputation acts as a strategic asset that fosters trust and enhances resource accessibility.

Specifically, the results underscore corporate reputation's role as a signalling mechanism (Myers & Majluf, 1984; Stiglitz & Weiss, 1981). Across both stakeholder groups, reputation reduces the uncertainties arising from information asymmetry, offering banks and auditors insights into firm reliability, governance quality, and ethical behaviour. For banks, a strong reputation may mitigate adverse selection in the ex ante phase and moral hazard in the ex post phase, resulting in greater access to loans and lower borrowing costs. These findings align with the insights of Camerer (1988) and Mishkin (1996), who emphasize reputation's ability to bridge information gaps in financial contexts.

In the auditing context, reputation reduces auditors' perceived risk of engaging with a firm, leading to lower audit fees and an increased propensity to offer non-audit services. These outcomes are consistent with the auditing literature (e.g. Houston et al., 1999; Ethridge et al., 2007), which highlights reputation as a critical factor in shaping auditors' risk assessments and pricing strategies.

Moreover, the findings suggest that corporate reputation operates as a dual-purpose asset, serving both as a resource enabler and a credibility enhancer. This duality reflects the theoretical underpinnings of legitimacy theory (Zimmerman & Zeitz, 2002; Suchman, 1995). In both firm-bank and firm-auditor relationships, reputation not only facilitates access to resources (loans, audit, and non-audit services) but also enhances legitimacy in the eyes of stakeholders. Specifically, by demonstrating adherence to ethical, professional, and societal norms, firms with strong reputations signal their legitimacy, thereby reducing stakeholders' uncertainties and fostering trust. This process is particularly critical in environments characterized by high levels of trust and risk, such as financial and auditing contexts (Bitektine, 2011; Cohen & Dean, 2005).

A more in-depth analysis of the results confirms the stakeholder-sensitive nature of corporate reputation, as its impacts vary significantly across different stakeholder groups. While both banks and auditors place substantial weight on corporate reputation ratings when engaging with a client (*Corporate_Reputation(1)* demonstrates a strong and significant association with leverage, cost of debt, and audit fees), the findings reveal notable differences in their sensitivities to other dimensions of reputation.

Banks are particularly influenced by the tone of media coverage surrounding the CEO (*Corporate_Reputation(2)* shows a strong and significant association with leverage and cost of debt), whereas auditors exhibit no significant association with this variable. Conversely, auditors appear to marginally consider the CEO's notoriety in their audit pricing decisions (*Corporate_Reputation(3)* shows a marginally significant association with audit fees), a factor that does not influence banks' decisions.

Shifting the focus to the different measurement methods, the findings emphasize that varying methods of measurement can yield different results regarding the impacts of corporate reputation, thereby confirming its measurement-sensitive nature. Notably, the hypotheses in the empirical analyses are consistently supported when corporate reputation is measured using the variable *Corporate_Reputation(1)*. However, the results differ when alternative variables, such as *Corporate_Reputation(2)* or *Corporate_Reputation(3)*, are considered, underscoring the influence of measurement approaches on empirical outcomes.

These empirical analyses contribute to the academic literature on corporate reputation and have practical implications for businesses. Firstly, this study adds to the understanding of the importance of reputational capital in relationships with individual stakeholders (Wartick, 2002), highlighting the relevance of this intangible asset in dealings with the banking system and the auditing market.

Secondly, given that the Italian business context heavily relies on bank credit as a primary source of external financing, companies can leverage the findings of this study to recognize the criticality of managing their reputation to strengthen their attractiveness to the banking system. The results underscore that firms can achieve this objective by also appointing top-level individuals, such as CEOs, who possess a favourable reputation in the market.

Thirdly, the evidence of this analysis informs firms on the crucial role of reputation in attracting expert auditors like the Big 4, which are perceived as more prestigious and reputed for offering higher audit quality in the market (Francis, 2004). This enhances the firm's market approval and credibility and thus positively impacts the firm's outcomes.

This analysis is not without limitations, which in turn highlights opportunities for future research on the topic. First, the sample size is relatively small, comprising 91 companies. Expanding the analysis to include a larger and more diverse set of firms, including non-listed Italian companies, would enhance the validity and generalizability of the results.

Second, while the study employs three distinct measurement methods for corporate reputation, the measurement-sensitive nature of the concept suggests that further analyses using alternative approaches are needed to corroborate and refine these findings.

Lastly, the analysis focuses exclusively on the Italian market, meaning that context-specific characteristics may have influenced the results. Future research could address this limitation by conducting similar analyses in different national contexts or offering cross-country comparisons to uncover potential similarities and differences, thereby contributing to a more comprehensive understanding of corporate reputation's impacts.

References

Abbott, L. J., Parker, S., Peters, G. F., & Raghunandan, K. (2003). An empirical investigation of audit fees, nonaudit fees, and audit committees. *Contemporary Accounting Research, 20*(2), 215–234. https://doi.org/10.1506/8YP9-P27G-5NW5-DJKK

Adams, F. G., Bedard, J. C., & Johnstone, K. M. (2005). Information asymmetry and competitive bidding in auditing. *Economic Inquiry, 43*(2), 417–425. https://doi.org/10.1093/ei/cbi028

Agarwal, J., Osiyevskyy, O., & Feldman, P. M. (2015). Corporate reputation measurement: Alternative factor structures, nomological validity, and organizational outcomes. *Journal of Business Ethics, 130*(2), 485–506. https://doi.org/10.1007/s10551-014-2232-6

Ali, I., Ali, M., Grigore, G., Molesworth, M., & Jin, Z. (2020). The moderating role of corporate reputation and employee-company identification on the work-related outcomes of job insecurity resulting from workforce localization policies. *Journal of Business Research, 117*, 825–838. https://doi.org/10.1016/j.jbusres.2019.02.060

Allen, R. D., Hermanson, D. R., Kozloski, T. M., & Ramsay, R. J. (2006). Auditor risk assessment: Insights from the academic literature. *Accounting Horizons, 20*(2), 157–177. https://doi.org/10.2308/acch.2006.20.2.157

Amato, S., Broccardo, L., & Tenucci, A. (2024). Family firms, management control and digitalization effect. *Management Decision, 62*(5), 1645–1667. https://doi.org/10.1108/MD-03-2023-0347

Asare, S., Hackenbrack, K., & Knechel, W. R. (1994). Client acceptance and continuation decisions. In *Auditing Symposium XII: Proceedings of the 1994 Deloitte and Touche/University of Kansas Symposium on Auditing Problems* (pp. 163–178).

Atkeson, A. (1991). International lending with moral hazard and risk of repudiation. *Econometrica, 59*(4), 1069–1089. https://doi.org/10.2307/2938174

Axelson, U., Jenkinson, T., Strömberg, P., & Weisbach, M. S. (2013). Borrow cheap, buy high? The determinants of leverage and pricing in buyouts. *Journal of Finance, 68*(6), 2223–2267. Scopus. https://doi.org/10.1111/jofi.12082

Bancha d'Italia. (2020). Relazione annuale.

Barney, J. (1991). Firm resources and sustained competitive advantage. *Journal of Management, 17*(1), 99–120. https://doi.org/10.1177/014920639101700108

Bednar, M. K., Boivie, S., & Prince, N. R. (2013). Burr under the saddle: How media coverage influences strategic change. *Organization Science, 24*(3), 910–925. https://doi.org/10.1287/orsc.1120.0770

Benedetti, C., Rovelli, P., Fronzetti Colladon, A., De Massis, A., & Matzler, K. (2025). CEO identity and media perception: The influence on family firms' brand importance. *Journal of Family Business Strategy, 16*(1), 100646. https://doi.org/10.1016/j.jfbs.2024.100646

Ben-Zion, U., & Shalit, S. S. (1975). Size, leverage, and dividend record as determinants of equity risk. *Journal of Finance, 30*(4), 1015–1026.

Berger, A. N., Molyneux, P., & Wilson, J. O. S. (2014). *The Oxford handbook of banking* (2nd ed.). OUP.

Bharath, S. T., Pasquariello, P., & Wu, G. (2009). Does asymmetric information drive capital structure decisions. *Review of Financial Studies, 22*(8), 3211–3243. Scopus. https://doi.org/10.1093/rfs/hhn076

Bitektine, A. (2011). Toward a theory of social judgments of organizations: The case of legitimacy, reputation, and status. *The Academy of Management Review, 36*(1), 151–179.

Blaskovich, J., & Mintchik, N. (2007). Post-Sarbanes-Oxley audit planning: Perceptions of internal control assessments and other institutional considerations. *The CPA Journal, 77*(10), 30–42.

Boesso, G., & Kumar, K. (2009). Stakeholder prioritization and reporting: Evidence from Italy and the US. *Accounting Forum, 33*(2), 162–175. https://doi.org/10.1016/j.accfor.2008.07.010

Burke, J., Hoitash, R., & Hoitash, U. (2019). Auditor response to negative media coverage of client environmental, social, and governance practices. *Accounting Horizons, 33*(3), 1–23. https://doi.org/10.2308/acch-52450

Cameran, M. (2007). Auditing in Italy: The development of a highly-regulated setting before and after the Parmalat case. In *Auditing, trust and governance*. Routledge.

Camerer, C. (1988). Gifts as economic signals and social symbols. *American Journal of Sociology, 94*(Suppl), 180–214. https://doi.org/10.1086/228946

Carcello, J. V., Neal, T. L., Palmrose, Z.-V., & Scholz, S. (2011). CEO involvement in selecting board members, audit committee effectiveness, and restatements. *Contemporary Accounting Research, 28*(2), 396–430. https://doi.org/10.1111/j.1911-3846.2010.01052.x

Choi, J.-H., Doogar, R. K., & Ganguly, A. R. (2004). The riskiness of large audit firm client portfolios and changes in audit liability regimes: Evidence from the U.S. Audit Market. *Contemporary Accounting Research, 21*(4), 747–785. https://doi.org/10.1506/RCBG-RWXT-QAVF-JDDW
Cohen, B. D., & Dean, T. J. (2005). Information asymmetry and investor valuation of IPOs: Top management team legitimacy as a capital market signal. *Strategic Management Journal, 26*(7), 683–690. https://doi.org/10.1002/smj.463
Cohen, J. R., Krishnamoorthy, G., & Wright, A. (2000). *Corporate governance and the audit process* (Working Paper). Boston College.
CONSOB. (2020). *Report corporate governance 2020—AREA PUBBLICA—CONSOB*. https://www.consob.it/web/area-pubblica/abs-rcg/-/asset_publisher/D4UvV7Ug51WY/content/report-corporate-governance-2020/11973
Conte, F. (2018). Understanding the influence of CEO tenure and CEO reputation on corporate reputation: An exploratory study in Italy. *International Journal of Business and Management, 13*(3), 54. https://doi.org/10.5539/ijbm.v13n3p54
Corbetta, G., & Salvato, C. (2012). *Strategies for longevity in family firms*. Palgrave Macmillan. https://doi.org/10.1057/9781137024589
Cronqvist, H., Makhija, A. K., & Yonker, S. E. (2012). Behavioral consistency in corporate finance: CEO personal and corporate leverage. *Journal of Financial Economics, 103*(1), 20–40. https://doi.org/10.1016/j.jfineco.2011.08.005
D'Aurizio, L., Oliviero, T., & Romano, L. (2015). Family firms, soft information and bank lending in a financial crisis. *Journal of Corporate Finance, 33*, 279–292. https://doi.org/10.1016/j.jcorpfin.2015.01.002
De Meza, D., & Webb, D. C. (1987). Too much investment: A problem of asymmetric information. *The Quarterly Journal of Economics, 102*(2), 281–292. https://doi.org/10.2307/1885064
Deephouse, D. L. (2000). Media reputation as a strategic resource: An integration of mass communication and resource-based theories. *Journal of Management, 26*(6), 1091–1112. https://doi.org/10.1177/014920630002600602
Dell'Ariccia, G. (2001). Asymmetric information and the structure of the banking industry. *European Economic Review, 45*(10), 1957–1980. https://doi.org/10.1016/S0014-2921(00)00085-4
Donelson, D. C., Ege, M. S., & Leiby, J. (2019). Audit firm reputational consequences of alleged non-accounting misconduct by clients: How bargaining power temporarily shifts around securities litigation. *Auditing: A Journal of Practice & Theory, 38*(4), 77–100. https://doi.org/10.2308/ajpt-52405
Ethridge, J., Marsh, T., & Revelt, B. (2007). Engagement risk: Perceptions and strategies from audit partners. Faculty Publications. https://doi.org/10.19030/jber.v5i4.2536
Fombrun, C. J. (1996). *Reputation: Realizing value from the corporate image*. Harvard Business School Press.
Francis, J. R. (2004). What do we know about audit quality? *The British Accounting Review, 36*(4), 345–368. https://doi.org/10.1016/j.bar.2004.09.003
Gabbioneta, C., Ravasi, D., & Mazzola, P. (2007). Exploring the drivers of corporate reputation: A study of Italian Securities Analysts. *Corporate Reputation Review, 10*(2), 99–123. https://doi.org/10.1057/palgrave.crr.1550048
Garzella, S. (2005). *Il sistema d'azienda e la valorizzazione delle «potenzialità inespresse». Una «visione» strategica per il risanamento*. Giappichelli.
Gungoraydinoglu, A., & Öztekin, Ö. (2011). Firm- and country-level determinants of corporate leverage: Some new international evidence. *Journal of Corporate Finance, 17*(5), 1457–1474. https://doi.org/10.1016/j.jcorpfin.2011.08.004
Hay, D. C., Knechel, W. R., & Wong, N. (2006). Audit fees: A meta-analysis of the effect of supply and demand attributes. *Contemporary Accounting Research, 23*(1), 141–191. https://doi.org/10.1506/4XR4-KT5V-E8CN-91GX
Hayward, M. L. A., Rindova, V. P., & Pollock, T. G. (2004). Believing one's own press: The causes and consequences of CEO celebrity. *Strategic Management Journal, 25*(7), 637–653. https://doi.org/10.1002/smj.405

Helm, S. (2013). A matter of reputation and pride: Associations between perceived external reputation, pride in membership, job satisfaction and turnover intentions. *British Journal of Management, 24*, 542. https://doi.org/10.1111/j.1467-8551.2012.00827.x

Hogner, R. H. (1982). Corporate social reporting: 8 decades of development at US Steel. *Corporate Social Performance and Policy, 4*, 243–250.

Holm, C., & Zaman, M. (2012). Regulating audit quality: Restoring trust and legitimacy. *Accounting Forum, 36*(1), 51–61. https://doi.org/10.1016/j.accfor.2011.11.004

Houston, R. W., Peters, M. F., & Pratt, J. H. (1999). The audit risk model, business risk and audit-planning decisions. *Accounting Review, 74*(3), 281. https://doi.org/10.2308/accr.1999.74.3.281

Hovakimian, A., Hovakimian, G., & Tehranian, H. (2004). Determinants of target capital structure: The case of dual debt and equity issues. *Journal of Financial Economics, 71*(3), 517–540. Scopus. https://doi.org/10.1016/S0304-405X(03)00181-8

Hummel, K., & Schlick, C. (2016). *The relationship between sustainability performance and sustainability disclosure—Reconciling voluntary disclosure theory and legitimacy theory* (SSRN Scholarly Paper ID 2595045). Social Science Research Network. https://doi.org/10.2139/ssrn.2595045

Igawa, K., & Kanatas, G. (1990). Asymmetric information, collateral, and moral hazard. *Journal of Financial and Quantitative Analysis, 25*(4), 469–490. https://doi.org/10.2307/2331011

Jackson, G., & Apostolakou, A. (2010). Corporate social responsibility in Western Europe: An institutional mirror or substitute? *Journal of Business Ethics, 94*(3), 371–394. https://doi.org/10.1007/s10551-009-0269-8

Jensen, M. C., & Meckling, W. H. (1976). Theory of the firm: Managerial behavior, agency costs and ownership structure. *Journal of Financial Economics, 3*(4), 305–360. https://doi.org/10.1016/0304-405X(76)90026-X

Jeppesen, K. K. (2019). The role of auditing in the fight against corruption. *The British Accounting Review, 51*(5), 100798. https://doi.org/10.1016/j.bar.2018.06.001

Johnstone, K. M. (2000). Client-acceptance decisions: Simultaneous effects of client business risk, audit risk, auditor business risk, and risk adaptation. *Auditing: A Journal of Practice & Theory, 19*(1), 1–25. https://doi.org/10.2308/aud.2000.19.1.1

Johnstone, K. M., & Bedard, J. C. (2003). Risk management in client acceptance decisions. *Accounting Review, 78*(4), 1003–1025. https://doi.org/10.2308/accr.2003.78.4.1003

Jones, F. L., & Raghunandan, K. (1998). Client risk and recent changes in the market for audit services. *Journal of Accounting and Public Policy, 17*(2), 169–181.

Kend, M., Leoni, G., Florio, C., & Gaia, S. (2021). *EU audit reforms: Analysing different impacts in the UK and Italy*. ICAEW.

Khalid, F., Sun, J., Guo, J., & Srivastava, M. (2024). Green corporate image: Assessing the effects of climate change management practices on corporate reputation. *Corporate Social Responsibility and Environmental Management, 31*(3), 1786–1801. https://doi.org/10.1002/csr.2663

Khalil, S. K., Cohen, J. R., & Schwartz, K. B. (2011). Client engagement risks and the auditor search period. *Accounting Horizons, 25*(4), 685–702. https://doi.org/10.2308/acch-50062

Kim, Y. A., & Liang, F. H. (2023). The effect of CEO prominence on cross-border acquisitions: An international entrepreneurship approach. *Journal of Business Research, 163*, 113950. https://doi.org/10.1016/j.jbusres.2023.113950

Kölbel, J. F., Busch, T., & Jancso, L. M. (2017). How media coverage of corporate social irresponsibility increases financial risk. *Strategic Management Journal, 38*(11), 2266–2284. https://doi.org/10.1002/smj.2647

La Porta, R., Lopez-de-Silanes, F., Shleifer, A., & Vishny, R. (1998). Law and finance. *Journal of Political Economy, 106*(6), 1113–1155. https://doi.org/10.1086/250042

La Porta, R., Lopez-de-Silanes, F., Shleifer, A., & Vishny, R. (2000). Investor protection and corporate governance. *Journal of Financial Economics, 58*(1), 3–27. https://doi.org/10.1016/S0304-405X(00)00065-9

Lafuente, E., & Desender, K. (2012). The role of enterprise risk management in determining audit fees: Complement or substitute (pp. 5–27).

Lancia, F. (2012). The logic of the T-LAB tools explained. Available at: http://www.tlab.it/en/toolsexplained.php

Laux, V., & Newman, D. P. (2010). Auditor liability and client acceptance decisions. *Accounting Review, 85*(1), 261–285. https://doi.org/10.2308/accr.2010.85.1.261

Leary, M. T., & Roberts, M. R. (2014). Do peer firms affect corporate financial policy? *The Journal of Finance, 69*(1), 139–178. https://doi.org/10.1111/jofi.12094

Lepore, L., Paolone, F., & Cambrea, D. R. (2018). Ownership structure, investors' protection and corporate valuation: The effect of judicial system efficiency in family and non-family firms. *Journal of Management and Governance, 22*(4), 829–862. https://doi.org/10.1007/s10997-018-9405-0

Lindblom, C. K. (1993). The implications of organisational legitimacy for corporate social performance and disclosure. In *Conference Paper, Critical Perspectives on Accounting Conference*.

Liu, A., Shu, C., & Xiao, Z. (2024). Entrepreneurial orientation, political ties, and corporate reputation: The moderating roles of institutional environments. *Journal of Business Research, 170*, 114347. https://doi.org/10.1016/j.jbusres.2023.114347

Love, E. G., Lim, J., & Bednar, M. K. (2017). The face of the firm: The influence of ceos on corporate reputation. *Academy of Management Journal, 60*(4), 1462–1481. https://doi.org/10.5465/amj.2014.0862

Miller, G. S. (2006). The press as a watchdog for accounting fraud. *Journal of Accounting Research, 44*(5), 1001–1033. https://doi.org/10.1111/j.1475-679X.2006.00224.x

Minichilli, A., Brogi, M., & Calabrò, A. (2016). Weathering the storm: Family ownership, governance, and performance through the financial and economic crisis. *Corporate Governance: An International Review, 24*(6), 552–568. https://doi.org/10.1111/corg.12125

Mishkin, F. S. (1996). *Understanding financial crises: A developing country perspective* (Working Paper 5600). National Bureau of Economic Research. https://doi.org/10.3386/w5600

Myers, S. C., & Majluf, N. S. (1984). Corporate financing and investment decisions when firms have information that investors do not have. *Journal of Financial Economics, 13*(2), 187–221. https://doi.org/10.1016/0304-405X(84)90023-0

Narayanan, M. P. (1988). Debt versus equity under asymmetric information. *The Journal of Financial and Quantitative Analysis, 23*(1), 39–51. https://doi.org/10.2307/2331023

Newman, D. P., Patterson, E. R., & Smith, J. R. (2005). The role of auditing in investor protection. *The Accounting Review, 80*(1), 289–313. https://doi.org/10.2308/accr.2005.80.1.289

Noe, T. H. (1988). Capital structure and signaling game equilibria. *The Review of Financial Studies, 1*(4), 331–355.

Parray, Z. A., Iqbal, J., & Mushtaq, R. (2023). Customer perception of corporate social responsibility and its impact on customer engagement: Critical significance of corporate reputation. *Corporate Communications: An International Journal, 29*(4), 592–606. https://doi.org/10.1108/CCIJ-05-2023-0063

Patten, D. M. (1991). Exposure, legitimacy, and social disclosure. *Journal of Accounting and Public Policy, 10*(4), 297–308. https://doi.org/10.1016/0278-4254(91)90003-3

Peruffo, E., Oriani, R., & Perri, A. (2014). Information asymmetries, family ownership and divestiture financial performance: Evidence from western European countries. *Corporate Ownership and Control, 11*(4), 43–57. https://iris.luiss.it/handle/11385/118993

Pierni, P., Montagna, D. M., & Maggi, M. (2022). Founding family ownership and firm performance: Some evidence from the Italian Stock Market. *Journal of Risk and Financial Management, 15*(5), Articolo 5. https://doi.org/10.3390/jrfm15050231

Power, M. K. (2003). Auditing and the production of legitimacy. *Accounting, Organizations and Society, 28*(4), 379–394. https://doi.org/10.1016/S0361-3682(01)00047-2

Rajan, R. G., & Zingales, L. (1995). What do we know about capital structure? Some evidence from international data. *The Journal of Finance, 50*(5), 1421–1460. Scopus. https://doi.org/10.1111/j.1540-6261.1995.tb05184.x

Ratzinger-Sakel, N. V. S., & Schönberger, M. W. (2015). Restricting non-audit services in Europe—The potential (lack of) impact of a blacklist and a fee cap on auditor independence and audit quality. *Accounting in Europe, 12*(1), 61–86. https://doi.org/10.1080/17449480.2015.1035290

Richard Baker, C., & Owsen, D. M. (2002). Increasing the role of auditing in corporate governance. *Critical Perspectives on Accounting, 13*(5), 783–795. https://doi.org/10.1006/cpac.2002.0566

Rindova, V. P., Williamson, I. O., Petkova, A. P., & Sever, J. M. (2005). Being good or being known: An empirical examination of the dimensions, antecedents, and consequences of organizational reputation. *Academy of Management Journal, 48*(6), 1033–1049. https://doi.org/10.5465/AMJ.2005.19573108

Rogers, J. L., Skinner, D. J., & Zechman, S. L. C. (2016). The role of the media in disseminating insider-trading news. *Review of Accounting Studies, 21*(3), 711–739.

Romenti, S. (2010). Reputation and stakeholder engagement: An Italian case study. *Journal of Communication Management, 14*(4), 306–318. https://doi.org/10.1108/13632541011090428

Rostami OstadKelayeh, S., Aghaei, M., & Biglar, K. (2024). Efficiency of business risk auditing approach in Iran based on the dimensions of legitimacy theory. *Journal of Management Accounting and Auditing Knowledge, 13*(52), 121–136.

Salvatore, S., Gennaro, A., Auletta, A. F., Tonti, M., & Nitti, M. (2012). Automated method of content analysis: A device for psychotherapy process research. *Psychotherapy Research, 22*(3), 256–273. https://doi.org/10.1080/10503307.2011.647930

Saviano, M., Caputo, F., Mueller, J., & Belyaeva, Z. (2018). Competing through consonance: A stakeholder engagement view of corporate relational environment. *Sinergie Italian Journal of Management, 36*. https://doi.org/10.7433/s105.2018.04

Simunic, D. A. (1980). The pricing of audit services: Theory and evidence. *Journal of Accounting Research, 18*(1), 161–190. https://doi.org/10.2307/2490397

Singh, H. (2024). Is corporate reputation associated with voluntary cybersecurity risk reporting? *Meditari Accountancy Research, 33*(1). https://doi.org/10.1108/MEDAR-02-2024-2329

Song, H., Yu, K., & Lu, Q. (2018). Financial service providers and banks' role in helping SMEs to access finance. *International Journal of Physical Distribution & Logistics Management, 48*(1), 69–92. https://doi.org/10.1108/IJPDLM-11-2016-0315

Stevens, C. E., & Makarius, E. E. (2015). Overcoming information asymmetry in foreign entry strategy: The impact of reputation. *Global Strategy Journal, 5*(3), 256–272. https://doi.org/10.1002/gsj.1099

Stigler, G. J. (1962). Information in the labor market. *Journal of Political Economy, 70*(5), 94–105.

Stiglitz, J. E., & Weiss, A. (1981). Credit rationing in markets with imperfect information. *The American Economic Review, 71*(3), 393–410.

Suchman, M. C. (1995). Managing legitimacy: Strategic and institutional approaches. *Academy of Management Review, 20*(3), 571–610. https://doi.org/10.5465/amr.1995.9508080331

Sun, X. S., & Habib, A. (2021). Determinants and consequences of auditor-provided tax services: A systematic review of the international literature. *International Journal of Auditing, 25*(3), 675–715. https://doi.org/10.1111/ijau.12244

Swoboda, B., Puchert, C., & Morschett, D. (2016). Explaining the differing effects of corporate reputation across nations: A multilevel analysis. *Journal of the Academy of Marketing Science, 44*(4), 454–473. https://doi.org/10.1007/s11747-015-0457-2

von Berlepsch, D., Lemke, F., & Gorton, M. (2024). The importance of corporate reputation for sustainable supply chains: A systematic literature review, bibliometric mapping, and research agenda. *Journal of Business Ethics, 189*(1), 9–34. https://doi.org/10.1007/s10551-022-05268-x

Wartick, S. L. (2002). Measuring corporate reputation: Definition and data. *Business and Society, 41*(4), 371–392. https://doi.org/10.1177/0007650302238774

Zimmerman, M. A., & Zeitz, G. J. (2002). Beyond survival: Achieving new venture growth by building legitimacy. *The Academy of Management Review, 27*(3), 414–431. https://doi.org/10.2307/4134387

Chapter 7
Conclusions, Limitations, and Implications

Who has not for the sake of his reputation sacrificed himself?

[Friedrich Wilhelm Nietzsche, German philosopher and cultural critic].

This book explores the multifaceted nature of corporate reputation, emphasizing its strategic significance, the processes involved in managing and measuring it, and its impact on organizational outcomes from two distinct perspectives: the organizational-oriented and stakeholder-oriented perspectives. Additionally, the book empirically substantiates the key assumption that has emerged throughout its chapters by conducting econometric analyses on a sample of 91 Italian-listed companies.

Chapter 2 offers a comprehensive review of the literature on corporate reputation, analysing the concept across a range of disciplines, including strategic management, organizational theory, accounting, marketing, economics, and sociology. This review identifies the key characteristics of corporate reputation: it is socially constructed, historically rooted, strategically valuable, stakeholder-sensitive, context-dependent, multidimensional, and dynamic. Furthermore, the chapter provides a refined definition of the concept, describing corporate reputation as a strategic, perception-based construct shaped by relationships with stakeholders and serving as an indicator of legitimacy. In doing so, this chapter contributes to the literature addressing the definitional problem of corporate reputation (Bigus et al., 2024).

Building on the insights from the literature review in Chap. 2, Chap. 3 presents a comprehensive framework for managing corporate reputation. This framework conceptualizes corporate reputation as a stock variable, influenced by a combination of four processes: reputation building, reputation acquisition, reputational risk management, and crisis management. The chapter also identifies the determinants that can either positively or negatively impact reputation capital, classifying these actions as either intentional or unintentional. As a result, this chapter contributes to the literature investigating the determinants of corporate reputation (Francesconi &

D. Vito, *Corporate Reputation as Strategic Intangible Asset*, SIDREA Series in Accounting and Business Administration,
https://doi.org/10.1007/978-3-031-93331-8_7

Dossena, 2009; Romenti, 2008; van Riel & Fombrun, 2007; Coda, 1991; Michelon, 2011; Basdeo et al., 2006; Helm, 2011; Basir, 2020) and strategies to manage it (Eccles et al., 2007; Coombs, 2007; Lamboglia & D'Onza, 2014).

Chapter 4, expanding upon the framework proposed in Chap. 3, delves into the outcomes of corporate reputation from a dual perspective: the organizational-oriented and stakeholder-oriented perspectives. From the organizational perspective, a strong corporate reputation is linked to enhanced financial performance, market performance, and competitive advantage. From the stakeholder perspective, it influences stakeholder decisions. The chapter underscores the interconnection between these two perspectives, highlighting their reciprocal reinforcement and positioning them as two sides of the same coin. Thus, this chapter contributes to the literature supporting the assumption that corporate reputation is a multidimensional concept (e.g. Money et al., 2017) that influences both organizational performance and stakeholders' decisions (Barnett & Pollock, 2012; Barney, 1991; Dierickx & Cool, 1989; Fombrun, 1996).

To complete the theoretical analysis, Chap. 5 addressed the challenge of measuring corporate reputation as accurate measurement is essential for evaluating the effectiveness of reputation management strategies and understanding the impact of reputation on organizational outcomes. Specifically, it explores various methodologies, including structured questionnaires, rankings, ratings, third-party indices, and media coverage. Each of these approaches has its respective strengths and limitations, with applicability varying depending on the specific stakeholder group under analysis. Consequently, this chapter contributes to the literature suggesting that corporate reputation is a measurement-sensitive concept (e.g. Vito, 2021).

Finally, Chap. 6 provides empirical evidence supporting the theoretical discussions presented throughout the book. By focusing on two specific, underexplored stakeholder groups (auditors and banks), the chapter demonstrates the impact of corporate reputation on variables such as leverage, cost of debt, audit fees, and non-audit services. The findings confirm the stakeholder sensitivity of corporate reputation, showing that its impact may vary depending on the particular stakeholder group. Additionally, this chapter corroborates the assumption that corporate reputation is measurement-sensitive, as the effects on organizational outcomes vary based on the measurement method employed.

Comprehensively, this book offers substantial contributions to academic literature on corporate reputation by offering an integrated and comprehensive framework for understanding, managing, and measuring corporate reputation. Its interdisciplinary approach, empirical insights, and practical guidelines provide valuable resources for both researchers and practitioners. By addressing the complexities and nuances of corporate reputation, the book enhances our understanding of how reputation influences organizational outcomes and stakeholder relationships, and it offers actionable strategies for effective reputation management in the modern business landscape. This comprehensive treatment of corporate reputation not only advances academic knowledge but also provides practical tools and insights that can help organizations navigate the challenges and opportunities associated with managing their reputational capital.

Despite its contributions, this study has also limitations that pave the way for future research.

Firstly, as this book focuses on two specific stakeholder groups, future research should explore the impact of corporate reputation on a broader range of stakeholders, including customers, employees, suppliers, and regulators. Additionally, comparative studies across different industries and geographical regions could provide a more comprehensive understanding of the factors influencing corporate reputation and its outcomes.

Second, the empirical findings of this book are based on the adoption of three distinct measurement methods. As highlighted in Chap. 5, the literature offers a range of methods, each of which may yield different results. Consequently, future research could address this limitation by exploring alternative measurement methods or developing and validating more robust tools, incorporating advancements in data analytics, machine learning, and artificial intelligence.

Moreover, with the rise of digital and social media, the landscape of corporate reputation management has significantly changed. Future studies should examine how digital platforms influence corporate reputation and how organizations can effectively manage their online presence to enhance and protect their reputation.

References

Barnett, M. L., & Pollock, T. G. (2012). *The Oxford Handbook of corporate reputation*. OUP Oxford.

Barney, J. (1991). Firm resources and sustained competitive advantage. *Journal of Management, 17*(1), 99–120. https://doi.org/10.1177/014920639101700108

Basdeo, D. K., Smith, K. G., Grimm, C. M., Rindova, V. P., & Derfus, P. J. (2006). The impact of market actions on firm reputation. *Strategic Management Journal, 27*(12), 1205–1219. Scopus. https://doi.org/10.1002/smj.556

Basir, N. (2020). Reputation enhancing through patent portfolios: An exploration of lapsed patents and IPOS. *Corporate Reputation Review, 23*(1), 42–56. https://doi.org/10.1057/s41299-019-00074-0

Bigus, J., Hua, K. P. M., & Raithel, S. (2024). Definitions and measures of corporate reputation in accounting and management: Commonalities, differences, and future research. *Accounting and Business Research, 54*(3), 304–336. Scopus. https://doi.org/10.1080/00014788.2022.2149458

Coda, V. (1991). *Comunicazione e immagine nella strategia dell'impresa*. Giappichelli. https://www.libreriauniversitaria.it/comunicazione-immagine-strategia-impresa-coda/libro/9788834806258

Coombs, W. T. (2007). Protecting organization reputations during a crisis: The development and application of situational crisis communication theory. *Corporate Reputation Review, 10*(3), 163–176. https://doi.org/10.1057/palgrave.crr.1550049

Dierickx, I., & Cool, K. (1989). Asset stock accumulation and sustainability of competitive advantage. *Management Science, 35*(12), 1504–1511.

Eccles, R., Newquist, S., & Schatz, R. (2007). Reputation and its risks. *Harvard Business Review, 85*(104–114), 156.

Fombrun, C. J. (1996). *Reputation: Realizing value from the corporate image*. Harvard Business School Press.

Francesconi, A., & Dossena, C. (2009). L'IT per l'analisi e la gestione della web corporate reputation. Un caso aziendale. 10o Workshop di Organizzazione Aziendale "Per lo sviluppo, la competitività e l'innovazione del sistema economico: il contributo degli studi in organizzazione aziendale", Cagliari.

Helm, S. (2011). Employees' awareness of their impact on corporate reputation. *Journal of Business Research, 64*(7), 657–663. https://doi.org/10.1016/j.jbusres.2010.09.001

Lamboglia, R., & D'Onza, G. (2014). Un modello di gestione del rischio reputazionale. Dall'identificazione al fronteggiamento. *Management Control*. 2013/3. https://doi.org/10.3280/MACO2013-003002

Michelon, G. (2011). Sustainability disclosure and reputation: A comparative study. *Corporate Reputation Review, 14*(2), 79–96. https://doi.org/10.1057/crr.2011.10

Money, K., Saraeva, A., Garnelo-Gomez, I., Pain, S., & Hillenbrand, C. (2017). Corporate reputation past and future: A review and integration of existing literature and a framework for future research. *Corporate Reputation Review, 20*(3/4), 193–211. https://doi.org/10.1057/s41299-017-0034-3

Romenti, S. (2008). Corporate governance e reputazione: Dallo stakeholder relationship management allo stakeholder engagement. *Impresa Progetto – Rivista on line del DITEA*, n. 2, 1–23.

van Riel, C. B. M., & Fombrun, C. J. (2007). *Essentials of corporate communication: Implementing practices for effective reputation management*. Routledge. https://doi.org/10.4324/9780203390931

Vito, D. (2021). La misurazione della reputazione aziendale: Un'analisi sistematica della letteratura. In P. Ferretti (Ed.), *La corporate reputation: Alcuni driver di sviluppo* (pp. 1–38). G. Giappichelli Editore.

The manufacturer's authorised representative in the EU is Springer Nature Customer Service Centre GmbH, Europaplatz 3, 69115 Heidelberg, Germany. If you have any concerns regarding our products, please contact ProductSafety@springernature.com

Printed and bound by CPI Group (UK) Ltd, Croydon, CR0 4YY
30/09/2026
02225577-0009